Apostolic Movement and the Progress of the Gospel

Joseph Mattera

Praise for:

"The Global Apostolic Movement and the Progress of the Gospel"

"Joseph Mattera's, *The Global Apostolic Movement and the Progress of the Gospel*, is a helpful addition to the knowledge regarding the Apostolic Network movements. I found great wisdom, insight, and clarification on important issues related to the Apostolic movement. There was lots of gold in the footnotes and in the bibliography. So many questions are addressed in the work and there is a lot of insight and wisdom. One difference I have with the author would be the following two sentences. "One valuable resource that I recommend is a book written by two solid Christian scholars, R. Douglas Geivett and Holly Pivec. The helpful book, "A New Apostolic Reformation? gives honest and scholarly insights into the high-profile NAR leaders, while examining their teachings."

"I intend in the future to publish a book that disagrees sharply with the conclusions of Geivett and Pivec. I did not find their book to be helpful, instead found it to be misrepresentative in some aspects and not scholarly insights into some NAR leaders which they named, myself included, who they did not interview to make sure they were reflecting accurately their positions.

"But this endorsement is for Mattera, not Geivett and Pivec so I will return to *The Global Apostolic Movement and the Progress of the Gospel*, overall, I liked Mattera and have found him in personal conversation to have a lot of wisdom and insight into the apostolic movement. I appreciate his humility and his language addressing the difference between office and function or office and gift. I believe his book will be helpful for those desiring to learn more about the apostolic movement. I enjoyed reading it and recommend it."

-Randy Clark, leader of the Apostolic Network of Global Awakening, president of the Global Awakening Theological Seminary, author of *Intimacy with God* and forty-seven other books.

"Most studies of the modern church lack understanding of today's apostolic movements. As a leader in this movement, Joseph Mattera provides his firsthand perspectives. He provides clarity on how many of these apostolic networks function and offers forthright challenges where many can function more biblically, working to bring more mature balance by reconnecting Word and Spirit."
-Craig S. Keener, F. M. and Ada Thompson Professor of Biblical Studies, Asbury Theological Seminary.

"In this dissertation-turned-book, Dr. Joseph Mattera has gifted the church with years of dedicated study on the nature and purpose of apostolic ministry. Loaded with good scholarship and research, this book will prove exceedingly helpful for people trying to faithfully recover the role of the apostolic person in the contemporary church. Highly recommended."
-Alan Hirsch, award winning writer of books on missional spirituality, leadership, and organization including The Permanent Revolution, 5Q, and The Forgotten Ways. Founder of Movement Leaders Collective and Forge Missional Training Network.

"As one who has studied apostolic ministry for over twenty years, I am delighted to endorse and recommend this book by Joseph Mattera. His insights into the Global Apostolic Movement rightly connects the dots pointing to God's saving mission through Jesus Christ. He understands that apostolic ministry is not about elevating gifted people or their ministries; rather, apostolic ministry is about pointing to and proclaiming the One who is already elevated on high. Rooted in sound exegesis, a comprehensive understanding of church history, and wise analysis of modern culture, this is an important book that will help keep us focused on the mission and goal of the gospel of Jesus Christ."

-Dr. Doug Beacham, International Pentecostal Holiness Church, General Superintendent and Presiding Bishop.

"This is Dr. Joseph Mattera's magnum opus, a critically important guide to a critically important subject. In fact, few subjects in the church are more important and yet less understood than the subject of contemporary apostolic ministry. What is the proper place of apostles today, and what are the potential dangers and abuses of apostolic ministry? Based on his decades of personal ministry experience, academic study, and leadership training worldwide, I can think of no better guide than my friend, Joe Mattera.

-Dr. Michael L. Brown, host of the Line of Fire radio broadcast, Bestselling Author.

"This book is a must read for every Protestant leader for understanding the origins, historical underpinnings, and ongoing impact of the Apostolic Movement. Mattera's insights are provocative, biblical, scholarly, and practical for equipping church leaders to move their constituents forward into building and expanding the Kingdom of God in the 21st century."

-Dr. Larry Keefauver, Bestselling Author and International Teacher

"In this dissertation and now excellent book, Dr. Joseph Mattera has rendered a valuable service to the entire Body of Christ. There is no more important movement taking place today than the new apostolic movement. It's influence is global and reaches not only its adherents but a vast number of Evangelical, Charismatic and Pentecostal churches. Furthermore, it's influence is felt in every branch of Christianity, Protestant and Catholic around the world. Dr Mattera has brought the excellence of doctoral scholarship to the plate of everyman in this splendid book. With a minimum of academic jargon, he has produced a milestone study of what this apostolic movement is and where it is today, and has traced the trail it took to get here. He has also produced a manual of best practices including a much needed glossary of key terms and not a few gentle reminders to keep the movement on track. Finally he has produced a guidepost to the future for the development of the movement and the genuine progress of the Gospel of Christ on the earth.

"I strongly recommend this book and commend its author. This book belongs in every seminary and university library, Christian or not, and on the shelf of every thoughtful minister of the Gospel."
-Ronald E. Cottle Ph.D., Ed.D., D.D. Founder and President Emeritus, Christian Life School of Theology.

The Global Apostolic Movement and the Progress of the Gospel

"This book attempts to give practical steps involved in the building of an influential national apostolic network as well as examining present-day theological challenges, paradigms, and the progress of the gospel."

Dr. Joseph Mattera

Published by BILD International, 2400 Oakwood Road, Ames, Iowa.
Printed by BILD. Distributed and sold by BILD in specified venues by permission of the author.

BILD is an acronym for Biblical Institute of Leadership Development—a training system and the leader of a global network of leaders working together to see the Church spontaneously expand by returning to the model of planting and establishing churches found in the New Testament. https://bild.org

Art Direction and Design: Kyle Watkins and Caroline Larson

ISBN: 978-1-7326986-4-2

Table of Contents

Preface

The Global Apostolic Movement and the Progress of the Gospel

This book is informed by a New Testament biblical theology. It incorporates the practical steps involved in the building of an influential national apostolic network, as well as integrating present-day theological challenges, paradigms, and the progress of the gospel.

The objective of this book: My reason for writing this book is because of the significant influence the burgeoning apostolic movement is having globally.[1] Most evangelicals in North America, as well as Western Europe, have relatively little knowledge of the history of the Apostolic movement[2] beginning from the time of the original apostles, to the church Fathers, to modern-day missionaries.[3] As a result, our current Church leaders are hindered in their ability to see and in turn articulate the importance of this revived expression of the church.

Evidence shows that this Apostolic movement is significantly impacting Christendom, resulting in a transformation of the current ways the Church is being viewed and expressed. Hence, the need for scholarly research, exposition, and insight from practitioners and scholars from within and without the movement. My hope is that this book will broaden the appeal of the Apostolic church among all Christian denominations, especially Evangelicals. In addition, it will serve as a pertinent resource for all practitioners in the Apostolic movement, as it inspires them to build according to the New Testament pattern and the way of Christ and His apostles.[4]

As one who has been involved in various apostolic networks and movements since the late 1980s, I have had a front-row seat as it relates to the subject at hand. I have also overseen various networks, initiated the establishment of a large apostolic network in Santo Domingo in 1993, planted a thriving New Testament Pauline patterned church in New York City,[5] birthed and currently lead Christ Covenant Coalition, a collective of apostolic leaders based on covenantal relationships[6] and currently oversee the United States Coalition of Apostolic Leaders (USCAL).[7] My goal has always been to build according to a biblical pattern as seen in Hebrews 8:5. Also, it must be said at the onset of this book that I am not a proponent of some of the teachings that have emerged out of the NAR because of my understanding of Scripture and the Way of Christ and His Apostles.

In this book I attempt to give a historical framework for the modern-day Apostolic movement, along with honestly assessing its strengths and challenges. My goal was to not only clearly distinguish between true and erroneous assumptions of apostolic function, but to give a practical blueprint that can help nurture emerging and established apostolic practitioners and give guidelines regarding how to build sustainable gospel centered networks and movements.

Considering this, I believe the way of Christ and His apostles is an informal disciple making methodology resulting in a missional church movement that advances the Kingdom of God through Gospel permeation in cities in every culture and context.

My hope is that some of those interested in reading this work would include: non charismatic Evangelicals interested in understanding more about this burgeoning Global apostolic movement and how it can possibly shape their own missional understanding of church planting and networking; Pentecostal denominational leaders who desire to comport their movements and churches to the New Testament pattern of church planting , disciple making and multiplication; Non-denominational charismatic network leaders who desire to ground their movements more biblically in the Pauline model of church planting, disciple making and biblical theology; Independent Charismatic leaders and movements that long to discover biblically based patterns of local church development and discipleship; Global apostolic leaders who are looking for a simple blue print to use for nurturing sustainable Gospel movements as well as training material for their seminaries and theological education.

All these potential readers have one main thing in common irrespective of their theological differences: They believe the Scriptures are the inspired word of God and as such serve as the highest standard for doctrine, reproof, and correction in righteousness that the person of God may be furnished for every good work. (2 Tim. 3:16,17)

By non-charismatic evangelicals, I am not referring to hardcore cessationists who strongly oppose the biblical legitimacy of the apostolic function and or the legitimacy of the use of the gifts of the Holy Spirit today (see 1 Corinthians 12:4-11). I doubt these would be interested in reading this book except to criticize it.

The Evangelicals I am speaking of may or may not be charismatic and or exhibit the spiritual gifts in their public assemblies – but there is a new wave of understanding and embrace of the term "apostolic" among their ranks since they hunger to replicate the amazing success of the first century church.

The classical Pentecostal denominations generally rejected the apostolic function in the past but today there is a new hunger among these expressions of the Body of Christ -starting in places like Australia but now affecting the whole world including North America.

Unfortunately, many non-denominational charismatics may use the term apostolic but generally do not replicate the Pauline model of church based theological education, disciple making, church planting and movement making. My prayer is that this work will greatly impact this group that is strong on signs and wonders and spiritual experience but weak in regard to biblical exegesis and theology.

Many thanks go to "Apostle" pappa John Kelly, an incredible global strategist who took me under his wing in 1989 and modeled for me apostolic networking, spiritual fathering, and the balance between administration and anointing.

Thanks also goes to Jeff Reed, the president and founder of Antioch University—a modern day apostle Paul who became the architect of a huge global network by strategically implementing his vast curricula to connect and help establish multiple thousands of churches in every continent of the world. He became a theological mentor since 1999 and helped me understand how to put a biblical theological framework and concepts to the church and networks I founded. He also introduced me to Roland Allen and his writings related to understanding the "way of Christ and His apostles" which is a major theme that runs through this work.

Glossary

Before proceeding, this Glossary and Abbreviations section is provided to assist the reader.

Apostle – The foundational ministry gift mentioned in 1 Corinthians 12:28 and Ephesians 4:11 that is assigned to a person uniquely sent out by the Lord Jesus to pioneer churches and or movements of churches.

Charismatic – A person and or historical denominational church that speaks in tongues and practices the other gifts of the spirit mentioned in 1 Corinthians 12:4-10.

Cessationist –A person and or sect of the body of Christ who contend that the gifts of the Holy Spirit , especially tongues and prophecy as well as the office of Apostle and prophet , ceased after the New Testament canon of scripture was completed . They believe that God only communicates through His written

4

word and any other mode of communication -whether by a word, impression in the heart, vision, dream or prophecy is adding to the word of God and is condemned by Scripture. (See Revelation 22:18,19)

Didache -The teachings of the New Testament letters that practically applied the life and sayings of Jesus to the post ascension church.

Epoch -A point of time marked by notable shifts in thinking and or ways of doing things.

Evangelical – A Christian who has received the risen Jesus Christ as Lord of their life and experiences the new birth for conversion -who believes the bible is the inspired word of God as their final authority for faith and life.

Fivefold ministry gifts = This is a reference to the five cluster gifts mentioned in Ephesians 4:11.

Incarnational – A spiritual leader and or church who focuses on being present physically in the lives and activities of their people and community.

Kerygma -the proclamation of the gospel.

Missional – A church that incorporates the command of Jesus to reach cities into their mission and purpose.

Movement -A cluster of churches that continually expand and multiply.

Network – A cluster of churches that are working together.

Pattern - The consistent practice, behavior or methods of a person and or church.

Paradigm -The lens by which a person or movement perceives reality.

Prophet – A foundational ministry gift mentioned along with the apostle with a unique calling to understand and discern the will of God for the sake of establishing the local church. (See I Corinthians 12:28; Ephesians 2:20; 3:5)

Pentecostal – a Christian and or denomination that believes in the second blessing of the baptism of the Holy Spirit with the evidence of speaking in other tongues. They also focus on preaching a gospel that includes salvation, healing and deliverance from demonic oppression.

Practitioner – A spiritual leader whose focus is on the practical application of the gospel regarding the spreading of the word of God and reaching their community for Christ.

Scholar – A spiritual leader who focuses on mastering the word of God, theology and other academic disciplines.

Wineskin -The structure and culture of a church and or movement.

Common Abbreviations

APEST = An acronym for apostle, prophet , evangelist, shepherd and teacher as found in Ephesians 4:11

NAR -an acronym for the so called New Apostolic Reformation; This was a phrase coined by the late Dr. C. Peter

Wagner to describe the post denominational apostolic age he believed started in the year 2001.

ICAL =An acronym for the International Coalition of Apostolic leaders that was founded by John Kelly in 1999 with the original name being ICA -International Coalition of Apostles. C.Peter Wagner eventually took it over in 2001 and led until he turned 80 years old when he gave the leadership of it back to John Kelly.

USCAL =An acronym for the United States Coalition of Apostolic Leaders that was launched as a component of ICAL by Joseph Mattera in 2015 (See USCAL.US)

Preface

Joseph Mattera is multi-lingual. He can speak to anyone on the spectrum of Pentecostals to Evangelicals. He calls Pentecostals to return to their roots of commitment to the progress of the Gospel. He calls Evangelicals to recognize the apostolic work in the world today. He summons all to go deeper than their own traditions in order to become fully aligned with the way of Christ and His Apostles. This is not an easy book to read. It challenges everyone at the paradigm level. Most of us are busy doing good things, but may be falling significantly short of the godly things that God intends for us. Whether you are comfortable with the language of an "apostolic movement" or not, Mattera helps you to understand this foundational concept from biblical, historical, and contemporary ministry perspectives.

Dr. Stephen J. Kemp
Founding Global Academic Dean
Antioch School of Church Planting and Leadership
Development

Forewords

by Jeff Reed and Mark Chironna

I have known Bishop Mattera for over thirty years. He was coming at his body of work from a Pentecostal tradition and I coming with my body of work from an evangelical tradition, but we were both moving towards the same center. We have discussed many, many seminal authors, both of us contributing to our growing conversation. When Joe entered our Ph.D. program, I carefully discussed, and discovered, his desire to write a Pentecostal theology for Global Pentecostal church networks and movements; he wanted it to make a significant contribution to evangelicals as well.

Conversations like this, at the right time in history and amidst many conversations as paradigms shift to new eras, are what Randall Collins, in *The Sociology of Philosophies: A Global Theory of Intellectual Change*, says produce whole new forms of thinking, followed by new forms of education—in our sphere, theological education.

In our doctoral program, this book is what we call an artifact. An artifact has dissertation level research at its base, but it does not stop as a formal dissertation on shelves of scholarly libraries. It is brought down to a tool that can be used by churches—in this case, church networks and movements. This artifact, in book form, is ten years in the making. During this time and prior, Joe has written many significant books for churches and church leaders, very practical books to be used in churches and by church leaders, with special emphasis on seeking the welfare of the city. When this was first submitted to us, Steve Kemp, our Global Dean, asked Joe to do more formal work on his biblical theology, specifically Pauline theology. So, Joe spent another two years doing just that, the essence of which has been included in this book.

Bishop Mattera is a very good theologian. But, I would like to suggest, he's a new type of theologian, doing what I refer to as "strategic practical theology." The early church prophets were the church's first theologians. I believe this book is the work of a prophet, the true meaning of prophet used by the apostle Paul when he said in 1 Corinthians, "first apostles, then prophets." For the last forty years, there has been a call for a new kind of theology—the inventing of a new theological encyclopedia, moving from the primarily academic theology of Western seminaries to a new theological process moving from biblical theology to theology in culture to strategic practical theology.

Pioneers in this field are such theologians as Don Browning in his books, *A Fundamental Practical Theology and Practical Theology: The Emerging Field in Theology, Church and World* (editor). I believe Bishop Mattera has accomplished his goal. He has written a strategic practical theology, solidly relevant to both Pentecostals and evangelicals, especially those from both camps who are tired of the old rigid divides of the two traditions. I consider this a pioneering work for all of us to follow. We intend on using this work in our global networks, especially the massive Global Pentecostal movements across the Global South, but in our Western network partners as well.

The term "strategic practical theologian" applies to Bishop Mattera for another reason. He has planted a very strategic church in Brooklyn; formed his own network of apostolic leaders, first in the greater New York City area and now globally; and plays a significant role in seeking the welfare of New York City, serving as a bishop in the city, which is recognized by many churches. This is not just theory. He has practiced these ideas at many different levels for decades.

Bishop Mattera is also the convener of the United States Coalition of Apostolic Leaders, which was previously known as the International Coalition of Apostles. He changed the name to the

United States Coalition of Apostolic Leaders in seeking to bring both traditions to the center, so all Evangelicals can embrace the movement.

I have written this foreword in both an academic and personal manner, shifting back and forth from Bishop Mattera to Joe, because I know Joe's heart and how we have both hoped this work will be positioned for leaders who carefully work through this book. I consider Joe to be a very humble leader and a personal friend. Although I have believed in "little a" apostles and "little p" prophets since my apprenticeship days in the early 1970s, thanks to Ray Stedman, I have learned a tremendous amount from Joe across the years. I consider it to be a privilege to write this introduction; I pray his book will have a significant impact globally.

I am sure Bishop Mattera will continue to develop and mature this book, producing future editions as he hears from global leaders of both traditions, because Joe is a committed lifelong learner. But it is clearly ready for global "prime time"!

And, by the way, Joe is also an accomplished jazz guitarist, with little time to play the guitar these days.

-Jeff Reed
Founder and President of BILD International
President of the Antioch School of Church Planting and Leadership

***

Much has been written by scholars on the issue of Primitivism, also known as Restorationism in relation to Protestantism. In its history in America alone, the world of Hughes and Allen is seminal. All the various denominations of Protestantism contain certain aspects and nuances of Primitivism / Restorationism. In some circles, there are areas far more pronounced, and certainly within the various streams of what began with Pentecostalism, which derived its impetus from Wesleyan Pietism and the Holiness Movement, the approach is far more exuberant and somewhat detailed, albeit with major flaws and misreadings of Church history.

At the same time, there has been an increased awareness of the genuine realities of the expressions of the Ascended Christ in relation to apostolic, prophetic, evangelistic, and pastoral-didactic function. The dangers of turning this into a form of hierarchy, creating power differentials is ever present, and falls short of something that Paul, John, or Peter contend for in the Sacred Text. There is no question that since the dawn of Pentecostalism, its evangelistic fervor has been perhaps the most noticeable of all the various sects within Protestantism. It could be argued that the future belongs to the heirs of the Pentecostal movement.

With that in mind, we need to come to terms with the fact that reform has been taking place in the Church since the most ancient of its beginnings. While the Great Reformation is touted as if it is the only Reformation, a careful study of church history from the apostolic age, the apologetic age, to the patristic age and beyond refutes such a claim. Is it that Restorationism or Primitivism is a call back to an earlier time, or a call forward to continue to course correct and engage the Sacred Text and the mission that we have been entrusted with in a way that passes muster, and is scrutinized by the ways in which we engage the Sacred Text here in the current post-modern era and culture where it seems everything is up for grabs?

My dear friend, Joe Mattera, is a student, a life-long student of both the Scriptures and Church history and is committed to the church local and the church global. His approach to these matters is thorough, thought-provoking, engaging, and challenging. We need to take this work he has written quite seriously and begin to wrestle with what we will do with what he observes, interprets, and proposes. I would argue that this work is a step in a much-needed direction and would serve us all well if it receives as wide an exposure as possible.

-Dr. Mark J. Chironna, Bishop, Church On The Living Edge,
Legacy Edge Alliance,
Mark Chironna Ministries
Longwood, Florida
October 2021

14

Introduction

The Restoration of Apostolic Ministry Today

As a foundational ministry, the apostle serves together with the prophet to lay the foundation for the entire temple of God, while receiving alignment and positioning from the cornerstone, Jesus Christ. Without the Apostle as a member of the ongoing foundation of the church, we cannot fully become the temple of the living God. The Apostle cannot be omitted as a primary member of the Body of Christ or as a foundational structure of the temple of God. The original Greek word translated apostle is *apostolos*. It comes from a root word, meaning one who is sent forth or sent away from one place to another to accomplish a specific mission. The word "Apostle" was used to mean naval officers or merchant mariners responsible for an entire fleet of ships. It was also used to refer to an emissary or ambassador; to a fleet of ships or an expedition sent with a specific objective; to the Admiral who commanded the fleet or to the colony that was founded by the admiral.[8]

Since the late 1940s, there has been a resurgence of attempts to activate the five-fold ministry gifts as found in Ephesians 4:11. Starting with the "Latter Rain movement" in Canada, various groups have arisen to proclaim the restoration of the Apostolic and Prophetic gifts.

The result has been the emergence of great movements of independent networks led by apostolic visionaries. As such, we have witnessed an explosion in Asia, Latin America, and Africa of these gifts. Such apostolic movements, being witnessed in those nations, represent the fastest growing segment of global Christianity. Furthermore, as a result of this, we are seeing that even Evangelical leaders and movements are embracing five-fold ministry language to describe the current church leadership. The primary reason for this is because the church is being taught by the Holy Spirit. The truth is that if the Church is going to replicate the amazing Jesus Movement of the first few centuries of church history,it has to go from a "pastoral" model of church to an "apostolic" model of leadership.

Truly, the Protestant Reformation which began in the 16th century is still taking place as the Reformed church is continually reforming itself. Evangelical leaders like the late Fuller Professor Dr. Peter Wagner, who crossed over to embrace the charismatic gifts in the 3rd Wave of the 1980s, became the catalyst for the wider Body of Christ to embrace this Apostolic restoration.

Although some of the earmarks of what Peter Wagner called the New Apostolic Reformation (NAR) have made many of us in the present Restoration movement uncomfortable,[9] it is still advancing. The reason for this advancement is because Jesus is the One building His church, through the magisterium of the Holy Spirit, Who is pulling the whole Body into the vortex of the New Testament pattern of Church.

(One great sign of hope related to the restoration of the church back to the way of Christ and His apostles is the global church based theological movement of BILD that is helping establish prominent church-based leadership and planting movements in every continent. -especially in the global south among huge Pentecostal networks and denominations. see BILD.org<http://BILD.org>)

Biblical Background

Jesus gave the title "apostle" to the original 12 disciples whom He entrusted the church to. Although He called them apostles, it was never to be used as a title. In fact, Peter, James, John, and Paul were referred to by their first names, and not with the prefix "Apostle". The term, Apostle was used to indicate a ministerial and governmental function. Although the New Testament refers to dozens of other leaders as apostles, when the original twelve passed away, out of deference to the original 12 apostles, their successors began to refer to them as bishops. Consequently, the Catholic Church perpetuated the apostolic function by consecrating bishops over cities and regions. These were the ones who walked in "Apostolic succession." To legitimize the bishop, they were granted genealogical documents that traced their succession back to at least one of the original 12 apostles.

After the alleged conversion of Emperor Constantine to Christianity, the Catholic Church became an institution. In the fourth century, we see the Church went from being called a "way" to being identified as an institution. The apostolic was no longer considered a function but was now considered an office, which was conferred upon a person by an institution. The office and function of the bishopric of the western church and the Patriarchs of the Eastern church became the glue that held the church together through the Middle Ages. This ensured that the power and voice of Christendom, over the nations in Eastern and Western Europe, held sway. This was important in the eleventh century when the official split between Roman Catholicism and Eastern Orthodoxy occurred.

Protestant Church History

Fast forward about five hundred years later and we see the rejection of the bishopric in the Protestant Reformation. One of the major reasons was because of the perceived corruption of the so-called princes of the church (Bishops, Cardinals, and Popes). Hence, Martin Luther and John Calvin rejected the apostolic succession of the bishopric, which led to a major leadership paradigm shift for the Church. One of the results of this was seen as the Church moved towards a two-fold ministry gift function of the pastor and teacher.

Another reason for the decline of the Apostolic office could have been that believers did not see a need for evangelism. The lack of a missionary, apostolic mindset, to reach new territories and nations could have been due, in part, to the fact that most people were infant baptized and as a result felt that their salvation was secured. Consequently, the glue that held the church together, the apostolic governmental function of bishops and patriarchs, was now discarded in Protestantism. This resulted in mass fragmentation, which eventuated in millions of independent churches and over thirty thousand denominations.

One of the major tragedies that resulted was of the loss of unity within the Church. As a result, Christianity eventually lost its influence in the public square, which resulted in various forms of secular humanism. Such embrace of human philosophies continues to hold sway in the political, economic and educational spheres of life in contemporary culture.

What God Is Doing Today

I believe that the present embrace of the five-fold ministry of the evangelical pastors in the USA can catalyze a global convergence. Such convergence is possible amongst the charismatic churches, Independent Apostolic networks, Evangelical networks, and ultimately even Evangelical bible confessing denominations.

The implications of this will be extraordinary! Some snapshots as to the consequences of this paradigmatic shift include the following:

1. The church will go from being pastorally led to apostolically led and prophetically inspired. This restoration of apostolic function in church leadership would, of course, comport with the original design of the church by Jesus when He chose twelve apostles to lead the church. Curiously, until fairly recently, I did not notice what now appears to me to be an inherent inconsistency in what

I had been taught; Our ideal was the church led by the apostles, but supposedly, no such apostles were to be found in our churches today! Having accepted such a premise, it would then become clear that we could replicate the first century church today only if the apostles were a trivial or relatively insignificant component of first -century Christianity. No biblical scholar I know, however, would affirm that. Apostles were a recognized key to the vitality of the Early Church.[10]

2. This emerging apostolic paradigm will shift the missionary focus from planting local churches to planting movements of churches. These would produce Christ followers who would permeate every facet of society fulfilling the mandate Jesus gave to His followers in Acts 1:8,9.

3. The apostolic paradigm will shift the focus from gathering crowds on Sunday to developing disciples who will manifest the reign of Christ from Monday to Saturday! This is what Jesus intended when he commanded His followers to make disciples (Matthew 28:19). In addition, it follows the Pauline model as shown in 2 Timothy 2:2.

4. The present apostolic paradigm will restore the church back to "the way of Christ and His Apostles". I believe that as we head into the 21st century, the denominational and pastoral paradigmatic structures would inevitably collapse under the weight of their inability to sustain themselves further into the 21st century.

5. The present apostolic paradigm will bring a course correction to the so-called New Apostolic Reformation (NAR). The Apostolic will no longer be viewed as an office, or a title, but will be used as an adjective, as a ministry function. This is consistent with Paul, who himself did not use the word as a title. In the introductions in Paul's epistles, the word apostle was secondary to his name, "Paul, an apostle,"

hence, apostle was an adjective more than an office or title.

6. The present apostolic paradigm will correct the autocratic top-down hierarchical leadership seen within the so-called New Apostolic Reformation networks. This paradigm shift will institute the servant leadership style so perfectly displayed by Jesus, who came not to be served but to serve and give His life as a ransom for many (Mark 10:42-45). Jesus modeled the New Testament way of having influence with people. In John 13, we see this displayed when He wrapped a towel around His waist and washed the feet of His apostles. This is how the Church is supposed to lead. Paul embraced such servanthood, often referring to himself as a servant of God (Romans 1:1; Titus 1:1). This servant leadership model, which he expressed in his letters, served as essential teachings of the burgeoning New Testament church. One of the key phrases in the Didache of Paul was the amazing poetic passage found in Philippians 2:4-12 which called the church to emulate the servanthood model of Jesus.

7. The present apostolic paradigm will not spout triumphalist Dominion Theology rhetoric. Instead of making declarations such as, "The church is called to take cities" it will instead be, "The church is called to love and serve our cities!" When the "Cultural Mandate" of Genesis 1:28 was given to the first Adam, the earth was not populated with humans. It stands to reason that Adam was called to have "dominion" over the created order. However, it was never about having dominion over other humans, but rather to steward the land, as well as the plant and animal kingdom.

The truth is that those who are best at serving become the greatest problem solvers and inevitably, the greatest leaders. Paul said that the Church is called to do good to all men and serve as a benefactor community to the cities they reside in (Titus 2:14; 3:8).

20

The Ultimate Goal

God said that the five-fold ministry gifts of Ephesians 4:11 will continue until we all come to the unity of the faith.[11] Jesus said the world will not believe He was sent by the Father until the Church is united as one in Him (John 17:20-24). It seems to me that the greatest hope we have of seeing the church become one is for the broader Body of Christ to embrace the Apostolic function as described in the New Testament. Unfortunately, many remain strongly resistant to this idea. Those who are resistant to this concept argue that I'm being heretical because I am speaking about the restoration of a personality or ministry rather than continuing the historic witness of the church. Others would say it is heretical because the Scriptures alone are sufficient to continue the apostolic ministry. To them I would argue:

First, the apostolic function (as well as the others in Ephesians 4:11) is a ministry expression and/or gift from Christ Himself. Therefore, it is a function of His Body which is His church. It is not a separate entity or personality outside the church, although it is encased in an individual leader. The New Testament was not a nameless and faceless movement; God used individual apostolic leaders in an extraordinary way to plant churches. This is displayed in the way He used Paul in the nineteenth chapter of Acts. As we see in Galatians 2:1-10, the individual apostolic leader has no authority outside of the cooperation and affirmation of the New Testament church. Hence, his role as a "sent one" is a missional extension of the Church. He is called as a leader to fulfill the Great Commission (Matthew 28:19).

The book of Acts is a catechetical treatise, serving as a prescriptive narrative for the missions of the church. It, therefore, stands to reason that it should still be the pattern for the contemporary Church.

Second, the restoration of the Apostolic function is based on the New Testament pattern of church ministry. As such, its restoration is necessary to ensure that the Church continues to follow the Scriptures. The model and methods laid out in the New Testament in regard to the Apostolic office must be used to bring about the necessary coarse correction to certain historic streams of the church that have neglected or denied this biblical norm. So, I would argue that we who embrace the restoration of this ministry function are more biblically grounded than those who reject or neglect it.

Third, the apostolic function has historically been the glue that has held the Body of Christ together -which goes along with one of God's goals for apostolic function as found in Ephesians 4:13 which has to do with attaining the unity of the faith. We see a pertinent example of this function in church history when in 1054 A.D. the Western and Eastern church suffered a schism and the unity of local churches remained largely intact. However, after the Protestant Reformation in the 16th century, the church fragmented largely because it's leaders -Martin Luther and John Calvin, jettisoned the episcopate -which was the main church office that held the body of Christ together regionally and beyond. (Historically the office of Bishop and or the episcopate, was recognized by the church starting in the second century as the succesors of the apostles. consequently, 1500 years later the protestant church has over 30 thousand denominations!)

Let's pray that the full restoration of the church takes place. It is necessary so we can reach the nations with the gospel and hasten the bodily return of Jesus, who will come to unite all things in heaven and on earth in Him (Ephesians 1:9-11). May the Lord Jesus, who alone can build His church, continue to restore His bride back to the biblical pattern as demonstrated by His original apostles in the New Testament. Amen.

Chapter 1

The New Apostolic Age

In this chapter, I desire to give the reader a bird's eye view of the first century missional church and then I fast forward to the past several hundred years of evangelicalism to contextualize the roots of the modern apostolic age. This will help the reader see the continuity of how the Holy Spirit has been patiently working to restore His church back to the original way of Christ and His apostles.

Dr. Peter Wagner states,

> *The First Apostolic Age lasted for another 200 years after the first of the New Testament apostles concluded their ministry. This is not to say that the church of Jesus Christ or the kingdom of God went into some kind of hibernation for 1,800 years—it most certainly did not. The true Church has been with us down through the ages, sometimes larger, sometimes smaller, sometimes stronger, sometimes weaker. In Matthew 16:18, Jesus said, "I will build my church," and He has been doing so for over 2,000 years through God's people on Earth as they preach the gospel, make disciples, and set captives free!"* [12]

When we think of the new apostolic age, we immediately have to go back to the first century church in which Jesus commissioned twelve apostles to build His church. Hence, the church was apostolic, and missional in nature since the true meaning of apostle has to do with "being sent" which is where we get our understanding of missions.

Since that initial age in which local congregations were founded primarily by apostles (1 Cor. 12:28) the Body of Christ began to veer away from this seminal foundation and by the fourth century became very institutional -which eventually stifled her missional impetus.

The apostolic age walks in the way of Jesus as found in the Gospels.

The Lucan gospel account gives a framework for the entire Book of Acts. In the very first verse of Luke's narrative, he states that his first account was concerning "all that Jesus began to do and teach". Hence, by implication, the Acts story recorded what Jesus continued to do through the narrative that was about to unfold. As we continue in this second Lukan narrative in Acts, we find that the primary agency called of God to continue the mission of Jesus was the Church. Acts chapter two records the actual birth of the church. The implication of this is profound because in this we see that Jesus always had the Church in mind as a corporate body that would be the conduit to continue His work on the earth.

A cursory reading of the Gospels clearly demonstrates this point. In John 14:12, Jesus told His disciples that they would do greater works than Him after He ascends to the Father. He went on to say that it was to the disciples' advantage that He should go away so that He can send the Holy Spirit to them (John 16:7). So, instead of Jesus being with them, the Holy Spirit will be inside of them (John 14:7). This would then enable them to do greater works than Jesus. In addition, the Holy Spirit would teach them all things and bring all things Jesus taught them into remembrance.[13] As we read the Acts narrative, we see the words of Jesus fulfilled regarding how He would build His church (Matthew 16:16-17), which would be through the guidance, leading and empowerment of the Holy Spirit (John 16:13-15).

What about the parachurch model?

The implications of Acts 1 means that Jesus' plan of building His church cannot be fully realized in a Parachurch model. Therefore, there should be a course correction to this model, especially since one of its unfortunate downfalls is that it separates the Gospels from the Epistles in its hermeneutics. That is, it attempts to make disciples apart from the centrality of the local church. Some Parachurch proponents may argue that Jesus made disciples before the local church was birthed. However, when the New Testament is read contextually, Jesus always had the church in mind. This was demonstrated in that fact as He was making disciples, He told them ahead of time that they would successfully continue His mission only through the power of the Holy Spirit, which came AFTER the church was born. In addition, it is also imperative to understand that the Gospels were generally written after the Epistles. The Apostles gave the Gospels after the churches were established. The Gospels were necessary because it completed the task of giving the Church a comprehensive understanding of Jesus as the culmination of both Israel's history as well as Gentile History.

Hence, I contend that without the Gospels, we cannot have a complete understanding of the Epistles nor understand the purpose of the Church. The church is a principal-agent of God in the ongoing meta-narrative of creation, fall, Israel, redemption, and God's reign through His kingdom. These are all fulfilled and culminated in the life, death, and ascension of our Lord Jesus Christ and applied in the world through His church. For these reasons, it is necessary that we embrace a Christological Ecclesiology as the proper underpinning of the Acts narrative and Pauline epistles.

Having a Christological Ecclesiology

Recently I've come into a deeper understanding of the fact that the church is His body; we, as Believers, are an extension of Jesus on the earth. For the church to fulfill the mandate of the Great Commission, it is necessary to reinterpret the way the church is currently viewed. It must be presented because the Church is the body of Christ. Its primary goal is to extend the life and teachings of Jesus in and through the faith and practice of His people. Paul the apostle focused a lot of his attention on the finished work of the cross and its implications in the life of the believer.

Some debate about whether Paul spent significant time in matters pertaining to the ethical and practical implications of the individual Gospels. They question whether Paul addressed their effectiveness or lack thereof of unpacking them ecclesiologically. The fact is that passages such as Ephesians 3:9, in regard to the administration of the mystery, address how the household of God should behave itself in light of the gospel (1 Tim. 3:15). These are referred to as the Didache or teachings and translate in the application of the gospel (kerygma) to the church as the family of families, through what is called by many "the household texts." These household texts are found primarily in Paul's middle Epistles such as Philippians, Ephesians, Colossians.

Unfortunately, most believers, especially Protestants, believe that the Gospel is only about the last six hours on the cross and the implications of Jesus' resurrection. However, the Gospel encompasses more than this. When we examine Mark 1, we see it clearly stated that Jesus began preaching the Gospel of the Kingdom. This implies that the Gospel at this point could not be referring to Jesus' death, burial, and resurrection, rather, the Gospel was about Jesus presenting the good news to his hearers.

The truth is that Jesus was the fulfillment of all the Hebrew Scriptures. This included the grand narrative which brought clarity and answers to the purpose of creation, along with the solution to the fall. In addition, the Gospel is viewed considering Jesus as the representative King, as well as Israel's priest. Jesus is the one who conquered His foes and inaugurated His kingdom as Israel's King through His death, burial, and resurrection.

To summarize, the Gospel is the totality of the life of Jesus as foreshadowed in the narrative streams of the Old Testament. Such truth has huge implications not just for the individual Believer, but for the Church. One such implication is that Christological ecclesiology should be one of our primary focuses. It is imperative that we look at each chapter of the Gospels with the understanding that it is relevant with regard to the terms of church practice, thought, belief, etc. In Galatians 2:19-21, Paul states that He does not live anymore but it is Christ that lives in him. He adds that this new life is lived by faith in the God who loved Him and gave His life for Him. In Philippians 3:1-4, Paul said he counted all things dung so that he may attain Christ. This means that his whole life was consumed and hidden with God in Christ.

Paul also said in Romans 8:29-30, that the goal that God the Father had in choosing the church was that they might be conformed to the image of his son. In keeping with the Apostle Paul's example and admonitions, the Church must understand that any church program, leadership training, practice, or discipleship process that doesn't ultimately lead to Christlikeness will always be done in vain. It does not matter if a multitude of people participate, how successful it is or even if community transformation occurs, if people are not led into conformity to Christ, it will not have an everlasting impact. The plumbline for all ministry and discipleship must be Christlikeness, not merely political engagement, economic empowerment, or community development, etc.

If we focus on the latter, without the former, merely using Kingdom principles without presenting the King, the real transformation of the heart will fail to occur. One of the results of this is that leaders, especially Conservative/Christian leaders who espouse Christian principles, end up living double lives and fall into a scandal.

The Way of His Apostles

In Acts chapter 1, we see the apostles and disciples begin to veer off course from the mission, and instead begin to delve into a Geo-Political Zionist eschatology. They did not want to be the oppressed minority who had to suffer for the gospel (Acts 1: 6-7). They were more interested in avoiding more persecution, obtaining comfort, and becoming the elite who possessed political and economic power. When they asked Jesus, "Are you at this time going to restore the Kingdom to Israel?" (Acts 1:6 NIV), Jesus did not even bother getting into the minutia of their eschatological question. He neither refuted their question nor ignored them. Instead, he got them fixated back on the primary mission, calling and purpose of their apprenticeship under Him. Jesus responded to them and said "[Y]ou will receive power when the Holy Spirit has come upon you, and you shall be My witnesses both in Jerusalem, and in all Judea and Samaria, and even to the remotest part of the earth" (Acts 1:8).

It's important to point out that receiving power was related to being His witnesses. This verse serves to bring a slight course correction to my Pentecostal brothers and sisters related to their focus on speaking in tongues as proof of the Spirit empowerment. Jesus did not say that they would receive power to speak in tongues but to be His witnesses. The Church must correct the mistake of focusing on existential realities above the main mission and purpose laid out by Jesus.

Also, Jesus mentioned bringing the gospel to cities and nations as the focal point of the mission as opposed to the construction of church buildings to facilitate gospel activity. Unfortunately, the post-Constantine church, which faced no persecution, began to do just that. They began to shift their focus from the main mission to the erecting of huge cathedrals and edifices. Another culprit for the move away from the true mission was the semi-Gnostic bifurcation of sacred and secular places. This resulted in believers focusing on the church place to the exclusion of the workplace. As a result, the true vision of permeating cities and nations with the power of the gospel was dimmed. The Jesus mission was to be His witnesses in Jerusalem (not in the temple), Judea, Samaria, and to the "uttermost parts of the earth." The goal was the earth realm.

Jesus told the apostles to start with Jerusalem. This represented their surrounding community - those who shared similar geography, religion, language, and culture. This mandate challenged Christ-followers to first be a witness of the gospel to those we are already in close contact with them. Jerusalem represents a monocultural, monolingual, and homogeneous church in which the congregation reaches out first to those they have the most in common with.

From this, we learn that if we cannot be His witness in our own surroundings, how can we be His witness in other places beyond? Jerusalem also represents for us the fact that our local churches should serve and impact our community. The church should not just serve believers who congregate inside the safety of a building for two hours on a Sunday!

Unfortunately, the Jerusalem church did not obey the mandate to go beyond Jerusalem into Samaria and beyond. This resulted in God allowing persecution, which caused the disciples of Christ to be scattered which then led to the Word being preached beyond Jerusalem into Samaria and Antioch. This, in turn, led to the planting of new churches. The Samaritans, who were half Jewish and half Assyrian, were at enmity with the Jews in Jerusalem (2 Kings 17:24-41). Jesus's admonition to go to regions like Samaria indicates his expectation that the church would go beyond their familiar cultural and comfort zone. He desired for them to go from homogeneity to heterogeneity to further His mission. This indicates that Jesus always intended for the "church gathered" to be the "church scattered." When this is enacted, Christ and His ways can then permeate every village, town, hamlet, city, region, and nation.

The Judean mandate exemplifies this mission. One of the original Church's mandates was that it would have an extra local impact; the impact would be felt from their city to their surrounding region. Hence, the implication is that Jesus expected His people to continue to progress from one territory and culture to the next. This is in keeping with the "apostolic nature" of the church. A regional influence is an apostolic influence. The apostolic influence is not merely concerned with serving the primary flock and immediate community, which is the primary role of a pastor. Rather, the apostolic influence is supposed to expand into the surrounding region.

Jesus' mandate to go to the ends of the earth was challenging for the early church. Implicit in said command were two things. One was that the disciples where to go to heathen nations where pluralism reigned and where the Jewish religion and culture had minimal influence. Hence it was a call for the disciples to go way beyond their comfort zone; it was a call for them to go to those they had absolutely nothing in common with. The present-day Church must seek to apply this component of the command. The Church must understand the need to become cultural anthropologists. The Church today must study other cultures so that it can relate the gospel to the people groups of every ethnic group, tribe, kindred tongue, and nation.

The second implication of Jesus' mandate of going to all nations was that the early church had to continue the task of multiplying disciples and leaders. This had to be continued since the original twelve apostle and their followers would never have enough numbers to effectively plant Jesus' communities in every city of every nation of the world.

To understand the way of Christ and His apostles we must first understand that Acts 1:8 is a continuation of Luke 24:47-48 when Jesus commanded them to be His witnesses to all nations and to wait in Jerusalem until they are clothed with power from on high. Both Luke's Gospel and the Acts narrative were recordings of carefully selected events that would serve to be catechetical in nature for the instruction of new believers. That the church is to be missional in nature is shown by the literary markers of Acts. It shows the progress of the gospel in different cultures and contexts having to do with the word of the Lord multiplying and spreading. Hence, it should be noted that it is necessary to understand the catechetical purpose of the Acts narrative as it serves as a prescriptive record for both the progress of the Gospel and the establishment of the Church. Consequently, because Acts is prescriptive and not merely descriptive, it is a necessary blueprint for the Church for all succeeding generations.

We can also see by examining the pertinent key marker passages, how the Holy Spirit played a key role in each successive forward movement for the Church. It is interesting to note that Luke records only key components necessary for the future church to understand it's missional purpose. Luke does not get into extensive biographies of any of the apostles. Luke has little interest in the exact nature of church government in each locale where the gospel was planted. In addition, there is no specific order related to how a person gets saved, filled with the Spirit, and how a church should be planted. Every church community was founded and functioned in different ways. What always stays the same though, was that the message of the Gospel (kerygma) and its application in

the teachings (Didache) were always centered around the person of
Christ and His Kingdom.

Consequently, the Acts narrative was to serve as a model for
the Body of Christ based on the overall picture given as it did not
give specific illustrations for any one church, ethnic group or city.

The Catechetical Element of the Acts Narrative and the Establishment of the Church

At the very beginning of the book, we see the progressive
nature of new converts. They went from being noted as those who
were "added to the church" or called "believers" to be categorized
as disciples. For example, we see in the sermon the apostle Peter
preached on the Day of Pentecost that those who received his word
and saved weren't yet called disciples. Acts 2:41 (ESV) says "So
those who received his word were baptized, and there were added
that day about three thousand souls," Acts 2:47 (paraphrased) it
says, "the Lord added to their number day by day those who were
being saved" and Acts 5:14 says, "And more than ever believers
were added to the Lord, multitudes of both men and women."
Worth noting is that Luke did not refer to any of the believers as
disciples up until this point. It was not until Acts chapter 6:7 where
we begin to see some increase in the leadership team and where
the word disciples is introduced: "And the word of God continued
to increase, and the number of the disciples multiplied greatly in
Jerusalem, "

From Believers to Disciples...

How did they go from being mere believers to becoming disciples?
Acts 2:42 illustrated that to be a disciple they had to submit to a
pattern of living and teaching, "And they devoted themselves to the
apostles' teaching and the fellowship, to the breaking of bread and
to prayer." This is a clear pattern for the making of disciples. Hence,

the early church, unlike our contemporary "attractional church model", did not merely attract crowds, but converts were submitted to a process whereby they could become committed disciples of the Lord. The fact is that Jesus built the church on Disciples, the apostles did the same, therefore, we must do the same.

The Apostles Made Disciples...

The pattern shown in Acts 2:42 reveals that the apostles made disciples in smaller groups (house to house). This is in line with what Paul commanded Timothy to do based on the Jesus model of setting apart 12 to be with Him as His disciple/apostles (Mark 3:13-15).

Jesus Made Disciples...

Jesus said to those He handpicked, "Follow me and I will make you to become fishers of men" (Mark 1:17). The key phrase here "to become" implies a process. It stands to reason that Jesus expects our churches to be process driven. This process includes the foundational discipleship elements such as teaching, accountability, small groups, and doing life together. This passage also speaks to the importance of accountability. It reveals the need for another person to speak into the life of his disciple. This must be done in the context of community, without which an individual's spiritual formation would be hindered. Jesus called his followers disciples. Jesus exemplified what this can look like, as He has a community of His disciples who sat under him as students. Today's leaders must model this Jesus method of disciple-making. Leaders must be careful to invest in only those who are serious enough to warrant them investing their time and resources into them.

The Way of The Apostles Regarding the Making of a Disciple

Paul instructed his protégé, Timothy, the attitudinal and capacity criteria for selecting a potential disciple to invest in. 2 Timothy 2:1-7 (ESV) says:

You then, my child, be strengthened by the grace that is in Christ Jesus, and what you have heard from me in the presence of many witnesses entrust to faithful men, who will be able to teach others also. Share in suffering as a good soldier of Christ Jesus. No soldier gets entangled in civilian pursuits since his aim is to please the one who enlisted him. An athlete is not crowned unless he competes according to the rules. It is the hard-working farmer who ought to have the first share of the crops. Think over what I say, for the Lord will give you understanding in everything."

Discipleship is tough. Disciples have to have the attitude and diligence of a soldier, athlete, and hard-working farmer. They also have to be faithful, capable, and able to communicate the gospel clearly to others.

Paul the Apostle Made Disciples...

Paul did not initially set out to plant churches but to plant the gospel by making disciples.

When the Apostle Paul entered new territory, he either looked for disciples and or made disciples. Acts 19:1 says, "And it happened that while Apollos was at Corinth, Paul passed through the inland country and came to Ephesus. There he found disciples.

Paul's Methodology for Establishment

Acts 14:21-23, 28 (ESV), illustrates the methodology Paul used to plant churches by first making disciples. "When they had preached the gospel to that city and had made many disciples, they returned to Lystra and to Iconium and to Antioch, strengthening the souls of the disciples, encouraging them to continue in the faith, and saying that through many tribulations we must enter the kingdom of God. And when they had appointed elders for them in every church, with prayer and fasting they committed them to the Lord in whom they had believed...when they arrived and gathered the church together, they declared all that God had done with them, and how he had opened a door of faith to the Gentiles. And they remained no little time with the disciples."

It seems like the basic pattern Paul used regarding the establishment of churches was:

1. Whenever he entered a city, he preached the gospel and either found or made disciples.
2. He planted a church community, based on his discipleship pattern, from the disciples he made.
3. He chose certain mature men to be elders whom he set as overseers of the church.
4. He left the church in the care of these elders and planted another church in a new city (usually a key strategic city of influence).
5. The churches he founded partnered in the gospel with him by supporting him financially and sending key representatives to accompany him on his apostolic missions (Philippians 1:5 and 4:14-19 regarding financial support and Philippians 2:25-30 related to ministerial support).
6. He then visited these churches again to see how they were doing (Acts 15:36).

If he could not personally see them, he would send a member of his apostolic team to be with them and help strengthen them in their faith (1 Thessalonians 3:1-6).

Generally, we see the Pauline pattern repeat itself in every city and in every one of his missionary trips. The Ephesian church planted other churches in Asia Minor (Acts 19; Revelation 2-3). The Corinthian Church was used by Paul as a hub of influence to reach the regions beyond (Acts 18:1-11; 2 Corinthians 10:12-18). The Thessalonian church sounded out the word of the Lord to all of Macedonia and Achaia (Acts 17:1-9; 1 Thessalonians 1:7-8). This pattern, to evangelize cities, make disciples, plant new churches, set in elders to oversee each of the churches, connect each of the churches through key churches in strategic cities, (like Ephesus, who became hubs of influence and church planting throughout their region) was paramount in the continuation of the establishment of Christ's Kingdom.

This stands in stark contrast with many of today's Church leaders, whose focus is on planning huge events, planting more churches divorced from the hard work of disciple-making. The fact is that when the goal is to merely plant a church, the main objective would be to gather a big crowd and build big buildings to house the masses. However, if the goal is to make disciples, then the focus would be to create a Jesus community whose goal would be to establish Christ's Kingdom and not man's. This community would inevitably become a significant church whose culture would be based on discipline, love, service, and missions.

The Apostles Brought Together the *Kerygma* and the *Didache*

Throughout the Book of Acts, we see how the *Kerygma* and the *Didache* were necessary for the establishment of the churches. In Acts 10:34-38 Peter preached the gospel (*kerygma*) to a group of Gentiles gathered in the home of Cornelius. Peter's sermon in Acts 2 and Paul's sermon in Acts 13 (both to Jewish people), where very similar in content. In Acts 11:26 we see that the apostles taught the believers for an entire year (*Didache*). The apostles rigorously protected the Gospel and its application in the *Didache*, as well as the unity of their movement of churches. This was demonstrated in the Jerusalem Council in Acts 15. The apostles and the first-century church were so successful in regard to spreading the Gospel, that Paul was able to say that it went to all of the known worlds in his lifetime (Colossians 1:6).

Some historians have estimated that by A.D. 100, the gospel had spread to nearly every Roman Province and region. Up until A.D. 50, the focal point of the church was Jerusalem and Samaria, however, within the next 50 years, the major concentration of the church was in Rome and Ephesus. The primary way the gospel spread was no longer the synagogue or the temple (Acts 1-6), but through house churches (Colossians 4:15; Romans 16:5; Acts 20:20).

Regarding the Apostle Paul, who was the focus of the Acts narrative (after chapter 11), he seemed to have a strategic plan of preaching the gospel to all the major cities and regions within his reach. We see this with a culmination of him reaching Rome through Spain (Romans 15:19-23). It is no accident that the Book of Acts ends with Paul in a Roman prison, preaching the gospel unhindered (28:30-31).

In summary, the church that was founded on the Day of Pentecost, obeyed the mandate given by Jesus in Acts 1:8-9, by going into all the known world. They accomplished this impossible task of reaching the world. Their strategy was not to set up bible colleges, mission agencies, and para-church organizations, but by making Spirit-empowered disciples who would form strong, established local churches. These local churches would unite and form complex apostolic networks with resourcing from stronger hub churches in strategic cities. The local churches would also remain connected with the founding apostles by financially supporting them and sending them men to serve as co-laborers on their missionary teams.

Through this pattern of apostolic connection, each congregation would always ensure that they would retain a global focus even though the church had a local focus. Vice versa, the apostolic leaders, like Paul, ensured that they retained their local influence by setting up church elders, while they continued their global missionary endeavors of spreading the gospel. As a result, the churches continued to exist after the earthly departure of the original apostles because they successfully passed the baton of leadership to the elders they chose from among the disciples (Acts 20:17-34). Also, Paul kept his legacy alive by instructing two of his primary apostolic protégés, as evidenced in his later epistles (1 and 2nd Timothy and Titus).

The Explosion of the Present-day Apostolic movement

Since the year 2000, men like Dr. C. Peter Wagner and David Cartledge have taught and written extensively concerning the huge shift the Body of Christ was made from a denominational (institutional) pastoral paradigm to a restoration of the New Testament Apostolic paradigm. Wagner also said, "My term for the new wineskin that God has provided for these churches is the "New Apostolic Reformation." It is a "reformation" because we are currently witnessing the most radical change in the way of "doing church" since the Protestant Reformation. It is "apostolic" because the recognition of the gift and office of the apostle is the most radical of a whole list of changes from the old wineskin. And it is "new" to distinguish it from several older traditional church groups that have incorporated the term "apostolic" into their official name.[14]

The Roots and History of The Modern Pentecostal Apostolic Movement

Since 1948 there has been a shift in the Church to rediscover the fivefold ministry gifts as evidenced in Ephesians 4:11. In this chapter, we will trace the history of this movement to our present Apostolic movement.

A brief overview of the roots of the Contemporary Apostolic movement:

The Importance of Pietism

In my reading of church history, it is evident to me that the root theological and methodological movement that eventuated in the rise of modern-day Evangelicalism and Pentecostalism was the Pietistic movement.[15] The Pietist subscribed to the teachings that said that every person had to have a personal, inner relationship with God. In addition, they had to have a witness of the Holy Spirit, which ensured that one was truly converted. This teaching was revolutionary in its day because it flew in the face of the formal, dry, Lutheran traditions which were focused on creeds, confessions, and catechisms. It also went against the belief that a person was born into the church by virtue of their parents' Church affiliation.

Consequently, Pietism was birthed in a time when the burden for missions[16] was non-existent as well as the lack of a large scale understanding of experiential faith. One of their students of Pietism was Nikolaus, Ludwig Count von Zinzendorf, (1700-1760). Count Zinzendorf was a person of wealth and prestige. He allowed persecuted Christian refugees to stay at his Herrnhut estate. At Herrnhut, the Spirit of the Lord fell as these persecuted Christians began to pray. This praying community of Brethren served as the impetus for a prayer meeting that lasted 100 years. Zinzendorf saw himself as a person continuing in the tradition of John Hus. His movement eventually became equated with the Moravian movement. This movement helped launch the modern Protestant missionary movement.

John Wesley

The Moravians had a direct impact on the First Great Awakening. John Wesley (1703-1791) and Charles Wesley (1707-1788 who wrote about 6500 hymns), as well as their friend George Whitfield (1714-1770), were used by God through their mass open-air preaching crusades to start a revival in England and in the 12 Colonies of the New World. Wesley recorded in his journal on January 25th, 1736, while on a storm-tossed ship headed to America about his observation of these German believers. He remarked that whilst the English passengers were screaming for fear of dying in the story, these Moravians were the only ones who exhibited no fear. In fact, they even sang hymns to God. The faith and behavior of the disciples of the Moravian movement directly made a lasting impact on John Wesley. Two years later, while attending a Moravian led meeting in London, Wesley had a personal encounter with His Savior.

John Wesley, and George Whitefield and Jonathan Edwards[17] were similar to the Pietists of Hernhut, in that they were not focused on the historic Creeds, Councils, rituals and church tradition. Rather, these revivalists were focused on seeing the Holy Spirit work in the hearts of individuals to bring about the conversion or "born again" experience.

In addition, there were many other moves of the Holy Spirit during this Awakening. These revivals would be shown to be the precursor to the Pentecostal revival that was to take place approximately 160 years later.

Interestingly, there are major points of similarity between the present charismatic renewal and the original American revival. Both movements were characterized by ecstatic spiritual experiences and unusual physical reactions to the power of the Holy Spirit. Being "slain in the Spirit", as Charismatics would call it today, was quite common in the Awakening. In both revivals, participants reported they had seen visions and felt that God had actually spoken to them...many among the clergy disdained and discredited such claims.[18]

Out of this Awakening came an incredible Apostolic movement of itinerant evangelists like Francis Asbury. Asbury used small groups to make disciples who then spread the Gospel all over the North American continent. After a spiritual lull, the Second Great Awakening burst upon the USA; Evangelist Charles Finney led this Awakening. While Finney continued in the tradition of the Pietists and Wesleyans, he initiated new measures, which the Church uses today. For instance, he instituted the "altar call" so that the sinner could demonstrate his new commitment to God. The impact of the First and Second Great Awakening brought significant moves of the Holy Spirit. The Methodist movement, with its focus on evangelism, discipleship, and holiness, birthed the Holiness movement. Such varied moves of the Spirit of God paved the birthing of the Pentecostal movement in the early 20th century.

Pentecostalism: The Birth of Modern Day Pentecostalism

"The Pentecostal and Charismatic movements in all their multifaceted variety probably constitute the fastest growing churches within Christianity today. According to often quoted controversial and undoubtedly inflated estimates, there were over 600 million adherents worldwide in 2010 found in almost every country in the world."[19]

The worldwide genesis of the more modern growth of Pentecostalism came in the early 1900s. "Historians often trace the origins of Pentecostalism in the American context to a revival that began on January 1st, 1901, at Charles F. Parham's Bethel Bible School in Topeka Kansas. [20]" It was here where the baptism of the Holy Spirit with the evidence of speaking in tongues fell on many of the students, spreading to others who came seeking the

Parham's ministry. Parham began traveling and ministering about the infilling of the Holy Spirit. He moved to Houston, Texas where he started a school.

One of the people directly impacted by Parham's ministry was William Seymour. Seymour was an African American preacher who preached Holiness. Seymour attended Parham's school and became "convinced of the truth of Parham's teachings on Spirit baptism.[21] Seymour took this teaching back to Los Angeles, to his Azusa Street Mission, a dilapidated building on Azusa Street in Los Angeles. As a result, revival broke out and the Mission and it became a hub of revival with demonstrations of the evidence of the Holy Spirit. "The ensuing revival at the Azusa Street Mission (1906-1909) represented an anomaly on the American religious scene. Blacks, Whites, and Hispanics worshipped together."[22] As a result of this massive demonstration of the power of God, "news of the 'outpouring' of the Holy Spirit spread across the nation and around the world"[23]

Unfortunately, in the same way, the Wesley brothers and George Whitfield were shunned by the Anglican Church for their unorthodox methods, Pentecostals, like Parham and Seymour, were initially shunned by the other Denominations. As a result, a new Pentecostal Denomination was birth. Some of the several denominations that arose were: The Assemblies of God; The Church of God and the Church of God in Christ. Unfortunately, some of these denominations eventually became divided along the lines of ethnicity.

Historical Movements Leading to the Present Apostolic Movement

"The Second Apostolic Age is a phenomenon of the twenty-first century. My studies indicate that it began around the year 2001."[24] In this section, I will refer the reader to the extensive research that's been done by others with regards to the past movements which have all contributed to the present-day Apostolic movement. We will briefly examine such movements as: The African Independent Churches; The Chinese House Churches; The Latin American Grassroots Churches; The U.S. Independent Charismatic Movement; The Latter Rain Movement; The Latter Rain Influence Roots of the Present Apostolic Movement.

The African Independent Churches: When one observes the contemporary African Independent churches, one can observe some functioning expressions of the Apostolic office amongst them. When missionaries first went to Africa, they brought with them a Gospel that was fashioned within their European context, "The first churches planted by Western missionaries throughout Africa closely resembled the churches back home in Europe that had sent the missionaries. They looked and functioned much like the churches of the German Lutherans, the British Anglicans, the Swiss Reformed, the New England Congregationalists, and others."[25]

However, it was a matter of time before the African believer's embrace of the Christian faith would take on an expression that was different from their European brothers, "As the second generation of Christian believers in these churches matured, they became aware of a lack of contextualization in the teachings coming from the pulpit. Consequently, many of them separated from these mission churches of their parents and birthed independent churches that not only put an emphasis on theological context but were also more compatible with African culture."[26] As a result, these new churches grew exponentially, taking on more of an Apostolic nature, "Governmentally, these African Independent Churches were apostolic in nature, although the title "apostle" was not uniformly employed. The subsequent growth of these churches has far outpaced that of "the traditional churches of the region.[27]

The Chinese House Churches. The phenomenal Chinese House Church Movement began when Chairman Mao's Cultural Revolution ended in 1975. Over the ensuing decades, the movement has produced an evangelistic harvest of epochal proportions. Some estimate that 10 percent of the Chinese are now believers, in spite of a government that is almost violently anti-Christian. These churches also operate in apostolic government, though they've only recently begun using the title.[28]

The Latin American Grassroots Churches. "Around 1980, the growth of the evangelical (a.k.a. Protestant) movement in Latin America began to increase exponentially, due to the emergence of grassroots megachurches in most Latin American metropolitan areas. These churches, of 3,000 to 10,000 members or more, are pastored by individuals who typically have had no personal mentoring from foreign missionaries and have never attended traditional seminaries or Bible institutes. Many of these pastors were called to plant churches while they held positions in the business world. These churches are completely integrated within the Latin American culture and are led apostolically."

The U.S. Independent Charismatic Movement.

As an offshoot of the Pentecostal Movement, independent charismatic churches began to multiply in the United States around 1970. "One of the major differences between the two was that Pentecostal churches were usually committed to democratically-based church government, whereas independent charismatic churches were apostolic in nature. By the mid-1980s the charismatic churches had become the fastest growing in America.[29]

The Latter Rain Movement

The Latter Rain movement constituted an important development and turning point for post World War II

Evangelicalism. This movement originated at Sharon Bible School in North Battleford, Saskatchewan, Canada. As many of the students gathered to pray and fast, an explosion of revival took place among many of them. As this outbreak of the Holy Spirit occurred, it started to spread outside that region. Myrtle Beall, pastor of Bethesda Missionary Temple in Detroit, Michigan attended the meetings in Canada and brought the revival back to her church. Another way in which the Latter Rain movement spread across the world was through a publication called "The Feast of Tabernacles" by George Warnock. Many looked to it for God-inspired insight, which provided the context of their movement. In addition to the publication, Elim Missionary Assemblies, associated with Elim Bible Institute, carried on the primary teachings of the Latter Rain movement.[30]

The Latter Rain Movement was characterized by many of the same spiritual phenomena of the early century Pentecostal awakening. The movement was marked by speaking in tongues, gifts of healings, as well as strong anticipation regarding the soon Second Coming of the Lord Jesus. It also introduced a new style of "singing songs in the spirit", and "prophetic presbytery" (when a group of prophetic elders prays over an individual to give them the "word of the Lord"). It espoused an understanding that the Kingdom of God manifests itself through supernatural power that should be demonstrated on earth. There was a strong emphasis on "the fivefold ministry" (a belief in all five ministry gift functions as mentioned in Ephesians 4:12). This became the precursor to the Charismatic Movement and the present-day Apostolic movement.

"[T]he charismatic Movement was an extension and an expansion of the Latter Rain movement. The Pentecostal movement was the early rain being poured out at the beginning of the end of the age of the mortal church. The Laying on of Hands movement was the Latter Rain of the last century church. The charismatic movement was symbolic of the outpouring of the former rain in the latter rain in the first month Joel chapter 2:23. All of the truths that have been restored since the beginning of the period of the great restoration have been propagated by the Charismatic Movement.[31]

The Latter Rain Influence Roots of the Present Apostolic Movement

Dr. Bill Hamon observes that while the Latter Rain Movement did not morph into one particular denomination, its influence is obvious in many thousands of local churches.[32]

"To this Present time there has been no denomination formed out of the latter rain movement. There are fellowships, ministerial Associations, and evangelistic associations. Because of the strong teachings regarding local churches, each congregation is autonomous and Self Incorporated with no legal or doctrinal ties with other local churches."

Dr. Peter Wagner, the father of the so-called New Apostolic Reformation movement, makes some observations about the Latter Rain Movement and other similar Movements, ("terms such as 'Latter Rain,' 'Restorational Movement,' 'Deliverance Evangelism' and 'Shepherding Movement' were used")[33] during that time period.

"In North America, God began to open doors for the emergence of the apostles of the Second Apostolic Age right after World War II. It was around that time when some churches began to recognize the office of apostle." However, he notes that those Movements were not able to materialize. "The leaders of those movements had great expectations that what they had started would reform the entire Church in their generation. But it didn't happen. The majority of those post-World War II movements of God no longer exist today; and those that do, have relatively little influence."[34]

However, it stands to reason that those movements were the impetus that God used to usher in the Reformation of the Apostolic office.

Kevin Connor who passed away in February 2019, was one of the primary theologians and scholars of the burgeoning Apostolic movement of the mid-20th century. He was greatly influenced by the Latter Rain teachings.[35] Connor's books personally impacted me in that they became the foundation for my understanding of the New Testament and Apostolic movement.

Some of these books are: *The Church in the New Testament*; *Foundations of Christian Doctrine*; *The Tabernacle of Moses and The Tabernacle of David*.

In summary, although "apostolic function" has been taking place throughout church history, the recognition and intentionality of moving towards an apostolic paradigmatic shift began to gain a lot of steam starting in the Latter Rain movement of the late 1940s.

Since then, there has been a major shift underway in the Evangelical church towards the embrace of all of the five ministry gifts mentioned in Ephesians 4:11. That being said, it is important that we understand more fully the biblical view of apostolic function. It is essential for us to embrace this gift since the future of Global church expansion is going to be dependent upon it.

Consequently, in our next chapter, we will explore the Apostolic function. This is necessary for the reader to understand in order to apply the principles found in this book and to walk out the way of Christ and His apostles.

QUESTIONS TO ASK YOURSELF ABOUT THIS CHAPTER

1. How would you define the new apostolic age?

2. What are some of the historical evangelical roots of the contemporary apostolic movement?

3. Who were some of the prominent leaders in early evangelicalism?

4. What connection does the early 20th century Pentecostal movement have with the new apostolic age?

5. What are some of the global movements that have contributed to present day apostolic function?

6. What was the "Latter Rain" movement and what did it contribute to the present apostolic age?

Chapter 2

Understanding the Biblical View of Apostolic Function

In this chapter, I will debunk some contemporary objections to present day Apostolic ministry- show some of the misuses of the ministry of "apostle" as well as illustrate some differences between true and false apostolic function. I also show vast differences in philosophy as it relates to building the local church according to contemporary models, historic denomination models, and the biblical model of the apostolic church.

Debunking Opposition to Apostolic Ministry Today

Throughout the years there has been much opposition to the restoration of Apostolic ministry. Having been educated in non-charismatic Bible institutes and universities, I have a very good understanding of those who misunderstand the global restoration of the fivefold ministry gifts as seen in Ephesians 4:11. As a result, The so-called New Apostolic Reformation (NAR) has received some critical analysis from various leaders in the Body of Christ. Such a critique of the NAR is much needed and important.

One valuable resource that I recommend is a book written by two solid Christian scholars, R. Douglas Geivett and Holly Pivec. The helpful book, "A New Apostolic Reformation? gives honest and scholarly insights into the high-profile NAR leaders, while examining their teachings. Whether a person agrees with the book's conclusions or not, it behooves all those related in some way to the so-called NAR, to examine their critiques in light of Scripture. Such examination is necessary as any move, old or new, within the Body of Christ, should always seek to comport biblically and recalibrate when necessary. Some of the concerns and topics that Geivett and Pivec write about include whether the Apostolic is an office, Spiritual warfare, the 7 Mountain mandate, and the Prophetic office. I will examine some of these below.

Is the Apostolic an office or a function?

Some in the NAR are calling the ministry of Apostle a present-day church office instead of a function. Geveit and Pivec agree with the official definition of the Assemblies Of God:

[T]he AG governing body holds that many people in the church today fulfill the ongoing 'ministry functions' of apostles. It allows for individual Assemblies of God churches to identify certain leaders as 'Apostles' provided they recognize that those leaders are not equal in authority to the original 'foundational apostles.' It argues that the foundational apostles were commissioned directly by the risen Lord not only to preach the gospel, as present day apostles do, but also to perform specific, unique roles in founding the church, including overseeing the writing of Scripture.[36]

I would agree with their perspective on this matter. Regarding the use of the word "Office" to describe the apostolic ministry, I would suggest that some clarification be brought to this. Those who are against the term "Office" are concerned because of the confusion it elicits as it seems to refer to Acts 1:20. The original group of 12 Apostles' use of the term as an "Office" was understandable because they were the pillars of the Body of Christ for the ensuing future (Ephesians 2:20). However, even if this particular passage in Acts (which is quoted from Psalms), referred to the apostolic as an "Office", I would argue that it should be used as a function and not an office, since that is how the N.T. seemed to define it. (Paul was referred to as "an apostle-not the "apostle Paul". See Galatians 1:1; Romans 1:1;1 Corinthians 1:1)

Strategic Level Spiritual Warfare

Another area of agreement I have with Geivett and Pivec is their concern when it comes to the practice of Strategic Level Spiritual Warfare within the NAR. "Strategic level spiritual warfare is the act of confronting powerful evil spirits that are believed to rule specific geographical regions, cultural groups, and societal institutions. These spirits are called "territorial spirits" because they control different territories or cultural spheres."[37] The belief is that these spirits must be demolished over a city or region in order to see a release of the power of God over the said location. It is common for many intercessors in the so-called NAR to identify and name principalities and powers ruling over a city. If this is accomplished through prayer, "Then entire nations of people will respond en masse to the gospel and the church will read the greatest harvest of souls in history."[38] Practices such as spiritual mapping are also used, "Spiritual mapping is the practice of researching a specific city or nation to discover the ways territorial spirits hinder the spread of the gospel in that particular geographical region."[39]

Personally, I have never agreed with this teaching, even after reading numerous books and attending countless conferences where this was taught. For one, I have never read one instance in the Scripture where any of the Apostles prayed against a principality by name.

It is true that many instances of evil spirits being cast out were recorded in the Scriptures. Jesus and the Apostles dealt with demonic entities that possessed individuals. For instance, Jesus named a spirit of infirmity when He healed a lady as noted in Luke 13; Jesus also cast out a legion of demons as we see in Mark chapter 5; Paul the Apostle cast out a spirit of divination as we see in Acts 16, etc. However, there are no New Testament Scriptures that indicate any of these demons were the kind of high-level principalities that influenced nations and empires, as we observe in Daniel chapters 10-12.

In the New Testament, Jesus and the Apostles primarily focused on preaching the gospel of the Kingdom, planting churches and casting out demons. As a result, we observe that eventually, the whole city and surrounding regions were transformed. In the narrative shown in Acts 19:27, there is no indication that Paul focused on confronting the ruling principality (which seemed to be the goddess, Artemis) of the city.

Jesus sent His disciples out to preach the gospel door to door and heal the sick. Even when Jesus said He saw Satan fall like lightning from heaven, there was not one commandment from Jesus to name demonic deities and pray against them. The practice of naming principalities and warring against them in intercession, as the so-called NAR teaches, was not employed by the disciples of Jesus, yet the power of the devil was broken over the cities as the disciples preached the Gospel (Luke 10:1-20).

Proponents of Strategic Level Spiritual Warfare often cite Paul's statement in Ephesians 6:12, where he states that "we wrestle not against flesh and blood but against principalities." They point to that as evidence that Paul engaged in high-level demonic entities directly. However, there is nothing in the text, nor in the letter to the Ephesians, nor in the Acts 19 narrative of the birth of the Ephesian church, that comports with their methodology of naming and resisting principalities and powers directly.

I tend to agree with the authors' conclusions that practicing strategic spiritual warfare the way their NAR brothers do is not something that the Body of Christ needs to embrace, "We see no indication that Christians have been given the authority or responsibility to engage territorial spirits directly..."Since there is no biblical basis for confronting territorial spirits directly, there also is no basis for spiritual mapping projects that seek to aid such confrontations through the identification of territorial spirits."[40]

It should be noted that the authors are not against spiritual mapping per se, or those who seek to only identify ruling spirits in a region. The task of spiritual mapping is a simple attempt to create spiritual profiles of cities and nations to provide a guide to pray.[41]

The 7 Mountains Mandate

Another common term used within the so-called NAR is the "7 Mountains". This refers to the major societal structures that have the most influence in shaping the heart of a nation. The NAR movement preaches that Christians must get involved in influencing these structures, "Many NAR apostles and prophets claim that God has revealed a new strategy for advancing God's Kingdom, a strategy they call the "Seven Mountain Mandate. According to this revelation, the way to take dominion is by taking control of the seven most influential societal institutions called "mountains," which are identified as government, media, family, business, education, church, and the arts."[42] The NAR teaches that because said institutions "are presently dominated by secular humanists and other opinion leaders who do not share God's values,"[43] it's imperative for Christians to become involved and infiltrate such institutions with their Christian values, "The church must take control of them if its to fulfill its mandate to advance God's kingdom."[44]

Many of the proponents of this mandate (several of these leaders are my friends), often focus on influencing politics and economics with a top-down strategy. Scholar and author, James Davison Hunter, in his significant book "To Change The World", says that culture will not shift unless and until the gatekeepers of society change.[45] He believes that problems can be taken care of more rapidly with a top-down approach. He advocates what he calls the "faithful presence" of the church based on God's command to Israel in exile as found in Jeremiah 29.

Personally, I don't necessarily subscribe to the top-down approach strategy for the church. I don't believe the best and quickest way for the church to demonstrate power is by leading in the political arena. When too much focus is put on politics, I've discovered that half of the country, as well as the Church, becomes alienated from each other. The fallout and division that arise when political affiliation is noted often presents a hindrance to many from receiving the Gospel from those who don't agree with them politically.

I believe the best way the Christian leader or pastor should approach the political issue is to teach biblical principles as it relates to the pertinent issues, allowing the listeners to come to their own conclusions. However, there may be times where a Church leader will have to be more outspoken on an issue. For instance, when a political candidate/official has blatantly opposed such things as free speech, traditional marriage or the sanctity of life, it may warrant a Christian leader to make a stance against this (especially right before an election). I believe that word of caution with regards to the 7 Mountain Mandate (7MM) is necessary. The Church should not view it as a doctrine. Rather it must be viewed as a strategy or a methodology in how to effectively reach a city or nation through the Christ-like principles of servanthood.

I fully embrace the truth that Christians should function as Salt and Light (Matthew 5:13-16) in the communities. They should be involved in various institutions, effectively working towards influencing and changing laws that would reflect the 10 Commandments or the Judeo/Christian worldview. I believe that the most effective way this can be accomplished is when each Christ follower begins to make disciples within their particular "people group". As this discipleship process is replicated, we will see more disciples of Christ who are able to walk out their God given purpose. If a disciple happens to hold a powerful position in politics, business, economics, education, science, music, arts, and entertainment, then they should spread the gospel and make disciples among their peers and spheres of influence. In that way, there is a concomitant movement of both a "top-down" and "bottom-up" effect that is Gospel focused and not politically focused.

The confusion among many adherents of the 7MM is that their view of "discipling nations" (the literal translation of Matthew 28:19 is making disciples among the nations"), is based on the current understanding of nation-states. This understanding comes out of a geo/political construct that is only about 500 years old.

The nation-state developed fairly recently. Prior to the 1500s, in Europe, the nation-state as we know it did not exist. Back then, most people did not consider themselves part of a nation; they rarely left their village and knew little of the larger world. If anything, people were more likely to identify themselves with their region or local lord. At the same time, the rulers of states frequently had little control over their countries. Instead, local feudal lords had a great deal of power, and kings often had to depend on the goodwill of their subordinates to rule. Laws and practices varied a great deal from one part of the country to another.[46]

Consequently, the historically contextual meaning of a nation in this passage has more to do with "people groups", tribes, and ethnic peoples. Given this meaning, this allows for a more granular approach in which people are released to make disciples in their own subcultures, as opposed to tackling a whole geo/political system all at once! The Geo/political view of disciplining nations is out of context with what Jesus was referring to in Matthew 28:19. Understanding the Great Commission to mean disciplining contemporary nations compels adherents of 7MM to tackle politics and economics first before any other cultural sphere since that is the quickest way to fulfill this command.

Geivett and Pivec point out that some Evangelical ministries not connected to the NAR have joined forces with NAR with the goal to influence culture by the use of the 7MM strategy. However, they note that "many of these organizations have adopted what appears to be a much-toned down version of the Seven Mountain Mandate. The toned-down version teaches that Christians must exert influence in seven societal institutions if they are to complete the Great Commission. It does not teach however, that workplace apostles must cast out territorial spirits that control these institutions."[47]

Again, I go back to the methodology and attitude as espoused in the teachings of Paul in his Epistles. Paul admonishes the church to do good to all men (Galatians 6:10), not just saved men. He also admonishes them to be committed to do good works for the profit of all men (Titus chapters 2,3). The focus is on doing good works for the community as a witness of Christ to the unbelieving world (Titus 2:10). When the church truly makes Christ following disciples, they will automatically impact their particular subcultures and spheres of influence. I believe that if this is fully embraced by the Church, entire communities can be turned upside down (Acts 17:6).

The Prophetic Office

Since the prophetic is not the focus of my book, I will share briefly regarding this topic.

Geivett and Pivec have raised concerns related to the practice and teaching of some identified as NAR prophets. Broadly speaking, one of their major concerns about NAR is that they refer to the person operating in the prophetic as a one who holds an "office", referring to them as operating in the "Office of the Prophet". Geivett and Pivec point out that this bestows a binding governmental office upon prophets in the contemporary church. They do not believe that prophets in the Old and New Testament functioned in a governmental position that warrants the term "Office of a Prophet." Again, I'm inclined to agree with Geivett and Pivec. Personally, I prefer to use the word prophet as a function or description more than a title.

Another criticism of many contemporary prophets surrounds their use of certain terms to label their prophetic utterance like "present truth" or "new revelation". Those terms often imply that those prophets' words are binding on the whole church to the same degree as the Scripture is. Neither I nor any prophetic leader I know in the Apostolic movement believes that our prophetic words are binding upon all believers and or equal to Scripture. That being said, we need to be careful how we speak and teach because, by innuendo, we may give the impression that a so-called prophetic word or teaching is inspired and on the same level as Scripture.

Also, prophetic leaders have to be careful when they say they have a prophetic word and or revelation for the broader Body of Christ. Sometimes these words, revelatory teaching, or a new strategy, may arise out of a council they have had with apostles and prophets. Often, these prophecies are proclaimed to be binding upon the church. Unfortunately, in such cases, these purported revelations or truths can be viewed by some as being equal to Scripture. This goes without saying that it would be erroneous and even heretical.

At the very least, I would caution prophetic people to prayerfully read these chapters and re-examine how they speak and teach. I would encourage them to examine what they believe the nature of their prophetic authority and function is and what their relationship to the broader church should look like. These must be examined in light of the clear teachings of Scripture.

Geivett and Pivec are right to be concerned with statements from prophetic leaders associated in the NAR who say things such as, "To reject God's prophets is to reject God...... and to fail to recognize the prophets or to keep them from speaking, is to refuse God permission to speak. The consequences of such rejection are dire...Whole nations have arisen or fallen based on their response to God's word through His prophets."[48] I agree that we have to be very careful with statements like the ones cited above.

Generally speaking, although it is not out of the realm of possibility that God can speak a directive word to a person, or nation, it is usually rare and must be received with caution. That being said, I teach that a believer should never be guided or receive direction from so called prophets or prophetic words. This would violate the role of the Holy Spirit who is sent to lead His children (Romans 8:14-16). Personally, it doesn't matter the caliber of the person who gives me a prophetic word, I will always test it by Scripture. I will not act upon that prophetic word unless/until I also receive a witness in my heart from the Lord that it is indeed a prophetic word from Him to me. (For more on this, please read my recent book "The Purpose, Power and Process of Prophetic Ministry")

Having framed the previous section with some valid concerns, as enumerated in "A New Apostolic Reformation," I will commence with my defense of the Apostolic function and movement.

The following are twelve arguments against the contemporary apostolic movement and my response to them.

1. There were no apostles after the original twelve.

The fact of the matter is, in addition to the original twelve apostles of Jesus, there were numerous people either cited as apostles or who were sent as apostles in the New Testament.

During the days of the early church, the word Apostle was a common word used to denote a person sent on official business to represent another person, nation or government[49]. Hence, when Jesus designated the original twelve disciples as apostles, the connotation was that they were being sent out to represent Jesus and the Kingdom of God.

We read in Luke 10:1 that Jesus sent (*apostolos*) out another seventy people. Thus, apostolic ministry expanded to a total of

82 disciples. Furthermore, there were others recognized as apostles besides those already cited:

- Apollos (1 Corinthians 4:6-13)
- Epaphroditus (Philippians 2:25; "messenger" is apostolos in the Greek)
- James, the Lord's brother (Galatians 1:19)
- Barnabas (Acts 14:4,14; 1 Corinthians 9:5,6)
- Andronicus (Romans 16:7)
- Junia (Romans 16:7)
- Titus (2 Corinthians 8:23; "messenger" is *apostolos* in the Greek)
- An unnamed brother (2 Corinthians 8:18,22,23)
- Silas and Timothy (1 Thessalonians 1:1; 2:6)

Consequently, this indicates that the apostolic ministry was not only not limited to the original twelve apostles, but that the ministry was meant to continue until the fullness of time (when Christ returns bodily a second time). To this, the Apostle Paul alludes to in Ephesians 4:11-13. He says all five cluster gifts will continue until the unity of the faith and until the church comes to the knowledge of the Son of God to a mature man, and to the measure of the stature which belongs to the fullness of Christ. Obviously, since this has not happened yet, we can expect God to continue to manifest these ministry gifts on the earth.

Because Scripture says that the Apostolic must continue until the fullness of time, it must be taken seriously. As mentioned in a previous chapter, Paul's teachings in Ephesians anticipate the apostolic age to commence with, but not end with, the original 12 apostles.

Apostolic Function throughout church history

In making the point that the fivefold ministry gifts (Ephesians 4) never ceased after the original 12 Apostles, author

Alan Hirsch states that history shows that within every mission, God always raised up "apostolically gifted people."[50] He provides the following evidence:

a. Columbanus, one of the key Celtic monastics, planted more than one hundred monasteries across Europe, which then sent thousands of church planters out across Europe.

b. St. Martin of Tours, known as the founder of Western monasticism, inspired the Celts to found missions and monasteries. He is sometimes called the patron saint of Europe because of his passionate missional vision and work.

c. Saints Cyril and Methodius pioneered the mission to convert the Slavic peoples.

d. Saint Hilda, the abbess who hosted the synod of Whitby, played a major role in the extension of the Celtic movement. Her apostolic influence extended to leaders, nobles, and kings.

e. Ignatius Loyola, founder of the Jesuits, in his own lifetime, had missionaries going to India, Japan, and South America, in addition to various parts of Europe. His writings are thought to have partly influenced Wesley.

f. Henry Venn invented the now famous and profoundly apostolic three-self principles and influenced the development of indigenous missions just about everywhere.

g. Hudson Taylor's work with the China Inland Mission is credited with laying the foundations for the growth of the Chinese church today.

h. Bishop Crowther is the first African bishop; he has indelibly shaped West African Christianity.

i. Joan of Arc was credited with bringing modern France into being.
A very influential teen!

j. Mary Slessor was a remarkable missionary who deeply influenced the course of West African missions.

k. John Lake and P. Le Roux are thought to have shaped most of African Independent Church development in southern Africa.

l. Nicholas Bhengu, referred to as the South African Billy Graham, personally planted more than one thousand churches and is thought to have inspired and fathered those who planted tens of thousands of churches.

m. Enoch Adeboya is the father of the fastest-growing denomination in the world today: the Redeemed Christian Church of God.

n. Aimee Semple McPherson was an outstanding female apostolic influence in early Pentecostalism. She founded the Four Square movement.

o. Gladys Aylward was a missionary in China whose exploits were made into a Hollywood blockbuster, "The Inn of the Sixth Happiness", starring Ingrid Bergman.[51]

It should then be obvious, based on this snapshot of church history, that God has always had a witness of apostolic function in His church since its inception. Some of the diatribes leveled at this apostolic movement are…

"*Super Apostles* are trying to overthrow the pastoral ministry."[52]

Although those in the so-called NAR teach that the church should transition from a "pastoral paradigm" to an "apostolic paradigm", it does not mean that the pastoral role has to be eradicated or overthrown. By nature, pastors are called to maintain, protect, and care for the flock, which may have initially been founded by the apostolic ministry. Hence, while the apostolic leader usually doesn't stay focused on one local congregation but exerts extra local influence in some capacity (after the local church is established), pastors are appointed to focus on the wellbeing of the local church.

Apostolic language refers to the Church's need to recapture the pioneering missional spirit of the first-century church that not only planted churches but planted movements. This is in keeping with the model displayed by Christ and His Apostles, as articulated in both the Gospels and Epistles. If we look at the apostle not as a governmental office (or a continuation of the big "A" Apostles of Christ) but as part of the five-fold ministry gifts that serve as a function, then it flatlines everything. It takes away the leverage any so-called "super apostle" may attempt to use to position themselves above their brethren. It should be noted that the term "super apostles" was used by Paul in a sarcastic manner in 2 Corinthians 11:5.

It stands to reason that there really aren't any upper level "super" apostles in the Body of Christ. God set forth apostles first in the church (1 Corinthians 12:28) for a reason. It was to ensure that the church will always have an entrepreneurial attitude of continuing to expand the influence of the Kingdom. By nature, apostolic leaders are visionary leaders called into territories not yet reached for Christ; they are used by God in the areas of church planting, networking leaders, creating coalitions and equipping the saints to serve Christ in the workplace, not just the church place. I believe that this is illustrated in the Acts narrative, where the church was ever-expanding and the word of the Lord always multiplying (Acts 6:7; 12:24; 19:20).

All fivefold cluster gifts, including apostolic and pastoral leaders, are called to work together and actually depend upon the other in order to function at their apex. In my extensive experience with Apostolic ministry, as a practitioner in New York City, I have observed firsthand that true apostolic leaders create networks and support systems to encourage, train, equip and galvanize pastors together. The goal is so that they can all fulfill their purpose in Christ. My observation is that most true pastors do not have the burden or the bandwidth to focus extra locally. Therefore, their connection to apostolic leaders enables their church and ministry to have a local focus with global participation while the apostolic leader has a global focus on local participation. This is similar to what we see modeled by the apostle Paul.

"Apostolic leaders are trying to have dominion over society."

One of the earmarks of the present global apostolic movement is a new focus on helping to redeem entire cities, not just individual sinners. This echoes Isaiah's vision of the Gospel recipients rebuilding ancient ruins, repairing ruined cities, and the desolation of many generations (Read Isaiah 61:1-4). Consequently, the gospel of the Kingdom of God (which John the Baptist, Jesus and Paul all preached), has to do with the reign of Christ spilling over from individual believers into their environment. This spilling over occurs because it is a natural overflow of their love and service in response to being Christ-like. Consequently, apostolic leaders are called to promote the cultural mandate of Genesis 1:28 which talks about stewarding the created order of planet earth. The language of Genesis 1:28 makes use of the word "dominion" with regard to creation, not people (this was before the earth was populated with people). Hence, man was supposed to exert dominion over creation, not over other human beings. Dominion in this context also has to do with managing and preserving, influencing, never abusing. The New Testament equivalent to dominion is illustrated when Jesus wrapped a towel around His waist and washed the feet of His disciple, calling on His followers to do likewise. He was saying that true influence and leadership arises out of service to others.

Apostolic leaders today believe, like Jesus who called His disciples the light of the world and salt of the earth, that the church should have a positive effect on their surrounding communities. They should emulate the book of Acts (chapters 8; 19) where we witness whole cities and regions reached with the Gospel. As a matter of fact, when the disciples went into a city, some cried out "these men who have turned the world upside down have come here also" (Acts 17:6). The early church positively affected the values, beliefs and the economics of a region (as seen in the city of Ephesus in Acts 19).

The primary reason Christianity transformed the surrounding culture was that they proclaimed that Jesus was the true Lord, not Caesar. This meant that Christ followers, refusing to contradict their faith, were putting Jesus before the Roman Emperor and the societal mores (Acts 17:7). As Paul wrote in Ephesians 3:10, the church became a living witness of the resurrection of Jesus, refused to deny the faith in the face of persecution, and assembled together as Jews, Gentiles, Slave and free. Such a witness manifested to the powers that be of the wisdom of God and that Jesus is the only True Lord. Jesus, as King of Kings, unlike the Roman Caesars, was able to bring various people groups together.

Neither the early Church leaders nor the present apostolic leaders I know and work with, preach that the institutional church should politically rule over cities and nations. Also, history has shown that to be problematic theologically as well as in civil life.

I believe in the separation of church and state (the way the Framers of the Constitution meant it). However, I don't believe in the separation of God and state. Individual believers as good citizens should bring their Christian values into the public square just as individuals with other values will attempt to do. Furthermore, I do not know one apostolic leader who thinks that the church will bring a full manifestation of the Kingdom before the second bodily return of Jesus.

"The NAR is a Global Conspiracy"

The so-called New Apostolic Reformation (NAR) has elicited a significant amount of fear and has become a catalyst for those who are against its teachings. Opponents contend that the NAR has conspired on a global level to overthrow pastors in their quest to take over the world.

However, further examination demonstrates that most people espousing the restoration of the five cluster gifts, do not even know what the NAR is or have never even heard the term used.

Dr. Peter Wagner, as a researcher and missiologist, in the last decade, coined the phrase, New Apostolic Reformation (NAR), to denote individual networks formed by visionary leaders. It is called a reformation because regional church cooperation was no longer being limited to denominational affiliation. Visionary leaders, not necessarily denominational leaders, were and are leading this Reformation. It never was nor is an "anti-denominational" movement, but a movement that transcends denominations. It is a unifying force whose goal is to reach the nations with the gospel.

Consequently, the skeptics are incorrect when they label it like an organized conspiracy. Rather, it's a sovereign, global move of God that uses words as catalysis to unify the body of Christ so that the world will believe that the Father sent Jesus to be the savior of the world (John 17:20-23).

To conclude this point, there are Non-Charismatics in this movement. It's a diverse movement whose members have various views on eschatology, ecclesiology, leadership style. As noted above, some members belong to traditional denominations, and some are nondenominational. If this diverse group was somehow organized by human ingenuity, it would perhaps be the greatest miracle any of us have ever seen! Rather, this global movement is being orchestrated by Father God to help prepare the Bride for the coming of His Son so that He can claim back the earth for His glory.

"So-called apostles are proclaiming authority over the Churches."

It is true that some Apostolic leaders in the past proclaimed themselves to be the Apostle to a particular city or an apostle to a particular nation(s). This has made many of us within the apostolic circles cringe! However, within the last forty years, I have heard this rhetoric used minimally, and within the last 10 years not at all. That being said, even if it is currently being proclaimed by some today, it is always unfair to categorize a whole movement by its radical fringe.

Based on the teaching of Saint Paul in 2 Corinthians 10:10-15, there is a geographic authority given to apostolic leaders to plant churches based on their particular assignment. Having such an assignment does not carry with it a call to "lord over" other believers, but a call to serve the Church. Paul makes it clear that the authority he was given by God was not to tear down but to build people up (2 Corinthians 13). Also, this teaching by Paul was given in the context of a time when the early Church was planting churches throughout the known world. So, it would be hard to follow what Paul meant exactly as it applies to our contemporary context given the fact that today there are numerous churches in every city and town in many nations. The general idea we can extrapolate from this passage is the fact that God gives a measure of authority to certain people for specific regions so they can carry out apostolic work. This may mean that they may not have the same grace or authority if they ventured outside the geographic boundaries of their God given assignment.

"Apostolic leaders have an autocratic leadership style."

While it is true that some apostolic leaders are title driven and hierarchical, truth be told, they were probably like that before they embraced the title apostle. The title or the global apostolic movement had nothing to do with it. Rather, their leadership style has more to do with such things as their own internal wiring- insecurity, their cultural context, or ecclesiastical culture.

While these are general observations, some leadership styles can be attributed to their culture. For instance, African leaders lead in the context of a historically tribalistic understanding of top-down leadership. This often spills over into the ecclesiastical structures of government in many African churches. Many Latino leaders lead out of the context of the Euro Conquistador attitude.

This has shaped the leadership style of both ecclesial and political methodologies in Latin America. In the USA, the leadership style is often more consumer-driven by a CEO type model of leadership. Consequently, in every culture and context, it behooves those of us in the apostolic movement to undergo a thorough examination of biblical theology to determine whether or not our ecclesial structures and leadership have been shaped by the "way of Christ and His apostles" or by our cultural frameworks and assumptions. Furthermore, the same accusations of autocratic leadership can also be said about Bishops, Pastors, and Doctors within the church. We don't react by doing away with the function of the pastor or bishop, do we? Of course not!

Those of us within the United States Council of Apostolic Leaders (USCAL.US), have made a concerted effort to ensure that our movement is one that is formed and function around real relationships and not titles. We are seeking to espouse the servant leadership style of Jesus (John 13; Philippians 2:3-12) as our example and endeavor to use our influence to build people up, rather than to tear them down (2 Corinthians 13:10).

"The apostolic restoration is against denominations."

As was already alluded, the global apostolic movement often includes leaders in most evangelical denominations.

Within USCAL, there are leaders in the Roman Catholic, AOG, Anglican, Methodist and Baptist denominations. They are all evangelical and biblical in their beliefs and practices. The New Apostolic Movement is not meant to eradicate denominations but to motivate them in their mission and practice as they seek to follow the way of Christ and His apostles.

Just a cursory look at many mainline evangelical leaders and movements reveals that they are utilizing "fivefold ministry" language. I believe that in the next five years it will be almost impossible for opponents of the apostolic restoration to differentiate between the groups because it will be mainstream in evangelicalism. Opponents of this new Apostolic movement will eventually have to categorize most of Evangelicalism as the NAR and part of a demonic conspiracy if they don't open their hearts to what God is doing today in the world!

"Apostles Are Self-Ordained."

Since the restoration of the apostolic in name is still relatively new, there have been numerous people who have proclaimed themselves apostles. This has been done primarily because there are no set recognized processes for ordaining a person as an apostle the way there is for the preparation and training for a person to become a pastor, bishop, or member of the clergy.

Many of us within the movement have been discussing how to remedy this issue, and possibly recommending guidelines to those functioning in apostolic ministry. One of the ways to avoid being accused of being self-proclaimed is when key regional leaders in proximity to the person functioning apostolically, refers to that leader as an apostle before the leader's elders and church members begin using the title.

Since many of us refer to the function as apostolic rather than using the title apostle, we would be more comfortable with hands being laid upon people recognizing them as apostolic leaders or consecrating them to serve in "apostolic function or ministry." We would only do so if and only if there was apostolic fruit that is demonstrated. Apostolic fruit would be such things as church planting, ministering to pastors and leaders outside their local church, overseeing a network of churches and or a movement of leaders. It is rather embarrassing to be called an apostolic leader or a bishop when there is very little fruit within a ministry or there is a meager following.

On a personal note, I was consecrated both bishop and Apostle in 2006 by a dual college of 12 bishops and 12 apostolic presbytery leaders. In addition, there were 50 national and local leaders who participated in my consecration. My consecration was initiated by several bishops in the NYC area who felt from the Lord I was supposed to be set in and recognized as a bishop for the sake of the work of the Kingdom in which I was involved with.

"Apostolic movements are personality-driven."

The function of the apostle is one of the fivefold gifts of the church (Ephesians 4) and is an extension of the mission of Jesus and His church (2 Corinthians 10:10-14). In the book of Acts, Luke often names extraordinary miracles and works done by apostles. The fact that he mentions specific Apostles' names doesn't separate them from being a part of the church but rather it enhances the activity and narrative of the mission of the church. Consequently, the Jesus movement is not a "nameless and faceless" movement but it is a movement led by five-fold ministry gifts that represent the various ministry functions of the Lord Jesus Christ.

The profile of the apostolic leaders in the Bible does not make it personality driven but part of the organic church that serves as the visible body of the invisible Christ.

While there may be apostolic people who lead movements that are personality driven, we can say the same thing about some prophets, evangelists, pastors, and teachers. This does that mean we do away with all these other functions as well. So it is with the Apostolic, we must not get rid of it because of those who abuse it.

"The apostolic tradition is continued by the Scriptures, not by new Apostles."

This argument is self-refuting because as already mentioned, the Scriptures themselves testify that the apostolic ministry is going to continue until the church matures into the fullness of Christ.

"Apostolic leaders are dividing the church."

While I have heard of some reports of apostolic leaders stealing pastors from other networks or movements this is not endemic of all apostolic leaders. The same concept occurs more frequently amongst pastors who "sheep steal", or the more polite phrase "transfer growth". In the quest to grow their churches, these pastors appeal to believers who are already committed to other churches. These pastors end up dividing the church. Any leader who has a pattern of intentionally luring committed people away from good churches or movements should be confronted (first in private). Division in the church is never good, but to blame the restoration of the apostolic for dividing the church is unfair and untrue. Pastors and leaders who seem to embrace and follow "the way of Christ and His apostles" by embracing the apostolic move of God should not be labeled as divisive by their colleagues and ecclesiastical fellowship who opposed their decision.

As leaders, our allegiance is to the Scriptures and to Jesus, not to ecclesiastical systems that oppose what God has ordained in His Word. Also, to be clear, mature apostolic leaders will never endeavor to divide the Church but will attempt to work together for the unity of the Spirit.[53]

"Today's apostles believe their prophecies are equal to Scripture."

I do not know of any apostolic or prophetic leader who teaches that their revelations or prophetic words are equal to scripture. That being said, anyone who does this is in great error because prophetic words only have validity if they are in accord with the tradition, pattern, principles, and authority of the Word of God. True apostolic leaders should always uphold fidelity to the Scriptures otherwise they should be labeled as false apostles.

Contrasts Between true and false apostolic leaders

The following are contrasts between true and false apostolic leaders. For the sake of brevity, I use the term apostle for the title of each point instead of my usual apostolic.[54] In the context of this writing, false apostles are ones that have wrong motives in ministry. It doesn't mean they are not Christians, rather, it could be that they may be immature or a carnal or ambitious leader.

1. True apostolic leaders edify the church and promote God's kingdom. The counterfeits use the church to build their own platform and enhance its own empire. All false leaders are only committed to that which benefits themselves.

2. True apostolic leaders live to serve others. Counterfeits have an entitlement mentality and use their ecclesial title to be served. True biblical leaders exhibit brokenness and humility, hence their primary function is as a servant leader. The false apostle attracts naive sycophants in his desire to get ahead in life by having people serve him. These sycophants are guilty of idolatry since they often tolerate it when their leader objectifies others for the sake of building their apostolic empire.

3. Mature, biblical apostolic leaders nurture Christ-followers. The counterfeits only point people back to themselves.

The true apostolic leaders are motivated to guide people towards becoming mature saints who look like Jesus (Colossians 1:28, 29). The counterfeit seeks to draw masses to himself. This can be evidenced in their promotions and branding which orbits around them as an apostolic leader or man of God. Counterfeits are motivated to produce faithful, committed, loyal followers who will live to serve them. They draw disciples onto themselves and not to Jesus (see Acts 20:30).

4. True apostolic leaders desire to have the influence to bring glory to Christ (Isaiah 42:8). They often risk their own monetary stability in order to advance gospel movements. The counterfeits use their platform of ministry merely for monetary gain. The counterfeits don't even begin an endeavor if they calculate it will not turn a profit. They even endeavor to get "spiritual sons" in the faith for the express purpose of getting their tithe (hence the primary motivation is finances rather than pouring into their lives).

5. True apostolic leaders sacrifice their life for the sheep. The counterfeits sacrifice the sheep for themselves since they only have one agenda-their own benefit! They will even hurt people to get ahead.

6. True apostolic leaders edify others. Christ-like apostolic leaders are committed to the success of others and make room for them to grow and flourish. The counterfeits use their authority to tear down others. This is contrary to the New Testament pattern (2 Corinthians 13:10). Those who get ahead by attacking and slandering their peers, they deem their competition are false apostles.

7. True apostolic leaders uplift Pastors and churches. The counterfeits usurp the authority of pastors and their churches. I know many apostolic leaders who live to serve and equip Pastors and churches but I have also observed a

small minority who works at undermining the authority of local Pastors. Unfortunately, I have had first-hand experience with this. In the late 1980s a false apostolic leader was brought in to help our church. He initially gained our trust but eventually attempted to undermine my authority as the lead pastor. He worked directly with our church elders behind my back to garner their allegiance to him, thereby compromising their loyalty to me. Eventually, the elders saw right through him and voted to distance ourselves from him.

8. True apostles are accountable. False apostles are unaccountable. Any apostolic leader who refuses to be accountable or be corrected regarding his life, ministry or questionable teachings is functioning as a false apostle.

9. True apostolic leaders work through teams and show apostolic fruit. The counterfeits usually work alone and lack fruit in their ministry.

   Those who operate as a lone ranger without working through teams for maximum effect are either insecure, immature, or even worse, are functioning as a counterfeit apostle. Of course, there are many fine and sincere leaders who are not good at delegation and only have the capacity to operate a church like a mom-and-pop shop. However, those with true apostolic abilities usually are gifted in working through teams. Team leadership is exhibited in the Acts narrative and demonstrated by Paul. Hence, to be a true apostle, one must have a propensity to raise up and work through a community of leaders. Such leadership collectively bear much fruit and can be described as apostolic. A refusal to delegate and build teams can keep one from walking in their apostolic calling and gift.

10. True apostolic leaders point the church back to the original 12 apostles of Christ. The counterfeits posture themselves

as equal to the New Testament apostles. Consequently, anytime a person puts themselves or their teaching on the same level of any of the original twelve apostles, they are prone to heresy and are dangerous.

The original apostles of the Lamb became the plumbline, as well as the foundation for the rest of us, according to Ephesians 2:20. In light of this, all the saints throughout church history are called to point back to the original 12 (including Paul) as their primary reference point for ministry. It should be noted that some of the New Testament writers such as Luke, Mark, James, and Jude were never noted among the original 12 apostles of the Lamb but were close companions of those in proximity to them. For example, Luke was Paul's fellow worker (2 Tim.4:11); Mark was the spiritual son of the apostle Peter (1 Peter 4:13) and may have merely written the Gospel of Mark based on what Peter dictated to him. Jude was the half-brother of the Lord Jesus and the apostle James (Matthew 13:55; Jude 1:1); James was the half-brother of the Lord Jesus (Matthew 13:55). Apostolic Leaders who equate themselves as equal to or lift themselves above the original apostles of Jesus are false apostles and not to be followed.

11. True apostolic leaders base their teaching on the Scriptures. Counterfeits either wrest the Scriptures exegetically or base their teaching on subjective experience. Thus, whenever a leader consistently bases their teachings solely on extra-biblical experiences (personal visions, dreams, writings, prophecies) instead of on the sacred writings of both the Old and New Testament, they are in dangerous territory; they are setting themselves up to be a counterfeit that will potentially deceive many. This is especially problematic when a so-called apostle gets "revelation" from God that

they claim is an extra chapter or book of the Bible or that they received instruction directly from one of the saints in heaven rather than from God. Such leaders are to be avoided because eventually these so-called extra-biblical revelations may contradict or be in competition with the Bible (i.e. the book of Mormon). At the end of the day, only the Scriptures can be fully trusted as inspired by God.

12. True apostolic leaders nurture sons in the faith. The counterfeits produce orphans. Unfortunately, I have seen counterfeit apostles leave a path of destruction behind their ministry as they use, abuse and orphan their followers whom they refer to as their "sons" and whom they abandon after they get what they wanted from them.

13. True apostolic leaders walk with God. The counterfeits walk in the flesh (Galatians 5:16-23). A so-called apostle who consistently walks in the flesh by losing his temper, cursing, slandering, or berating their staff, lacks the fruit of the Spirit; he disqualifies himself according to the leadership standards set up by Paul the apostle in 1 Timothy 3:1-12 and Titus 1; 2. Jesus said in regard to false prophets that you will know them by their fruit (Matthew 7:20).

14. True apostolic leaders proclaim biblical doctrine. Counterfeits teach heretical doctrine. By heretical I am referring to any doctrine or teaching condemned by the New Testament writers as well as the early church councils (ex., Nicea, Constantinople, Chalcedon, Ephesus, etc.). Jude 3 speaks about the obligation we have as believers to earnestly contend for the faith that was once and for all was delivered to the saints. True apostolic leaders uphold this biblical faith. The false apostles promote that which contradicts cardinal doctrines such as salvation by faith alone in the finished work of Christ; the deity and Lordship of Jesus over all;

the need for all people to go through Jesus for eternal salvation; the reality of heaven, hell and eternity; the triune Godhead of Father, Son, and Holy Spirit.

When an apostolic leader deviates away from any of the cardinal doctrines they are a false apostle. Paul even said that if we or an angel preach any other gospel than the one they originally received let them be eternally condemned (Galatians 1). The church should have the courage to test those who claim to be apostles so we can discern between the true and the false, and thereby be able to bless, build and protect the Body of Christ.

In the next chapter we will explore the vast sociological implications and effect the missional apostolic church has had upon Western civilization. My hope is that the more the contemporary church comports to the way of Christ and His apostles -the more we will participate with Jesus in the renewal of all things.

QUESTIONS TO ASK YOURSELF

1. Is the apostolic an office or a function?

2. What are some erroneous teachings that have been connected to the apostolic movement?

3. What are some of the objections to the present apostolic movement?

4. What is the NAR?

5. Is the NAR a global conspiracy?

6. What are some of the contrasts between true and false apostolic leaders?

Chapter 3

The Historical Roots and Paradigms of Doing Church Relative to the New Testament Pattern of the Apostolic Church

In this chapter I will illustrate the vast societal impact of the historic, missional apostolic church. It is important to understand the amazing contributions of the church and its positive effects upon every aspect of culture when she is in forward motion out of obedience to Jesus commands (See Matthew 28:19,20)

We will also explore the major paradigmatic stages and epochal shifts the church has experienced so we can better understand the roots of our own particular Christian context.

A Brief Historical Overview of the Post Acts Apostolic Church

Ask of me and I will give you the heathen for your inheritance, the ends of the earth for a possession.
(Psalm 2:8 paraphrased)

What really holds together the twenty centuries of Christian history and tradition, which are so tremendously contradictory? The answer, here too an elementary one, can only be: it is the name of that Jesus who through the centuries has been called God's eschatological prophet and emissary, God's representative and son. The name of Jesus Christ is rather like a golden thread in the ever-renewed fabric of Christian history, which is so often torn and dirty; the binding primal motif in Christian tradition, liturgy, theology, and piety which is never simply lost, for all the decadence."[55]

Since its birth, the church has done a massive amount of benevolent, reforming, and cultivating work. Consequently, those who don't believe the church should be involved in societal reform insult the centuries of reformers and saints who used the Bible as their blueprint when they gave their lives to the civilization and cultivation of nations. Because these works of the church are so voluminous, I will only cite a few accounts to illustrate the theme of this paper.

The fact is, with or without the use of the title apostle, there have always been functional apostles in the church since its inception. Paul said all the ascension gift ministries will function until we all come to the unity of the faith (Ephesians 4:11-16). There is no other explanation for the prodigious amount of effective work done by the church, which has impacted all facets of society throughout history.

Peter Wagner says that when one observes history, it becomes obvious that many of the great church reformers were true apostles, "great men such as Gregory Thaumaturgus, Martin of Tours, Patrick of Ireland, Benedict of Nursia, Boniface, Anselm of Canterbury, Savanarola, John Wyclif, Martin Luther, Francis Xavier, John Knox, John Wesley, William Booth, William Carey, Hudson Taylor, and others throughout the centuries."[56] Wagner references a book written about Dwight L. Moody whose subtitle states, "A Tribute to the Memory of the Greatest Apostle of the Age."[57] The men and women apostles in the history of the Church were able to leave an indelible mark in society, bringing reformation to various institutions.

The church has primarily made a mark on society with works of compassion to the community. Acts 6 records how the church multiplied after assigning deacons to oversee the distribution of food. Christianity spread in Egypt in the second century because "the Christian women working together formed a team. Some went into the streets and collected abandoned babies while other women nursed the babies. The Christians also collected abandoned rotting corpses in the garbage dumps and gave them a proper burial."[58]

The eradication of slavery within the Roman Empire can be attributed to the power of the Church. "By the time of Christ, slaves made up an estimated seventy-five percent of the population in ancient Athens and well over half of the Roman population. Slavery was also widely practiced by many tribes of the American Indians long before Columbus set foot on the shores of the new world."[59] In Ancient Greece, slaves did all of the menial and skilled labor.

The strong anti-slavery theme within the Bible is evident. The book of Exodus is about God redeeming a whole nation from slavery. Leviticus chapter 25 speaks about the year of Jubilee when all slaves are freed and forgiven for their debts. Jesus speaks about those who come to Him as being "free" (John 8:31-34). Paul speaks about people becoming free of slavery if they can possibly do so (1 Cor. 7:21). He also states that we are "not to be entangled with a yoke of slavery" (Gal. 5:1). The most powerful verse is the egalitarian verse seen in Galatians 3:28. Here, slaves are placed on the same level as free people in the sight of God, thus giving the impetus for freedom on the basis of common human worth. In the book of Philemon, Paul exhorts Philemon to receive his runaway slave as a brother in the Lord, not as a slave. All of these biblical passages laid the groundwork for the abolishment of slavery for all time.

"During the second and third centuries, the freeing of slaves was performed in church in the presence of the bishop. Constantine, in A.D. 315, imposed the death penalty on those who stole children to bring them up as slaves."[60] St. Augustine saw slavery as the product of sin and as contrary to God's divine plan.[61] St Chrysostom, in the fourth century, preached that when Christ came, He annulled slavery.[62] Of course, anti-slavery sentiment continued many centuries later.

In the West, we see men like William Wilberforce in England and evangelist Charles Finney in America leading the way to abolish slavery. William Wilberforce labored for over fifty years to abolish the slave trade as an esteemed member of the English Parliament. His success in 1807 encouraged leaders of the American abolitionist movement who were converts of the Finney revivals, such as Theodore Weld, and the Tappan brothers. The Tappan brothers used their vast wealth to support Finney and the reform movements. They were not only against slavery but against any semblance of one group lifting itself above other groups, whether it be based on ethnicity or economics. Later in the mid-20th-century, Christian activists like Dr. Martin Luther King led the way for the civil rights of Blacks in America because of his understanding of the liberation narrative of redemption in the Scriptures.

The Fall of Rome and the early formation of the modern Western European nations

In 1796, the General Assembly of the Church of Scotland stated that converting barbarians to Christianity was ill-thought out. They stated, "To spread abroad among barbarians and heathen natives the knowledge of the gospel seems to be highly preposterous, insofar as it anticipates, nay even reverses, the order of Nature." However, despite statements like this, the church has historically been the key agent for civilizing the barbaric peoples and cultivating what we now understand as modern nations.

Starting around A.D.376 to A.D.476, Germanic tribes began to attack the Western part of the Roman Empire. "It took the barbarians nearly 100 years from the time the Visigoths crossed the Danube in A.D.376 to the fall of Rome in A.D.476 to conquer the western part of the Empire.[63] The decline of Rome was due in part to this invasion. "The Goths matter to us because their crossing of the Danube frontier in 376 and subsequent settlement inside the empire symbolize the beginning of the process which since the time of Edward Gibbon we have known as the Decline and Fall of the Roman Empire."[64]

In the middle of the fifth century, Attila the Hun turned his face toward Rome and began to brutally sack and pillage Rome. However, it was the intercession of Leo I (some call him the first official Pope) who stopped Attila and saved the city. Eventually, the barbarians conquered every province of the western part of the Empire: Italy, North Africa, Spain, Gaul, the Netherlands, and Britain. The empire fell, but the church survived. Many of the barbarian tribes had accepted Christianity and respected the bishop of Rome. The position of the church was improved by the successes of the bishop of Rome in protecting the people to a certain extent from the worst excesses of the barbarians when the emperor had not been able to protect them. When the smoke and dust cleared, there stood, intact among the blackened ruins of the Empire, the church ready to bless and educate the barbarians who had caused this ruin.[65]

The church now faced a monumental task. After the Church was legalized, it rapidly grew with its urban-based house churches. Early in the first century, the senior priest would be elected to oversee the surrounding churches in the area. The church was organized around dioceses that were based on city-states. A bishop's importance was based on the kind of city he was overseeing. Thus, the bishop of Rome was very important. This was the structure in place prior to the legalization of Christianity. When the Roman administration fell apart and abandoned their post, the only one left in the city was the bishop. As an act of service to the city, the bishops picked up the pieces of the Roman administrative structure.

In the past, the church evangelized civilized people in the Greco-Roman culture. With Rome overrun by the barbarians, they faced people largely uncivilized. From this point forward the church not only Christianized but civilized, the nations.

By the year 1000, the nations of Europe were Christianized. By the year 1500, all these new nations developed their own cultures with a Christian worldview. Regarding the center of gravity for Christianity during these tumultuous times, Philip Jenkins said:

> By the time the Roman Empire granted the Christians toleration in the early fourth century, there was no question that the religion was predominantly associated with the eastern half of the empire, and indeed with territories beyond the eastern border. Of the five ancient patriarchates of the church, only one, Rome, clearly stood in the west. The others were at Constantinople, Antioch, Jerusalem, and Alexandria—three on the Asian continent, one in Africa. If we can imagine a Christian center of gravity by around 500, we should still be thinking of Syria rather than Italy. Africa, too, had its ancient Christian roots. Apart from Egypt, much early Christian history focuses on the Roman province known as Africa, roughly modern Tunisia. This was the home of such great early leaders as Tertullian, Cyprian, and Augustine, the founders of Christian Latin literature.[66]

Great missionaries influenced the formation of the Church

Saint Augustine of Hippo, a bishop, was born in A.D. 354 in Tagaste, North Africa. Augustine was perhaps the most influential early church father in the history of Christianity. His monumental work, The City of God, was his philosophy of history. It served as a defense of Christianity after many blamed the fall of Rome on the ascendancy of Christianity. Augustine said that humanity was divided into two cities, one earthly and the other heavenly. He observed that after Cain killed Abel, Cain went on to build a city that was based on safety and security.

In contrast to this earthly city, there is a heavenly city. It is based on a spiritual reality in which its inhabitants, though part of the spiritual city, also live in this earthly city. However, they never in their heart, feel at home in this worldly city. In God's providence, there will always be two cities. As we are led to the consummation of all things, the spiritual city will ultimately have the ascendancy and the most influence on humanity. Augustine was the prime influence on Emperor Charlemagne, Luther, Calvin, Abraham Kuyper and a host of others. As a result of his enormous impact, he is one of the only influential leaders in history that both the Catholic Church and Protestant Church have claimed as one of their own.

Saint Benedict was a reformer, the father of monasticism, and one who left an indelible impact on the Christian faith. "Benedict (A.D.529) started a monastery organized around a 24-hour day of six hours of work, six hours of worship, six hours of study and six hours of sleep. He organized laypeople and sent them into the worst, most violent places in Europe, where they converted people and developed economies and communities."[67]

Saint Patrick. Christianity was not spread by military conquest or political pressure, rather legitimate missionary endeavors help to spread Christianity. St. Patrick was an admirable example of character. In fifth-century England, he was kidnapped by Irish slave traders, but he came back to the continent that kidnapped him and went back to those who enslaved him, bringing them the gospel. Ireland was a pagan land, "In order to understand the significance of what Patrick [did] in Ireland we need to know pre-Christian Ireland. Celtic paganism and druids universally practiced human sacrifice. Skulls were bashed in; people were drowned and strangled.... It is a rather brutal religion."[68] Even the Romans considered the Celtic religion brutal and barbaric. Saint Patrick gave his life to bring Christ-like love to such a pagan culture. By the time of his death, the church was firmly established in Ireland.

One of the many ways in which Christianity impacted the Irish were education. Saint Patrick understood that in order for

Christianity to survive, the people had to be able to be versed in languages, especially since the pagan Celtic religion prized knowledge.[69] "It was Patrick's Christian mission that nurtured Irish scholarship.[70] [T]he first Irish Christians also became the first Irish literates." As a result of this, Irish literacy included the mastery of Latin and Greek. "Within a generation...[t]hey devised Irish grammars, and copied out the whole of their native oral literature....They began to make up languages (barely a generation after the Irish had become literate), could write to one another in impenetrably erudite, never-before spoken patterns of Latin called Hisperica, Famina, not unlike the dream-language of Finnegans, Wake or even the languages J.R.R. Tolkien would one day make up for his hobbits and elves."[71]

The Irish became to be recognized as a learned people, "Wherever they went the Irish brought with them their books, many unseen in Europe for centuries and tied to their waists as signs of triumph, just as Irish heroes had once tied to their waists their enemies' heads. Wherever they went they brought their love of learning and their skills in bookmaking. In the bays and valleys of their exile, they reestablished literacy and breathed new life into the exhausted literary culture of Europe."[72]

Saint Boniface: Boniface was the greatest of the early English missionaries, who Christianized barbaric Germany.[73]

Boniface was radical in His love for God, which translated in him destroying idols, establishing monasteries and confronting the evils of paganism. In Germany, he cut down a sacred oak tree dedicated to Thor, the god of lightning. The heathens expected Boniface to be struck dead by lightning and when nothing happened to him, they converted to Christianity. "When the pagans who had cursed saw this, they [stopped] cursing and, believing, blessed God."[74] Boniface then used the oak to erect a chapel. Boniface brought about significant reforms within the ecclesiastical realm.

Charlemagne. Charlemagne (Charles the Great) became emperor on Christmas day A.D.800. He became one of the greatest figures in all of the Western Civilization. Influenced greatly by The City of God, he stood for three things: law and order, the civilization of culture, and Christianity. He succeeded in establishing all three of these for the people of Western Europe. He established security by establishing wise laws and enforcing them. He established schools throughout the kingdom. He even became a pupil in a school he established in his palace. He was a great warrior who conquered the fierce Saxon tribe and forced them to convert to Christianity with the sword. "He imported scholars to aid in his goal of educating his empire. The most influential of these was Alcuin....Under Alcuin's influence, the king issued a series of edicts in the 780s, which stipulated that monasteries had to provide for their member's intellectual nourishment as well as spiritual... Charlemagne commanded that monasteries had to establish schools where all boys could be educated, not just those living at the monastery.... In 797 Charlemagne ordered priests to establish schools in every community, where all children could be educated for free."[75]

Within the next 300 years this movement eventually led to the formation of the universities. The first one was the University of Bologna, formed around 1088 (In Oxford University, teaching first took place in the church but eventually moved to various houses and eventually dorms. Some of the first universities were Christian in nature, in the curriculum, and in purpose. From the twelfth century forward, many universities were birthed in Italy, Germany, France, and England. Out of these universities, Christianity produced some of the greatest minds in history: Anselm, Peter the Lombard, Albert Magnus, and perhaps the greatest mind of all, Thomas Aquinas. Aquinas' massive work, Summa Theologica, is a synthesis of classical and Christian thought and was largely based on the philosophy and ethics of Aristotle. This book is still referenced by theologians and is the foundation of Catholic doctrine today.

Urbanization was rising, the population was rising, trade is rising, and the church was working on reforming itself as well through the monasteries. There became an increase in the demand for education, so education left the monasteries and was shifted to the cathedrals. Cathedral schools developed a worldview working from the base of the Irish, called platonic humanism. This belief is different from secular humanism. It is the belief that the world comes from God and the world can lead us back to God. Human beings have God's mind, and we can study the world. We can know the mind of God better by studying the world instead of using miracles to determine the truth and using reason to judge people on trial. As bishops had more and more administration, they couldn't keep up with the cathedral schools and so they started guilds of students in universities. Scholasticism is a method of study that led to a vision of the world that comes from God, ordered and integrated. Scholasticism resulted in a search for the 'grand synthesis' which was to attempt to structure all knowledge under God in an interlocking, totally unified vision of the world with theology as the queen of the sciences.[76]

This grand synthesis paved the way for the biblical worldview that integrated all knowledge under God. Modern science and the scientific revolution were based on medieval science and platonic humanism, making sense of the world because it came from God. Learning a biblical worldview is very important. In the church in America, consumerism, superficial culture, and anti-intellectualism are part of society and the church. The American church is like the arrival of the Irish coming to the church after the fall of Rome. We desperately need to recover the vision of the Christian worldview.

Centuries later, Christianity continued to lead the way and produce the greatest centers of learning through the universities. Calvin, the great reformer who set up the Christian government in the city of Geneva, established the Geneva Academy in 1559, a university that enjoyed the highest reputation from its inception. Soon, almost a thousand boys enrolled, and preachers were released throughout all of Europe, as this became the center of Protestantism. Calvin's influence thus spread to Italy, Hungary, Poland, and Western Germany. In addition, the church set up by Calvin in Geneva, became the pattern for the Huguenot church in France, the Reformed Church in the Netherlands, and the Presbyterian Church in Scotland.

Among those influenced by Calvin was John Knox, who adapted Calvinism after visiting Geneva. He helped Thomas Cranmer establish the Forty-Two Articles Protestant creed, adopted by the Church of England in the mid-sixteenth century. Everywhere he went, his preaching was explosive and caused iconoclastic parties that destroyed religious idols. In 1560, within just a few years after arriving in Scotland, the nation officially changed their religion from Catholic to Protestant. A Calvinistic confession of faith was adopted and by the year 1570, the Presbyterian Church was fully established. John Knox was responsible for changing the church and the nation of Scotland within one generation. The Puritans who founded the Thirteen Colonies were also Calvinistic and their preaching prepared the way for the Christian Commonwealth that became the underpinning for the Declaration of Independence and the U.S. Constitution.

From the days of the Greek centers of learning to John Calvin's Geneva to Ivy League schools like Harvard, Yale, and Princeton, education has been one of the main catalysts for cultural transformation and for the advancement of Christian civilization. Both Martin Luther and John Calvin attempted to interpret all of life through the lens of Scripture because they regarded the Gospel as truth. This truth was directed to all realms of society and was not relegated to only the Church or just spiritual things.

These early universities had as a goal to produce not only educated clergy but Christians who would become leaders in the fields of politics, law, economics, and education. Harvard was established in 1636 by Puritans. John Elliot, the founder, was called the Apostle to the Indians. Yale (1701) and Dartmouth (1769) were founded by Congregationalists. Princeton was founded by Presbyterians. Kings College (Columbia University) was founded by Anglicans. Brown began in 1764 by the Baptists. Rutgers began in 1766 by the Dutch Reformed.[77] Duke University had a Christian beginning with a goal of teaching students to assert their faith in the eternal union of knowledge and religion set forth in the teachings and character of Jesus Christ, the Son of God.

When Harvard began to drift away theologically, Yale was founded in 1701 to counter that. The founders of Yale required students to learn the Westminster Confession in Latin, "Yale in the early 1700s stated as its primary goal that every student shall consider the main end of his study to wit to know God in Jesus Christ and answerable to lead a godly, sober life."[78] Education in New England was for the express purpose of equipping young men and women with a superior education in the relevant disciplines with divinity serving as the centerpiece and queen of the sciences.

Unfortunately, today's church has been more focused on the rapture and last day's teachings than educating Christian leaders to fulfill the Cultural Mandate. The disastrous result has been that the church has abandoned the culture to secular humanism and to those who think that the slaughter of the unborn is their civic right. Harvard, Yale, Princeton and most of the Ivy League schools have strayed away from their Christian roots and have embraced humanism. While they have gone on to produce the most influential people on earth, including most U.S. presidents, they have allowed secular humanistic forces to rob Christianity of its inheritance and mandate to have cultural influence on the earth. While today's liberals are supposedly the stalwarts with regard to compassion for the powerless and needy, we must remember that the church has been the primary catalyst for charitable works and compassion ministry since its inception.

As I close this section, it is impossible for me to cite all that Christianity contributed towards the progress of humankind since its inception with regard to quality-of-life. For example, the understanding that the universe was not the result of "matter in motion" and mere "randomness" but was indeed the result of an intelligent designer, caused many scientists to study the works of God as a way of discovering and understanding more of His glory (Psalm 111:2; Psalm 19; Romans 1:19-22). That Christianity and Christians at one point dominated the field of science is without refutation. World-famous Christian scientists include William of Occam (1285-1347, who postulated Occam's Razor), Leonardo da Vinci (1452-1519, physics, human anatomy), Blaise Pascal (1623-62, the first adding machine), Galileo (1564-1642, astronomy), Roger Bacon (1214-1294, empirical method of scientific experimentation), Nicholas Copernicus (1473-1543, astronomy), Isaac Newton (1642-1727, discovered laws of gravity and calculus, among other things), Louis Pasteur (1822-1895, discovered bacteria), and George Washington Carver (1864-1943, discovered various ways to utilize peanuts to name a few).

Today eminent scientists like Stephen Meyer and Jonathan Wells and others, have become notable Christian apologists with regard to making a strong case against naturalistic evolution as proponents of a theistic view for the origin of the cosmos. Consequently, I believe that Christianity alone has the necessary worldview that provides a rational basis for all the sciences. I believe the church will continue to develop the world's leading thinkers and as the sciences continue to develop, they will also continue to be faced with the reality that the world does not make sense without a creator who designed life.

My hope is that the church will be at the center of all cultural thinking including education, music and all the sciences, as we begin to understand the reality of the reign of God inaugurated by Jesus Christ. Of course, this fits in line with the statement by Saint Paul in 1 Timothy 3:15 in which he says that the Church is the ground and pillar of the truth. He is not only referring to church doctrine but rather he is referring to all truth. Jesus said He is the Truth, referring to the fact that He is behind all truth as the Logos and Genesis of the universe. I believe the church should produce the main cultural prophets, critics and ethicists, since we represent God's truth and kingdom to this world.

The Roots of Contemporary Church Models, Including the Current Restoration Movement (To the Way of Christ and His Apostles)

Examples of paradigm changes in theology include the first-century church going from an apocalyptic Jewish paradigm during Jesus' time to the Hellenistic paradigm of Origen (when the church had to grapple with Greek Philosophical influence and Gnosticism); from Hellenistic to Latin with Augustine when the church had to deal with Pelagianism and Donatism (Augustine emphasized the central role of the church over the individual); To the crisis of Augustinianism that led to Thomas and his Aristotelian orientation of Theology. We went from there to Luther and Calvin with a biblical Christocentric conception of theology that rejected the allegorizing of Origen. The religious wars and intolerance led to the liberal theological paradigm of Schleiermacher; which then led to the neo-orthodoxy of Barth; Thus, historical processes are complex in their causation, initiation, and development in the theological community and are rarely accomplished by just one individual.[79]

90

In this section, we will explore the roots of contemporary church models.

The Jerusalem Model: Mono Cultural

The first model of the early church was focused on reaching only Jewish people in Jerusalem (Acts 1-8). This mono centrality seemed to ignore the Great Commandment given by Jesus that called the disciples to reach all nations and cultures (Matthew 28:19). Unfortunately, even contemporary churches and denominations can fall into a cultural comfort zone and focus on one ethnic group. The Church is not called to preach an ethnocentric gospel but a Christ central gospel. God was so displeased at this mono-ethnic model, that He allowed horrific persecution to shake up the church in order to disperse believers and spread the gospel (Acts 8, 11).

The Antioch Model: Multi-Ethnic, Trans-Cultural/ Missional

The Antioch church started when Jewish believers were forced to leave Jerusalem. Eventually, this church became influenced by the Apostle Paul and became the hub for reaching the nations of the world (Acts 13-28). The leadership of this church was multi-vocational and multi-ethnic, as we see in Acts 13:1, 2 (Barnabas was into real estate, Manaen was a politician, Saul was a religious leader as well as a tentmaker, and some leaders were African). Furthermore, according to some historians, walls divided the city to separate ethnic groups. As a result, believers would climb these walls just to get to church because they knew the blood of Christ united all peoples. Consequently, the Antioch church replaced the Jerusalem church as the primary apostolic model based on the Great Commission mandate. Modern churches and movements that are multi-ethnic and mission-focused instead of ethnically homogeneous are drinking from the fount of the Antioch church.

The Greek Model: Individualism

After the Romans ransacked Jerusalem (AD 70 and AD 130), believing Jews were dispersed and the church became primarily non-Jewish. Apologists like Justin Martyr (2nd Century) wore the attire of a Greek philosopher and began to apply the gospel to the Hellenistic culture, "This turn towards a Hellenistic paradigm of Christianity resulted in going from the temporal salvific scheme related to the cross and resurrection and the earthly life of Christ to thinking primarily from above downwards in a cosmic spatial scheme of pre-existence as the Son of God and Redeemer."[80]

Consequently, the church went from a corporate, holistic, Hebraic mindset to an individualistic, Eastern mind-set, "Instead of the faith being explained in simple narratives, language, hymns, baptismal confessions, the relationship of Jesus to God is now explained in the essential, ontological concepts of contemporary Greek metaphysics...Instead of reflection on the dynamic revealing activity of God in the history of this world, the focal point of reflection shifted to a more static contemplation of God in Himself in his eternity."[81]

The Jews looked for the perfect city as in Isaiah 65:17-25 and the Greeks were looking for the perfect human as per the writings of the classical Greek philosophers, "Instead of the faith being explained in simple narratives, language, hymns, baptismal confessions, the relationship of Jesus to God is now explained in the essential, ontological concepts of contemporary Greek metaphysics."[82]

In the next century, the great Church father, Origen of Alexandria, wrote the first-ever systematic theological treatise and introduced a subjective form of biblical interpretation called the allegorical method, which sought to understand the hidden, spiritual meaning behind the plain text of the Scripture. Origen enabled Christianity to be the religion of the future because of his combination of faith and science, theology and philosophy, he attained the theological turning point which made possible the cultural turning point (the combination of Christianity and culture) which in turn made possible the political turning point of the alliance of church and state, which was achieved just over 50 years after his death! The coming Hellenistic paradigm was historically necessary if Christianity wanted to remain relevant and acculturate which would not have been possible without the new spiritual and ecclesial self-understanding on the part of Christianity as embodied by Origen.[83]

Roman Catholicism vs. Eastern Orthodox Claim to Historical Ecclesial Legitimacy

Adherents of Roman Catholicism lay claim to historical legitimacy due to their claim of Apostolic Succession, whilst the Eastern Orthodox Church lays claim to historical ecclesial legitimacy due to the fact that out of it arose the Councils and Creeds that defined true Christian belief and the church.[84]

So, questions arise for both adherents:

1. Does Rome have a legitimate claim to apostolic succession and the right to demand complete allegiance to it as the only real and legitimate carrier of the Christian faith?
2. Does the Eastern Orthodox have a much better claim to legitimacy than all other models based on the fact that its influence came from the Hellenistic era and was the most responsible for defining the faith with the Creeds and Councils, and defending the faith from Gnostic heresies?

In my opinion, Rome does not have a legitimate claim for apostolic succession because the Didache does not say that a person lays claim to the apostolate merely because another apostle laid hands upon them and or made them a bishop. The criterion for being an Apostle is the same as the criterion for an elder. Peter called himself an elder (1 Peter 5), which leads us to the writings of Paul in 1 Timothy 3. Furthermore, the apostolic gift (Ephesians 4:11) is handed down to the church according to the measure of the grace gift of Christ. This is the determining factor of becoming an apostolic leader (Ephesians 4:7-11). Hence, whether it is the Roman or Eastern Church, historical legitimacy is not enough. We need to have a constant flow of apostolicity[85] to perpetuate the faith and continually verify the claims of the risen Christ, from one generation to the next.

The Eastern Orthodox Church is still influenced by its historic roots, including the allegorical method as well as individualism (as contrasted to the Hebraic corporate mindset). The modern Evangelical/Charismatic church still reeks of rampant individualism and the subjective private interpretation of Scripture nineteen hundred years later. This is totally contrary to the holistic, corporate focus and framework laid out by Paul in the Didache (this is especially seen in the dissemination of the gifts of the Spirit in the context of the Body (1 Corinthians 10:16-14:35).

Summary of the radical changes that took place when the church went from a Hebraic to a Greek cultural mindset.[86]

First, starting in the 2nd century the church became a bearer of culture, reaching the intellectual elite because of the sophistication of apologists like Clement of Alexandria, Origen and others who mimicked Greek philosophers in their presentation of the gospel, which was more than a match for any anti-Christian pagan philosophical presentation and/or concept. Furthermore, after the conversion of Emperor Constantine, only Christians began to be upwardly mobile and cultured; non-Christians were looked down upon as unenlightened and uncultured.

Also, as the Roman Empire continued to disintegrate, more and more of its citizens looked to the Christian religion to fill in the gaps. This resulted in increased conversions with a subsequent Hellenization (influence of Greek culture) in the church.

Second, even as Christian apologists scorned pagan religions, they looked with favor upon Greek philosophical systems and concepts. This resulted in a growing tendency to define the faith more precisely and systematize its doctrines like Greek philosophers systematized concepts (e.g. resulting in the creeds of the church).

Thus, salvation went from the Hebraic understanding of emphasizing a historical event or narrative (e.g. the Exodus of the children of Israel; the death, burial, and resurrection of Christ) to salvation through knowledge. The church went from the Hebraic emphasis on experience to the Hellenistic emphasis on enlightenment through the rational understanding of true knowledge. God's revelation was no longer understood in the context of events, but as the communication of truth regarding the being and nature of God.

This is best exemplified by comparing Jesus' Sermon on the Mount (Matthew 5-7) with the Nicene Creed. This sermon by Jesus is all about ethics and totally devoid of metaphysical speculation; the Nicene Creed is all about doctrine and says nothing about ethics. Furthermore, later in church history, Hellenistic influence resulted in more of an emphasis on truth being communicated through images (plastic arts, visual arts and paintings, and even the icons of the present Eastern Orthodox Church) rather than the Hebrew emphasis on communicating truth through the spoken word (Romans 10:17).

In summary of this point, the Hebraic original gospel presents the reign or Kingdom of God as an event by which people should believe and repent; the Greek mindset presents the reign of God as rational truth to be believed. In the Hebraic mindset, the Kingdom of God is in stark contrast to the present contradictions of the present pagan world and serves as a deposit of what is yet to come in its fullness.

The Greek mindset presents the reign of God as a truth to be comprehended as something already fulfilled or complete. Thus, in Paul's understanding, Christ ratified rather than fulfilled the Old Testament because the end is still to come (Romans 15:8). But in the Greek mindset, all is already fulfilled in the cosmic Christ. Faith in God's promises yet to be fulfilled was replaced by the already consummated Kingdom of Christ; Christ's resurrection was a completed event and not viewed as the first fruits of the resurrection of all believers (1 Corinthians 15:20).

Third, because of the first two points, the historical continuity and hermeneutic between the Old and New Testaments were ignored. With the Greek mindset, the historical element of the Old gave way to an allegorical (spiritual, subjective or mystical) interpretation of the Old Testament as a prelude to the New Testament event of Christ.

Fourth, historical thinking gave way to metaphysical categories. Believers began to espouse a vertical relationship between time and eternity resulting in focusing more on heaven rather than on this age and God's involvement in history—looking towards eternity more than on a future restored earth.

Christologically, this resulted in an emphasis on the pre-existent Jesus as the Logos (John 1:1) which spiritualized the Christ event, rather than emphasizing the historical Jesus; the emphasis became Jesus' origin and identity rather than why He came. Speculation on the nature of the incarnation of Jesus shifted from Him identifying with the plight of humanity to metaphysical discussions on the incarnation regarding whether He had one or two natures.

Fifth, the Hellenistic (Greek) approach resulted in shifting the gospel's impact. Instead of eventually transforming the earth realm into a future "new heaven and a new earth" (Revelation 21), the Greek approach emphasized the relationship of the individual soul to God in a spiritual context. Thus, the Hebrew concept of salvation (*yasha*) for this world shifted to the Greek concept of being rescued from material burdens and one's bodily existence, or salvation from this world. Thus, in the Greek mindset, the Christian religion saves people from this earth instead of transforming the earth!

Hence, involvement in this world increasingly took upon itself the form of charity. Even Holy Communion was looked upon as medicine for immortality in the midst of a corrupt world. Communion became the primary way of connecting believers historically to the event of Christ.

The emphasis went from God's involvement in history through the church to merely using earth as a place for individuals to secure rewards for the next life in heaven. The more good deeds an individual performed, the more prayers prayed, the more the individual soul would move towards spiritual perfection and be secured a place in heaven. Many believers even suffered martyrdom so they could escape hell and be rewarded with heaven!

Sixth, Gnosticism (a Greek philosophical understanding of salvation from the material world through knowledge) made inroads into the church even though, by-and-large, the church withstood the heretical elements of Gnosticism (e.g. the heretical beliefs that Jesus never had a physical body, or that the Old Testament God is an evil materialistic god and the New Testament God is a God of love and spirit). Gnosticism's over-emphasis on ontological dualism is still alive in the church today: the difference between the temporal and the eternal, the physical and the spiritual, the earthly and the heavenly, the flesh and the spirit, etc.

Seventh, the church went from a missions movement empowered by the Holy Spirit and led by apostles, prophets and evangelists in the first century to a church in which the Holy Spirit was merely the Spirit of truth, of light, love, and life meant to build up and sanctify the church so that ecclesiology (doctrine of the church) became its sole purpose rather than expanding the kingdom and transforming the world. The church became the mystical universal body of Christ that already actualized the kingdom as the spiritual elite of the universe.

The church became an institution for salvation and Greco-Roman culture. Even when it expanded it did so through church propaganda. For example, those outside the church were uncivilized pagans; evangelization became associated with the spread of civilization and culture. The monks, who practiced ascetic separation from the world, succeeded the martyrs as the heroes of the faith and were the ones most instrumental in civilizing the barbarians who took over the Roman Empire.

Eighth, after the Edict of Milan (AD 313) granted religious equality to Christianity, the church's focus on the heavenly Jerusalem made it possible for the Roman Emperor to have free reign when it came to temporal things. By the time the First Council of Nicaea took place in AD 325 Christ was viewed as a majestic king who granted an audience with His subjects during the liturgy of the church service, done increasingly in majestic cathedrals with Roman architectural designs. This resulted in a compromise of the church in which Christ was to rule in eternity and the emperor was to rule in time. Whereas Jewish monotheism (belief in one God) conquered pagan polytheism (belief in a multiplicity of gods), the Roman monarchy (one king to rule the empire) conquered polyarchy (numerous leaders ruling diverse territories). The unity of the faith would depend upon the unity of the Roman Empire. Thus, the objectives of the church became the objectives of the empire and vice versa.

In summary, the church had to go from a Hebraic to a Greco-Roman cultural approach so that it could evangelize the known world and not remain limited within the narrow confines of Jewishness. The Hellenistic approach was especially helpful in allowing the church to reach cultural elites and intellects.

This approach also led to utilizing art to preach instead of only the spoken word, and to the ordering of biblical beliefs into systematic theology: doctrines and creeds to protect from heresy without and to bring clarity within.

As already stated, this also resulted in a Gnostic view of dualism in which spiritual and physical things were separated. Faith became focused more on the metaphysical understanding of truth rather than on the historical actions of God. The result of this was that preachers began to abandon the hope of an eschatological renewal of this world (Revelation 21:1). Instead, an emphasis was placed on the individual soul escaping the earth and going to heaven. The Church became passive with regard to reforming culture or challenging political rulers. Instead, the Church settled into merely performing acts of charity as its primary act of participation in this world.[87]

The Creedal Model: Consensus Faith

To battle the heresies of Arianism (similar to modern-day Jehovah's Witnesses) and Gnosticism, the church was forced to articulate their beliefs regarding the nature of the Godhead, the Church, and the Gospel, in the form of Creeds (example, The Apostles and Nicene Creeds). This was done through ecumenical gatherings of several hundred Bishops who wrestled with Scripture together until they reached a consensus. To keep the unity of the faith and to differentiate true believers from false, the Creeds were to be recited every Lord's day during congregational assemblies. Contemporary ecumenical efforts to reach an Ecclesial consensus in theology and practice have been influenced by this model in church history.

(In my opinion, there is nothing wrong with this way of keeping consensus in the contemporary church - given the fact that there was also a formulaic confessional means of defining the faith

even in the N.T. Didache. See formulaic sections of Scripture in 1
Corinthians 11:23-26;13; 15:3-8; Philippians 2:5-11; 1Tim.3:16
to name a few)

The Roman Model: Institutional/Papal

After the conversion of the Roman Emperor, Constantine, the
church went from being a persecuted group to a privileged elite;
this resulting in it becoming an Ecclesial institution. Also, through
a series of events, after the Barbarian invasion of Rome, the bishop
of Rome ascended to power (the throne of the Apostle Peter, as
the Vatican states). His authority placed him over the Bishops of
other prominent cities. Hence, the Church went from leadership
through consensus (through the ecumenical councils of Bishops),
to Bishops and Prelates submitting to Papal rule.

The contemporary Roman Catholic Church is still unpacking
the implications of this sixteen hundred years later, "The
development of (Christianity) took place almost in accordance
with sociological laws: the small communities become a large
organization, the minority becomes a majority, the underground
church becomes a state church, the persecuted become rulers, and
the rulers often in their turn become persecutors...which century is
the truly Christian century.[88]

This inorganic method and view of Church becoming an
institution in conjunction with secular political systems is totally
against the thesis of this work which has to do with the church
going back to "The Way of Christ and His Apostles". Jesus never
said, "I am the Institution", rather, He said, "I am the Way" (John
14:6). Christianity has to do with a way of life. This was a common
description for the first-generation Christ-followers (Acts 5:21,
9:2; 19:9, 23; 22:4; 24:14,22).

Reformation Model: Confessional/Scripture Focused

The Protestant Reformation was a move away from Papal authority, extra-biblical traditions, and institutional hierarchical titles (Bishop, Cardinal) and positions. In place of Church canon law and tradition, the focus was on the Bible as the only standard of the faith. There also arose healthy respect for historic church councils and creeds during the first six centuries, as well as the writings of the historical Church Fathers. In addition to the above-mentioned councils and creeds, there was also a focus on the development of confessions, theological writings, and catechisms. The rejection of the office of Bishop took away the only form of ecclesial government that was able to keep the church united. Consequently, after the Reformation leaders "threw the baby out with the bathwater" and rejected the Apostolate as passed down through the bishopric, the church eventually divided into numerous denominations.

Autonomous churches arose that compromised the ability of the church to speak authoritatively, as one voice, to the culture. The Bishops, in the apostolic tradition, were the only ones able to maintain the unity of the churches (Ephesians 4:11-14); this is why, even after the split between the Eastern and Western churches, the divide was limited only geographically. The number of independent churches and denominations were contained since both entities kept the Bishopric in the form of bishops and patriarchs. This 16th century Reformation was the root of all present-day historic Protestant denominations (Lutheran, Reformed, Presbyterian, etc.), as well as independent fundamentalist churches (ex. Independent Baptist churches).

Pietistic Model: Personal /Subjective Faith

In response to the dead, corporate state churches of Protestantism, a movement arose in the 17th century called

Pietism. It emphasized individual salvation with a personal witness in the Spirit that gave assurance of a believer's salvation. Pietism de-emphasized the need for church creeds, councils, and confessions, and prioritized the Bible and prayer to cultivate an intimate personal relationship with Jesus.

This movement eventually became the catalyst for the Moravian movement (in the lineage of Jan Hus, which eventuates in the movement led by Nicholas Von Zinzendorf), which led a 100-year prayer movement. This movement was called "The Lord's Watch" in the 17th century that resulted in the modern-day missionary and revivalist movements. Pietism is also the root of present-day Christian "mystics " and even the 20th-century Christian version of Postmodernism (as espoused by theologians like Soren Kierkegaard).

While the Pietist encouraged the Believer to have a vibrant personal faith as opposed to mere appearance and nominal faith (something condemned in the Didache, 2 Tim.3:5), the downside was that it fed into the rampant individualism. (This individualism started with the shift from the Hebraic to the Greek worldview in the Church beginning in the second century).

Enlightenment Model: Liberal Christianity

In the 17th century, Isaac Newton discovered "natural law" and demonstrated that truth can be discovered without divine revelation. This had vast implications. It led to the separation of truth from scripture and the dividing of science from faith. This was referred to as the "Enlightenment". This eventually led to belief systems such as Deism and naturalistic Evolution (which framed reality without the existence and or participation of a divine being).

Out of this arose liberal theologians and theology. The emphasis was placed on natural knowledge, culture, and the sciences and became the primary lens in which to interpret the Bible. Hence, the values and discoveries of society trumped the eternal values of Scripture. This eventually led to professing Christians denying the supernatural elements of the Bible, including a denial of the bodily, historical resurrection of Jesus Christ.

Thus, the Enlightenment model is the root of the present-day departure from the faith in many, if not most, historic Protestant denominations, which infiltrated segments of the Lutheran, Methodist, Reformed, Presbyterian, Episcopal church and beyond. The revised standard version of the Bible produced in the early 20th century highlights this liberal perspective with their translation of 2 Tim. 3:16 wherein it reads "all scripture that is inspired by God" instead of "all scripture is inspired by God". Such an incorrect translation leaves the door open to parse through and deconstruct the Bible. Such deconstruction reduces the Bible down to merely another cultural artifact, equal to humanistic literary works such as those featured in the Great Books of the West collective.

Revival Model: Awakening/Renewal/Pentecostal

Out of the 17th century Pietistic Moravian movement arose a revival model of Christianity, that was advanced by the first Great Awakenings that revolutionized both England and the colonies of present-day USA. Both John and Charles Wesley were converted by Moravian missionaries, who also impacted George Whitfield. All three of these men preached an individual form of salvation, de-emphasized the State Church and Creeds, and saw revivals that forever altered the Body of Christ. This revival model became the root of the 19th-century holiness movement, the 20th-century Pentecostal movement, the mass evangelistic crusades of Evangelists like D.L. Moody of the 19th century and Billy Graham of the 20th century, the 1950's Charismatic Movement that swept through every denomination including Roman Catholicism as well as modern-day Evangelicalism, and beyond.

With regards to Protestant Missions, David Bosch's book, Transforming Mission, gives us great insights on the development of faith and practice from the Reformation to the present Evangelical church. The following is a summary of Bosh's book:

The Reformers and Mission[89]

-The churches of the Reformation were involved in a battle for sheer survival...

-The Protestant Reformers were weak in extending the faith through Missions because the starting point of their theology "was not what people could or should do for the salvation of the world, but what God has already done in Christ...

-Luther, in contrast to the Roman method- was completely against the use of force to Christianize people.

-Protestants saw their principal task as that of reforming the church of their time, which consumed all their energy and efforts.

-Protestants had no immediate contact with non-Christian peoples.

-They were focused on survival and only after the Peace of Westphalia in 1648 were they able to organize themselves properly.

-In abandoning Monasticism, the Reformers had denied themselves a very important missionary agency and it would take centuries before anything remotely competent would emerge in Protestantism.

-Protestants were themselves torn apart by internal strife and dissipated their strength in reckless zeal and in endless dissensions and disputes – thus little energy was left for turning to those outside the Christian fold.

- While The Catholics prided themselves in the unity and visibility of their church, Protestants' preoccupation was with the right doctrine. This resulted in defining the church based on what happened inside the four walls of a building, not in terms of its calling in the world. This church of pure doctrine approach resulted in a church without mission and its theology more scholastic then apostolic.

-They did not believe the Great Commission passages of Mark 16 and Matthew 28 were still binding – the church had no business getting involved in a mission to the heathen since the Apostles already completed the task of world evangelization. The emphasize lie more with God and His sovereignty and initiative.

-The Lutherans believed that nobody could be excused before God by reason of ignorance because God had revealed Himself to all people through nature as well as through the preaching of the apostles. They believed that the whole world already had the gospel preached to them and that those who were still not Christian should not be given a second chance.

-The Great Commission was for the Apostles only and the pagan nations are savages who are impervious to the Gospel.

- Pietism changed the nature and view of the church in regard to salvation and mission. Under Pietism, the formally correct, cold, cerebral faith of orthodoxy gave way to a warm, devout union with Christ. Concepts such as repentance, conversion, the new birth, and sanctification received new meaning. A disciplined life rather than sound doctrine, subjective experience of the individual rather than ecclesiastical authority, practice rather than theory were the hallmarks of Pietism.

-Zinzendorf opposed the idea of group conversion and emphasized individual decisions for Christ.
-Mission was for him not an activity of the church but of Christ Himself, through the Spirit. Pietism introduced the concept of voluntarism in mission. They believed in the church within the church – which would do missions – this was one step towards mission becoming the hobby of special interest groups, which is the modern Para church movement.

-The Pietistic influence resulted in mission no longer being considered the duty of colonial governments; Mission was no longer limited to rulers and church hierarchy – but was an enterprise with which ordinary Christians could actively participate; Pietism ushered in the ecumenism in missions that transcended the boundaries of nations and confessions; Pietism showed what total commitment meant in a way not seen since the monastic movement.

-Eventually, the Puritan movement which came out of Calvinism added to missionary goals a union of church and state that resulted in a theocracy – which was a socio-political order in which God Himself would be the real ruler; Their eschatology was more post- millennial which shaped the way they viewed mission which was ultimately the gradual improvement of human conditions through Christian benevolence, educational programs and political leadership which would eventuate in the nations being Christianized culminating in the return of Christ.

Restoration Model: The Way of Christ and the Apostles

Epochs are periods of time signified by a drastic paradigmatic change in theology.

These Epochal upheavals shape the history of theology, the church and the world as a whole. Neither the individual theologian nor theology as a whole can simply create a paradigm. Rather a paradigm takes shape in an extraordinary complex of various social, political, ecclesiastical and theological factors. It grows out of them and matures in them. Every theologian must face the question of whether the paradigm of theology still corresponds to the paradigm of his time. The given society is the theological change that occurs within the community of theologians in a university or a base community, in the context of believers in the church and in the background of human community. The paradigm of theology has to be seen in the context of the paradigm of the church against the background of the paradigmatic changes in society; Theologians must not ignore the findings of science but the dialogue between the two must be on the basis of equal rights; The philosophical debate with the theory of paradigm change forces theology for its part to clarify the relation between rationality and irrationality.

The first-century churches of the New Testament book of Acts and the Epistles were decentralized institutionally but united in heart and mind to advance Christ's Kingdom (Acts 2:42-47; Ephesians 4:11-16).

The Way Back to the First Century Apostolic Model

Missiologist missionary to China, Roland Allen (1868-1947), was the one who originally coined the phrase regarding the need for the contemporary church to "go back to the way of Christ and His apostles," he wrote seminal books that greatly influenced the founder of BILD, Jeff Reed. Some of his book titles include:

The Spontaneous Expansion of the Church, Missionary Methods: St. Paul's or Ours?, and more.

Also, around 1948 in Canada, there arose a movement called the "Latter Rain Movement" that began preaching the restoration of the Ascension Ministry gifts (Ephesians 4:11), the gift of prophecy (1 Corinthians 14:1-5), prophetic presbyteries (1 Timothy 4:14), the gifts of the Spirit (1 Corinthians 12:4-8), as well as the Kingdom of God.

This movement has continued to grow exponentially (the name "Latter Rain" is no longer used). Presently, the fastest growth of Christianity globally is Charismatic, Independent, Christian networks led by apostolic and prophetic type visionaries who desire to mimic first century New Testament Christianity. Although this movement is Bible focused and robust, it still walks in the individualistic Greek paradigm as opposed to the Hebraic corporate mindset evident in the original Jerusalem and Antioch church models. This has resulted in numerous Independent apostolic type leaders and movements. Unfortunately, these leaders tend to be territorial, rarely collaborating with other apostolic leaders and networks.

I believe the next phase will be earmarked by a focus on a Christo-centric focus on the Kingdom of God. This model will have the ability to unite all expressions of Christianity, including Charismatics, and non-Charismatics, Evangelicals, Evangelical Roman Catholics, Orthodox, and Anglicans. This Kingdom focus will eventuate in a Jesus Reformation, in which the ongoing and evolving focus will be on the King of the Kingdom more than merely on the work of the Kingdom. This will prepare the way for the glorious church Jesus is returning to receive (Ephesians 5:27) and the consummation of human history in which all things will be united in Christ (Ephesians 1:9-11), who in turn will be subject to the Father so that God will be all in all (1 Corinthians 15:24-28).

In conclusion, these various church paradigms show us the importance and power of how ideas and concepts have generational consequences. What happened in the first to fifth centuries is still influencing and impacting the church world today. This should provoke Believers to become a student of Church history so that we may be able to frame our future. The fact is that for many of us, our present view of Christianity has been colored by the lens of culture or many have been influenced by various past movements that may or may not have had a proper biblical warrant. Of significant importance to me is to see how much the Greek philosophical influence has shaped my thinking, theology and reasoning. It has caused me to realize our thinking, practice, and preaching would change if we were more influenced by the original Hebraic - Apostolic first century model.

In the next chapter I will attempt to contrast contemporary and denominational church models from the New Testament model with a hope to provoke major shifts back to the way of Christ and His apostles.

QUESTIONS TO ASK YOURSELF

1. What are some of the ways the historic church has impacted western civilization?

2. Who are some of the prominent leaders who have influenced western civilization?

3. Name some of the scientists who positively affected civilization?

4. What are some of the roots of contemporary church models?

5. What is the primary root of your contemporary church model?

6. How does the way of Christ and His apostles challenge your contemporary church model ?

Chapter 4

Comparing the Contemporary and Denominational Church Model from the New Testament Apostolic Church Model

In this chapter, we will show the vast differences in philosophy related to building the local church according to contemporary models as well as historic denomination models and the biblical model of the apostolic church.

David Cannistraci, in his book, *The Gift of Apostles*, observes that the fact that Denominations exist is a testament to the need for Churches to cooperate and be unified. However, he notes that "[H]istory's harsh lessons have revealed that the structures upholding most denominations often undermine the purpose of unity, thus creating division and breakdown."[90] He goes on to note that because of this, there is a decline in denominationalism. He states, "Many people now mistakenly equate organized religion with evil and resist any structure at all. Both developments are unfortunate."[91] Cannistraci heralds the rise of Apostolic networks, saying, "Apostolic networks are different from most denominations because, in networks, relationships (not policies and rules) are the main source of organizational strength. Only minimal legal and financial controls are imposed."[92]

The Difference between the Apostolic Church Model and the Contemporary Church

We have already examined the historical roots of many of the most common contemporary churches and movements. In this chapter, we are going to broadly examine the primary differences between the Way of Christ and His apostles as shown in the original church of the New Testament and the most common denominational expressions of Christianity today.

As has already been illustrated in this book, the first century Church, founded by the Apostles, was the most effective in history as it turned the known world upside down and transformed the Roman Empire all within three centuries. Conversely, the modern era methods of reaching the world with the gospel are replete with fatal flaws. This is evidenced in many Para-Church models as well as the typical contemporary local church/denominational model.

To frame this section, let me say that in my opinion, the Parachurch often tries to make disciples apart from the local church family structure, while the typical Denominational Evangelical Church attempts to spread the gospel often in ways alien to the New Testament model.

Contrasts between New Testament Apostolic Church Models and Denominational Church Models

While pastors and board of trustees lead denominational churches, apostolic and prophetic leaders along with a team of elders lead the New Testament church. Seen within the New Testament church model are multiplicities of ministries. The New Testament pattern for church government is seen in Ephesians 4:11; 1 Timothy 3:1-15, as well as Acts 15 in which the general council for church deliberation is seen to be comprised of apostles, prophets and elders.

1. While Denominational Churches are often egalitarian in church government, the Apostolic church government is vertical in nature as the elders and leaders try to discern the will of God while regularly waiting upon the Lord in prayer (See the catechetical missional narrative that the Apostle Luke provided in Acts 13:1,2).

2. While Denominational/Contemporary churches want to attract more members and draw crowds, New Testament Apostolic churches seek to nurture mature sons in the faith (Romans 8:19-22; 2 Timothy 2:1 Corinthians 4:15).

3. Denominational church leadership are often driven by positions, titles and are hierarchical in nature. Churches patterned after the New Testament model is driven by organic relationships. Jesus called his disciples to be with Him, not merely to do bible studies with Him. As we see in the Gospel accounts, Paul often called those who walked with him his sons (II Tim. 1:2; Titus 1:4). Of course, this is because both the Old and New Testaments adopt the family structure for their governmental model (1 Tim. 5:1,2; Hebrews 1:1).

4. Denominational church structures compartmentalize and isolate foreign missions, church planting, and evangelism. The Acts narrative illustrates that Apostolic churches are missional in nature. They are proclamation communities who continually send out leaders. What Jesus commanded His disciples before His ascension illustrates the nature of the church and the fact that the church should never be separated from its missional assignment. In Acts 1:8-9 Jesus said, "You will be my witnesses and to the ends of the earth." This defines the Apostolic kerygmatic community. Furthermore, we see how Paul's method of evangelism was based upon the capacity of the local churches he planted; there were no separate evangelistic crusades. In II Corinthians 10:13-16, Paul made it clear that his missiology was expressed through a robust ecclesiology related to his prescribed methodology of evangelism.

The context of the following snapshots from the book of Acts shows how evangelism emanated out of the local churches:

- Acts 6:7: And the word of God increased, and the number of the disciples multiplied in Jerusalem greatly, and a great company of the priests was obedient to the faith.
- Acts 9:31: Then had the churches rest throughout all Judaea and Galilee and Samaria, and were edified, and walking in the fear of the Lord, and in the comfort of the Holy Ghost, were multiplied.
- Acts 12:24 - But the word of God grew and multiplied.
- Acts 16:5 - And so were the churches established in the faith and increased in number daily.
- Acts 19:20- So mightily grew the word of God and prevailed.

Hence, the present method of having evangelistic crusades with a visiting gifted evangelist does not fit the Pauline model. According to the New Testament model, the Gospel was spread through established local congregations who were empowered to plant the gospel outside of their region (1 Thessalonians 1).

5. Denominational churches often are separated from those they send out apostolically. New Testament churches partner with and stay connected to their overseeing apostle through the following ways:

A. Financial Resources: They partnered financially with their apostolic leader and also sent apostolic teams to support the apostle. Every one of the churches Paul started had a commitment to continue their partnership with Paul as the founder, by financially supporting his apostolic ministry. This is evident in the following passages. In Philippians 1:1-5 Paul said of the Philippian congregation, "I thank my God upon every remembrance of you, Always in every prayer of mine for you all making request with joy, For your fellowship in the gospel from the first day until now"

In 2 Corinthians 8-9 we see how a cluster of churches Paul founded supported his missionary benevolent project for another city church. This indicates that even their giving was missional and apostolic in nature.

B. People Resource: In addition, many of these congregations also supplied people who would serve alongside Paul on his apostolic team (Philippians 2:25-30; 2 Corinthians 8:16-24; Romans 16:1-2). Paul said in Philippians 2:25, "Yet I supposed it necessary to send to you Epaphroditus, my brother, and companion in labor, and fellow soldier, but your messenger, and he that ministered to my wants." Again, we see in II Corinthians 8:16-18 Paul says, "Thanks be to God, which put the same earnest care into the heart of Titus for you. For indeed he accepted the exhortation; but being more forward, of his own accord he went unto you. And we have sent with him the brother, whose praise is in the gospel throughout all the churches." Paul goes on to speak of others who helped such as Phebe, Priscilla and Aquila (In Romans 16:1-4).

6. Denominational as well as Evangelical churches often separate themselves governmentally from their Apostolic leader who often becomes trans-local. New Testament churches remain under the Apostle's oversight. Hence, the local church remains committed to the global expansion of the gospel by partnering with their itinerant apostolic leader and the apostolic leader stays connected to the local church through the congregational elders.

7. Denominational churches are held together by common creeds, rituals and by sharing resources. New Testament churches organically relate based on common doctrine, common missional call, and connected spiritual households.

8. Denominational churches are often held together legally by central property ownership, funding for projects, and hierarchical ecclesial structures. Apostolic New Testament churches are primarily voluntary associations of congregational clusters that form complex apostolic networks. They echo the Pauline methodology as demonstrated in the Acts narrative:

   - Each church planted in a major resource city and became a church planting hub that eventually formed complex networks of churches and apostolic teams that edified one another.
   - Paul planted the church in Ephesus. Acts 19 says the Word of the Lord went out to Asia Minor. This resulted in the birthing of the seven churches (spoken about in the book of Revelation) as well as the churches in Melitus, Assos, Troas, Hierapolis, Colossae. Hence, if we follow the New Testament Pauline pattern of church planting, we will not merely plant local churches, but we will create movements of disciples in strategic cities and locations.

9. Denominational Churches equip leaders for Sunday ministry. New Testament churches equip leaders to influence their marketplace assignments for the Kingdom.
   Since the early church did not meet in huge edifices, the Christian movement did not gain cultural credibility by filling Cathedrals with huge crowds (this started after Constantine favored Christianity starting in 313 A.D. in the Edict of Milan). The only credibility this New Testament House Church movement had was based on their witness, benevolence, and spirit of excellence in the marketplace. This is why Paul laid so much importance on Christians doing good for their surrounding communities as we see in the Didache (Titus 2:14 and 3:8).

10. Denominations are driven by tradition, canon law and policy/The N.T. The apostolic church is motivated by vision and mission.

    This is why the primary catechetical narrative for missions is called "The Book of Acts"- not "The book of Truth or theology"! The missional flow of the Acts narrative is meant to be a prescriptive (not merely a descriptive) account of the normal life, values, and ways of the original Jesus movement.

11. Denominations are usually theologically, sociologically and culturally motivated in biblical interpretation. The Apostolic hermeneutic is missiological in nature and motivation. Unfortunately, often the hermeneutic of historic Protestant denominations is more in line with contemporary cultural mores, anthropology, psychology, as well as the social frameworks related to human sexuality and family than the Hebraic worldview of the biblical authors. Since those in the present Apostolic restoration are informed by the Bible as the authoritative word of God, and not anthropology, psychology, and various social frameworks, they tend to take the Scriptures at face value which naturally catalyzes a burden for missions, evangelism, and church planting.

12. Denominations focus on the glory days of the past. Apostolic movements emphasize the present move of God in season. It is unfortunate that most of the historic Denominations' best years are behind them, (with the exception of some major Pentecostal denominations and a few others). Hence, they have to constantly go back to their past to justify their present in order to attain a glimmer of hope for their future. In contrast, those currently involved in the Apostolic Restoration Movement are excited about their past, present, and future. They find their inspiration from the Holy Spirit as they move towards the mission, vision, and purpose of His kingdom.

13. Denominations emphasize the religious institution. The Apostolic emphasizes the movement. Although there is nothing wrong with churches starting entities that become institutions in society (hospitals, universities), the local church itself should never be calcified but forever function as a movement. It should be like a river instead of a swamp. After the conversion of Constantine in 312 A.D., the persecuted church became the powerful elite, the decentralized "saints driven" house church movement became a clergy-led institution that began to build famous cathedrals and "The Way"[93] became an institution that went from being the prophetic voice to become subservient to the Roman emperor and his empire. Hence, the Church allowed the leaven of Herod (Mark 8:15) to permeate and transmute their mission and essence. As a result, the once-powerful Apostolic church became merely a cultural-religious institution (of course after Rome fell great apostolic missions movements led by people such as St. Patrick started converting the Barbarians of Europe).

14. Denominational clergy are assigned by their superintendent or bishop. Apostolic leaders are led by the Spirit in regard to their ministry assignment. The present-day denominational structure gives the responsibility to bishops or superintendents of assigning pastors to a particular parish. Some denominations (ex. Roman Catholic and Methodist) give their priests and pastors a new geographic assignment every few years. This ensures that the denomination always maintains more power over their parish than an individual leader. Conversely, the Apostolic Church leader is led by the spirit and guided by the elders as to their ministry assignment (Acts 16:6-10; 13:1-2).

15. Most mainline Denominations believe in a higher critical view of biblical inspiration. and place anthropology,

sociology, psychology, empirical science and cultural norms on the same level or elevate them higher than scripture. Apostolic leaders generally believe in biblical inerrancy and or have a very high view regarding the inspiration of Scripture.

This makes a huge difference due to the fact that those who actually believe the Bible is the word of God are more obligated to obey it's mandates since they cannot explain it away by saying it's commandments are archaic or no longer culturally relevant.

16. Denominations emphasize committees to implement strategic plans. The Apostolic emphasizes the power of Christ and faith to fulfill their mission. Although the Apostolic Church is not against the use of committees and implementing strategy, they are not shaped by the present corporate CEO model that is often utilized by Evangelical churches. Instead, they wait on the Lord in prayer, and fasting, exercising faith together as elders and leaders in order to get divine guidance and grace to fulfill their God-given mission.

17. Denominations utilize seminaries to train clergy. Apostolic utilizes the local church as their primary training ground to develop leaders. As we see from the New Testament Didache, especially the Gospels, Acts and Epistles of Paul, the local church (functioning as the Jesus community of disciples) was the primary methodology of leadership development.

Sending a potential leader out to a Bible school or university to prepare them for church leadership apart from the local church would be as silly as having an intern perform heart surgery without conducting surgery with an experienced surgeon. Just accumulating mere knowledge and obtaining a master's degree is no guarantee a person has the capacity to lead in the context of the cauldron of human relationships. When the Church adopted the methodology of the Greek Academy and forsook the methodology of the New Testament pattern as seen in II Timothy 2:2, it failed to produce the scale of leaders necessary to keep up with the global expansion of the gospel. Sending someone off to Seminary is expensive for most burgeoning believers, (especially in the developing world). It has also proved to not be wise to separate a person for several years from their apostolic oversight and pastoral covering.

Elders, overseers, and all church leaders were developed in the early church in the context of their congregations, which is why they were able to multiply disciples. Whatever is not practical is not spiritual. This is why the criterion for church leaders was that they were required to manage their own household well and have a good reputation in the marketplace (1 Timothy 3:1-8).

Even in my own experience, I have found that individuals with extensive marketplace experience lead many of the most influential churches and movements in the world. This perhaps because of their ability to integrate spirituality with practical real-life issues related to leadership, management, strategic planning, working off budgets and outcome-based goals, causes them to understand how to apply their faith in a way that impacts their church and community. After all, Jesus did not choose one religious leader as one of His 12 apostles. Instead, they were all versed in the marketplace arena related to either money (one was a tax collector), politics (one of them was a zealot) and business (at least four of the brothers had their own fishing business). Consequently, the concept of using the theological academy to nurture top church leaders is not necessary to the New Testament Apostolic pattern for the development of mature disciples who are to permeate whole cities with the gospel.

The Challenge of Parachurch Ministries

Parachurches are ministries that operate outside of the context and the oversight of the local church. Although they may partner with local churches, their ministry does not emanate from and through the local church unless it is a local church network, movement or collective.

Many parachurch ministries tend to separate the gospels from the epistles because they reason that Jesus made disciples of 12 men before the local church was born. However, those with this line of reasoning fail to understand that Jesus always had the Church in mind when building His disciples. Acts 1:1-2 implies that Jesus continued to do and teach through the apostles who subsequently formed the church. Acts 1:1-2, says, "The former treatise have I made, O Theophilus, of all that Jesus began both to do and teach, Until the day in which he was taken up, after that he through the Holy Ghost had given commandments unto the apostles whom he had chosen." Most of the gospels (except for Mark) were written after the Epistles of Paul were written. They were written for the purpose of collecting the written and oral sayings of Christ. They compiled the synoptic Gospels to give context to the church when catechizing their new converts. In Luke 1:4 the Greek word for teaching is the root word for catechism, hence the gospels were used to help establish people and churches in the kerygma (the simple proclamation or gospel of Christ). So, the Gospels were always connected to the church. A person should never think they could make disciples outside of a local congregation.

Contrasting Institutions and Movement

It might also be helpful at this point to make a contrast between an institution and a movement. Denominational churches tend to participate more in an institutional structure, whereas Apostolic Churches and networks tend to participate more in a movement (though they have the potential in their ensuing generational cycles to become institutionalized).

Timothy Keller in his masterful book, Center Church, portrays a stark contrast between the two. (I've included his words below, without the graph form, which is how Keller presents it in his book).

Institutions are held together by rules and procedures. Movements [are] held together by common purpose and vision.

- *Institutions*: a culture of rights and quotas; a balance of responsibilities and rewards
- *Movements*: a culture of sacrificial commitment

- *Institutions*: Changes in policy involve a long process, all departments, much resistance and negotiation
- *Movements*: Vision comes from charismatic leaders; accepted with loyalty

- *Institutions*: decision made procedurally and slowly
- *Movements*: decisions made relationally and rapidly

- *Institutions*: values security and predictability
- *Movements*: values risk, serendipity

- *Institutions*: emphasis on tradition, past, and custom. Future trends are dreaded and denied
- *Movements*: emphasis on present and future; little emphasis on past

- *Institutions*: jobs given to those with accreditation and tenure
- *Movements*: jobs given to those producing best results[94]

In summary, the first century Apostolic Church had the following as a general template:

- A leader was sent out of the city church as an apostle.
- The apostle would plant other churches in other cities.
- In each church the apostle would leave and plant another church after a strong eldership team was raised up to care for the flock.
- These churches had a global apostolic vision by continuing to stay connected to their apostle with financial support, praying regularly for him, supplying co-workers for the apostolic team, and staying accountable and keeping regular communication with him.
- The apostle continued to have governmental rule without ministerial proximity and hands-on leadership.

In the next chapter, based upon my four decades of experience, I will share practical ways to build an apostolic local church , a regional network and a global apostolic movement .

QUESTIONS TO ASK YOURSELF

1. What are some of the primary differences between the New Testament apostolic church model and denominational models?

2. What was one of the negative results when the church adopted the methodology of the Greek academy and forsook the New Testament pattern?

3. Does your church properly utilize marketplace leaders? If not why?

4. What are some of the conceptual challenges of para church ministries?

5. What are some of the contrasts between institutions and movements?

6. What are some of the changes you will make as a result of understanding the way of Christ and His apostles?

Chapter 5

The Process of Building an Apostolic Local Church, A Regional Apostolic Network, and a Global Apostolic Network

In this chapter, I will relate how I founded a local Apostolic Church, a regional Apostolic Network,[95] and a national Apostolic Movement in the USA. I will also show their connection to a vast international Apostolic Movement. Additionally, I will unpack the Pauline model of being both a "master builder and a thought leader". In my model for ministry, I always endeavor to replicate Paul's work based on my God-given DNA and my affinity for the Pauline model of apostolic leadership.

This topic has been shaped by the work I have done as both a church planter and builder of coalitions. Let's start by delving into the New Testament topic of master building and relate it to our contemporary situation.

PREAMBLE:

Understanding Master Builders, Builders and Thought Leaders

During my leadership journey since the early 1980s, I have noticed various gifts amongst leaders that are not necessarily understood or even taught, neither in seminary nor in theological or leadership books. For example, when I peruse through some of the writings of New Testament Scholars, (even those whose focus is Pauline writings), the concept of a "Master Builder" never even comes up, even though it was how the Apostle Paul described himself (1 Cor.3:10). I surmise that the reason for this is because our knowledge base, insight, and vocabulary are largely based upon the knowledge we use, not mere head knowledge or abstractions.

Consequently, great theologians and New Testament scholars will speak about Paul's theology with great expertise while at the same time bypassing his main missional call, which is that of a "Master Builder." This is not a criticism but a realization that many of our greatest teachers are not practitioners of what they teach. As a result, their limited practice creates a limited framework of biblical interpretation.

While the Apostle Paul described himself as a master builder, he was also a thought leader (theologian). Sometimes, on rare occasions, there is overlap. Some examples of this can be seen in great leaders in history such as Martin Luther, John Calvin, St. Augustine, Abraham Kuyper, John Wesley. Some of our contemporary leaders follow this pattern. Thought leaders and Master Builders often leave a huge imprint with their ability to think biblically and apply Scripture to the building of Gospel movements. However, more often than not, leaders focused on building movements are not necessarily thought leaders and vice versa. The following are delineations between master builders and thought leaders

Master Builder

The Greek word for Master Builder is architekton (1 Cor. 3:10), which is where we get our English word for an architect. This refers to a master builder, expert builder, and director of works.

Paul also said that he was a "wise" master builder. The Greek word for wise is Sophos which means a clever, skillful, experienced, wise, expert. Hence, Paul was not only a builder but a wise master builder. We can see this illustrated in Acts and the Epistles, which shows that he planted churches in over thirty key cities of the Roman Empire. Out of this emanated a vastly complex network of churches and leaders who worked together to do mission in both local and global arenas.

Paul and other Christian missionaries went to great cities because when Christianity was planted there, it spread regionally (cites were the centers of transportation routes) it also spread globally (cities were multiethnic, international centers and converts took the gospel back to their homeland) and finally it more readily affected the culture (the centers of learning, law, and government were in the cities)...the importance of cities for Christian mission today is, if anything, even greater.[96]

This network included the use of apostolic teams, financial support, apostolic leaders, and prayer support to ensure that Paul was able to fulfill his apostolic mandate.

On a local level, the network was held together by the disciples they made and by the elders and deacons that Paul and his team placed as overseers over each of the local churches they planted in each of the cities (See the pattern exemplar in Acts 14:21-23). Paul was a unique apostle! Nowhere else in the New Testament do we see any other Apostle referred to as a "Master builder" not Peter, nor James, nor John. While they all might have been builders, not one of them had the kind of capacity to build complex networks and launch a missionary movement the way Paul did.

In my own personal observation, I have seen only a few contemporary Master Builders in the body of Christ. There are many teachers, mentors, and builders but few Master Builders.

By a Master Builder, I am referring to a person who not only has the message of Jesus but is also able to implement a Holy Spirit inspired method. This method then aptly applies the gospel in such a way as to garner the support of others (through evangelism, discipleship, and networking of other believers and leaders), which then creates networks and gospel movements.

These Master Builders are not only visionaries that influence and attract other great leaders, but they are able to harness the energy and excitement that arises from their vision. This is done through a strategic framework that perpetuates vision and creates movement and momentum that catalyzes systemic change in the church place and workplace.

Master Builders not only have a vision, but they are able to create systems that create other systems and subsystems. With multiple wheels in motion, it is sometimes hard to tell who the overseer of the movement is. They understand that the key to any movement is the distribution of labor. Some examples of Master Builders in the workplace are the entrepreneurs who take the idea of the "mom and pop shop" hamburger and make a franchise out of it (McDonald's); They take the formula for soda and design a world-class brand out of it (Coca Cola and Pepsi).

These master builders are also able to create the blueprint for a network or coalition effortlessly because it is in their wheelhouse or sweet spot. Some of them can put the blueprint for earth-shattering movements on a napkin while having an informal meal. One of the weaknesses of a Master Builder is seen in a high "D" personality type (Doers). Master Builders can tend to be frustrated when they are around other leaders who only know how to give a good talk but have no practical understanding or ability to implement their ideas.

Hence, they become sick of talk because they have the need to only do.

Builders

Builders are those who can create a network or coalition, but mostly a self-contained network with limited success or influence (perhaps with a community rather than a national or international dynamic). They may even be an effective church planter who can give themselves to one or several churches for the rest of their life, without creating momentum for a citywide or extra-local network or movement. Hence, what distinguishes Builders from Master

Builders in the context of this preamble is the fact that Builders have a more limited scope of building as opposed to the Master Builder who creates a movement way beyond the local context.

While Builders can create systems, Master Builders can create systems that spawn other systems, subsystems, and movements. In my opinion, this Builder emblem is the category most successful church planters, nonprofit leaders and workplace leaders fall into.

While builders are gifted leaders, in that they are able to create a blueprint for a building, (like a typical architect), it is usually limited to a house. On the other hand, a Master Builder is able to build an apartment complex for hundreds of families.

Thought Leaders

Thought leaders are the thinkers, scholars, theologians, and communicators of information that have the gift of conveying their ideas in such a way as to be a prophetic voice and a trendsetter. Because of their unique assignment, most of their time is focused on research, serious study, giving lectures and getting their content out in the form of books and all forms of social media. While they have a great ability to influence the thinking of thousands, even millions of people, they themselves do not have the capacity, nor the divine assignment, to build anything more than a teaching platform. Their greatest burden is to receive insight from information and serious study and to present it to as many people as possible. They are their happiest when they are giving a talk or preaching at a large or influential conference of leaders, finishing a cutting-edge book, or communicating their thoughts before thousands of people via social media.

While those called to be master builders and builders would be frustrated if all they did was to distill information and speak at conferences, the thought leader thrives in those situations. Thought leaders can still have a huge impact, especially if within their audience are builders and master builders who understand how to put their ideas into practice and implement a strategic plan for movement. Thought leaders can sometimes feel discouraged or frustrated when they hear the criticism of others who tell them that they never built anything. What others fail to understand is that these thought leaders would not be as effective if they had to focus on building an entity or movement because the building would require administrative or managerial responsibilities that would take much of their time and focus away from contemplation, prayer, and study. This would greatly dissipate their ability to stay on the cutting edge of prophetic ideas.

Whenever I see a thought leader being placed in an administrative role or see him attempt to build a network, I know that it is only going to last a short time, failing to succeed. They cannot attempt to do what builders are gifted to do, rather, their primary focus should be focused on inspiring master builders, builders, and other thought leaders. A biblical example of a great communicator who was not a builder was Apollos (Acts 18:24-28). He came to the city of Ephesus to preach and teach and won several disciples to Christ. However, it wasn't until Paul came to Ephesus and found disciples (probably the same disciples Apollos won to Christ), that a church was planted, and a gospel movement was launched that shook all of Asia Minor (Acts 19:1-23). Paul said it best when he told the Corinthians "I planted, Apollos watered, but God gave the increase" (1 Corinthians 3:6). Here Paul wisely shares the importance of making room for both teachers and builders. Also, in the First Testament, we can see how Ezra was the primary teacher and Nehemiah was the Master Builder whom God used to bring about the restoration of Jerusalem (see the books of Ezra and Nehemiah).

In conclusion, we should never undervalue the significance of the thought leader who communicates the Word, whether it be via book, social media, or in person. Paul said that God manifested His Word through the preaching that was entrusted unto him

(Titus 1:3). We should also begin to recognize the extraordinary function and significance of the Master Builder function not often spoken about, but one that is desperately needed, if we are going to not only proclaim the gospel but create Gospel movements.

Now that I have laid the groundwork for what I deem is the master building concept laid out by Paul, I will now chronicle how global and national apostolic networks were launched.

The Genesis of the International Coalition of Apostles (ICA)

The following accounts are based on my first-hand knowledge of the organization and key people connected to the said organization, as well as the fact that I was a member of ICA since 2000.

Sometime around the year 2000, several leaders of networks around the world met in Singapore for several days for unifying the global apostolic movement. After their gathering, they agreed that it was necessary for this group to form a coalition. Among those present was John Kelly, who was nominated by the group to lead the newly formed "International Coalition of Apostles." After leading the group for almost three years, Kelly asked Dr. C. Peter Wagner to take the lead as the international Convener. He asked him for a number of reasons, one of which was due to his name recognition and another because of his ability to garner a critical mass of members identified with the apostolic movement. Kelly's foresight proved to be true since, under Dr. Wagner's leadership, the movement grew to a peak of approximately five hundred Apostolic leaders, representing hundreds of thousands of churches across the world, spanning every continent. [97]

Dr. Wagner, in accord with his role as a researcher, sought to give practical/theological definitions to the term Apostle so that the potential membership of ICA would fit the criteria to be considered an Apostle. Wagner defined Apostle as:

[A] Christian leader gifted, taught, commissioned, and sent by God with the authority to establish the foundational government of the Church within an assigned sphere and/or spheres of ministry by hearing what the Spirit is saying to the churches and by setting things in order accordingly for the expansion of the kingdom of God...Apostles, by definition, have been given the spiritual gift of the apostle by the grace of God...Some are territorial apostles to whom God has given authority covering a certain geographical area such as a neighborhood, a city, a state or a nation. Others have authority in a certain societal arena such as government or finances or media, etc...Among those with the gift of apostle, some have the ministry of vertical apostle. This means that they are in an apostolic leadership position over a network of churches and ministries or a network of those who minister in a certain affinity sphere such as women, prayer, youth, worship, etc. Others are horizontal apostles, who have a ministry of convening and connecting peers such as other apostles or pastors or prophets, etc.[98]

Dr. Wagner, as a renowned missions expert, stated that his research showed that ICA had become the largest expression of the Apostolic movement in the world! When Dr. Wagner turned eighty years old, he turned over every organization he oversaw, including ICA, to various spiritual sons and daughters. Consequently, Kelly was chosen by Wagner in 2012 to take back the helm of oversight as the convening apostolic leader of ICA. Within a few years, Kelly began to release apostolic leaders to start their own national coalitions. Such action caused the movement to go from primarily a U.S. based leadership association to a global movement. As a result, it grew from several hundred members to several thousand members in a short period of time. Currently, it had approximately 15 national coalitions.

The launch of USCAL

In 2014, I was approached by the International Council of ICA and asked if I would be willing to launch a coalition that would specifically focus on the United States. I accepted this request under the condition that there would be a name change; instead of International Coalition of Apostles, it would be called, The International Coalition of Apostolic Leaders. This was important to me because I did not feel comfortable using the title Apostle as an office since I viewed the ministry gifts mentioned in Ephesians 4:11 more as functions than as offices of ministry. The council, after a brief deliberation, unanimously agreed to change the name since many of the leaders, including Kelly were of the same persuasion. Consequently, the way was paved for the coalition to be called "The United States Coalition of Apostolic Leaders" (USCAL) as opposed to "The United States Coalition of Apostles".

The first year after my commissioning to launch USCAL, I focused on setting up backend systems, (formed an administrative team, a website, bank account and a 501C3), and national council. This council was made up of about 70 national and regional apostolic leaders in the church place and the workplace. (This council included some of my close associates like John Kelly, Jeff Reed), Harry Jackson, Dale Bronner, and more). They would be the core leaders responsible for driving the movement forward. It was important to include marketplace leaders, since, in my view, the reign of Christ is not relegated just to church buildings but is demonstrated in the marketplace of ideas; it works in the societal spheres of politics, business, economics, education, science, music, art, media, family, etc.

This council also represented a diversity of ethnic leaders, male and female, young and old, and other nuances meant to represent the Kingdom of God. In addition to the council, I instituted a Leadership Initiative Team (LIT). This team consisted of 18 significant leaders with a national influence that would function as a sort of board of directors in the initial stages of our development. Also, so we would have the capacity to represent and reach all communities in the cities of America, I invited Bishop Dale Bronner to be the Co-Convener of the movement. Presently I am in the process of starting a Hispanic arm with another co-convener, who will lead this endeavor. Furthermore, out of the LIT group I appointed Steve Fedesky as the "Chief strategic officer" of the movement. John Kelly serves as my primary mentor, helping me lead the movement.

After several years of developing USCAL's infrastructure, in 2018 I launched an executive team to aid in the strategic implementation of operations. With the consultation of the team, we created a mission statement to help guide everything we do so that it aligned with my own DNA, vision and my record of accomplishment in ministry.

It should be emphasized that the importance of coming up with a compelling vision cannot be overstated. Timothy Keller said, "A vision consists of an attractive vivid and clear picture of the future that the movement and its leaders are seeking to bring about. A movement states "if this is where you want to go, come along with us."[99]

> USCAL's 4R Vision statement:
> R - *Restore the church to the mission and method of the way of*
>   *Jesus and the apostles*
> R - *Reconciliation between ethnic leaders and churches*
> R - *Revive the church to expand kingdom influence*
> R - *Reformation of* society and the discipling of the nations

Restoration of the Church

The idea of the restoration of the Church was made popular by the notable early 20th-century missiologist Roland Allen. Allen focused primarily on Acts and the Pauline corpus to recapture the

Way of Christ and the Apostolic teachings. Such teachings were in opposition to the unbiblical methods of the 19th and 20th Century Western missionary model.[100]

USCAL's first goal is to help restore the church to the "Way of Christ and His Apostles." Doing so means restoring the simplicity, authenticity, and effectiveness of the Apostolic New Testament Church model. The Apostolic Church in the first century was marked with rapid growth; such growth penetrated every aspect of culture. This resulted in the transformation of the Roman Empire within three centuries! Some of the characteristics that are universal, transferable, and applicable that we, as a coalition are attempting to recapture in our context are:

1. The restoration of functional fivefold ministers as stated in Ephesians 4:11,12: Those functioning in the ministry gift of apostle, prophet, evangelist, pastor, a teacher with or without the title, who are called to equip the saints to fulfill their vocational calling to glorify God in every cultural sphere.

2. The restoration of the New Testament pattern related to the development of autonomous local church governance under the "set one" (pastor), out of which will arise, functional elders, deacons, administration, and the ministry of helps. These will then become the core leadership team of every congregation (1 Corinthians 12:28,29; 1 Timothy 3:1-8).

3. The visionary apostolic leader that convenes and galvanizes other churches and marketplace leaders in their region to produce a movement resulting in flourishing communities and cities.

4. Voluntary associations between autonomous local congregations, organizations, and associations that function interdependently through covenant, under the leadership of apostolic leaders, without denominational limitations or control.

5. Complex apostolic networking that produces hubs of leaders, local churches and marketplace entities that interface with other similar hubs in other geographic locations. This would result in a cohesive national Christian movement affiliated internationally through ICAL. (One great resource to understand this concept would be to read *The Churches of the First Century: From Simple Churches to Complex Networks* by Jeff Reed published by BILD. org<http://BILD.org>)

Reconciliation

The prayer of Jesus in John 17:20-23 shows us that the world will not believe the Gospel as long as His church is fragmented and divided. In the present church, there is ethnic and denominational division. In addition, there are a plethora of independent evangelical churches that are non-affiliated and in essence, if not consciously, building their own empire instead of God's Kingdom.

It is the goal of ICAL and USCAL to model the prayer of Jesus and encourage apostolic leaders in each nation to build bridges and cross-ethnic and denominational lines. It is only when apostolic leaders cross-pollinate and enter into Kingdom partnerships, that the Body of Christ can be one, thus having significant kingdom influence in each nation.

The famous passage related to unity spoken by Jesus in John 17:20-23 does not merely imply organizational unity but rather spiritual ontological unity. The passage is referring to believers being one with God in heart and mind (2 Peter 1:4) and the believers being of one heart and one soul (Acts 4:32; 1Corinthians 1:10). It is interesting to note, as it relates to the importance of recognizing the continued function of the apostolate, that the Eastern and Western Church split in the 11th century did not fragment the Church. They continued to recognize the office of the bishop, which was a continuation of the function of the apostolic ministry as far as church government goes. This contrasted with the Protestant Reformation, which rejected the bishopric and only recognized the function of pastors and teachers. This resulted in the vast fragmentation we see today in the global church because only apostolic leadership could hold the church together!

Revival

ICAL and USCAL work to see local churches and all Believers infused with the passion and power of God, according to the promise of Acts 1:8, to reach every nation for the Lord Jesus!

Only a vibrant church can awaken sinners and usher in the glory of God in nations. Every generation has to experience a true, heaven-sent revival, or else they will resort merely to man-centered strategies in the quest to expand kingdom influence. Evangelism and church growth merely through the use of technology, marketing schemes, and cultural relevance, without the manifest power and presence of God, will result in a weak, ineffective church. ICAL and its affiliate coalitions endeavor to promote true revival in every nation!

Reformation

By reformation I am referring to participating with Jesus for the renewal of all things. Revival in and of itself is not enough. Merely awakening sinners and filling churches will not bring systemic change to society. ICAL (and USCAL) espouses the original "Cultural Mandate" of Genesis 1:26-28. This mandate obligates apostolic leaders (in both the church and marketplace), to think through issues related to stewarding the earth and reforming nations. Truly, revival brings people into the church, while reformation equips the saints and commissions them to go into every sphere of society to reflect the Kingdom of heaven on earth (in heaven every person and system is aligned under the Lordship of Christ). Merely reviving the church without a goal for reformation is limiting; it will often result in megachurch growth but have little influence in culture.

Jesus, as the "Last Adam" (1 Corinthians 15:45), pointed us back to the original "cultural mandate." He commanded us both to win the lost (Mark 16:15-17) and disciple people groups/nations (Matthew 28:19, 20). Isaiah 61:1-4 teaches us that the good news that comes to the poor, heals the brokenhearted, and brings liberty to the captives, should also result in repairing ruined cities and healing the devastation of generations. Consequently, the proof of the gospel is not only transformed lives but also flourishing cities and nations. Finally, according to Isaiah 2:2-4, God's goal is not only for individual conversions but also for nations to adopt His moral laws for institutional transformation. This is the mission that ICAL and USCAL seeks to accomplish.

The Launch of Christ Covenant Coalition

In 1999, around the same time in which ICA was launched, fellow leaders urged me to consolidate the vast network of pastoral relationships I had developed. I was encouraged to start a formal association/coalition. After one year of meeting with key apostolic leaders of churches and networks, I launched Christ Covenant Coalition (CCC). CCC was started with a team of 12 key pastors who, at the time, were also emerging apostolic leaders. We initially met only once every quarter. For the past twenty years we have developed, within CCC, many deep relationships. Many of the leaders have developed their own apostolic networks. This was something that I intentionally sought to encourage because I believe as leaders, we are called to replicate ourselves in those we lead. I believe that by replicating what you do, you are not merely creating a coalition but a movement.

Eventually, we became a "network of networks" and evolved into having a criterion that allowed only those walking in apostolic function in the church place or workplace to join. We keep the movement together by having monthly zoom video meetings for mutual prayer, edification, and teaching. In addition, we have an annual conference, retreat and other gatherings. It is the closest thing I have ever seen to the book of Acts as we have done life together and have developed deep relationships. Several of us go on vacation together. Some have even joined the preaching team of our local church campuses so that I can be released to do extra-local ministry and to oversee USCAL.

Recently, we launched a church campus in the borough of Staten Island N.Y., in 2018, without a full-time pastor. However, the campus was run with a team of leaders and at least two of the apostolic leaders of CCC preaching twice per month. These CCC apostolic leaders not only preach but help develop the leaders in both our Brooklyn as well as our Staten Island campuses.[101]

The Launch of an Apostolic Church

By "Apostolic Church" I am referring to a church that makes disciples, sends them out, reaches and serves their surrounding community, networks other churches and community agencies, and is a flashpoint for what is happening as the center of the life of the community they reside in.

Another important feature is the fact that said church has a "Kingdom agenda" that transcends their own empire/building; that is to say, they are concerned about the wellbeing of the gospel being proclaimed by the Body of Christ at large and that they work to serve His Body for the sake of the expansion of His Kingdom influence.

Resurrection Church

In 1984, we were sent out by my local church to start a church in the very challenging community of Sunset Park, Brooklyn New York. After about twelve years of intense ministry, forging partnerships with other churches, community leaders and nonprofits, we saw our at-risk community of about 165 thousand people (high school dropout rate of almost 50 percent), experience a complete quality of life transformation. It should be noted that this was done without gentrification.

In addition, in the past thirty-plus years, we have sent out many high impact leaders who planted other effective churches or launched ministries that are effectively impacting youth throughout the nations. We also instituted "City Church" meetings once per month in which hundreds of leaders and people from other churches gather for a night of teaching, renewal, and worship. In addition, my wife Joyce launched a nonprofit[102] that reached a few thousand at-risk children (with about 350 children being bused into our church building once per week for about 18 years). This eventually expanded to include holistic educational programs that helped break the generational cycles of poverty for untold thousands of Hispanic and Asian children in Sunset Park.

In analyzing how these coalitions and churches were built, I have the following principles that are applicable to others desiring to launch a similar movement:

20 Things to Consider When Planning an Apostolic Network of Networks

"Again, the kingdom of heaven is like a net that was thrown into the sea and gathered fish of every kind" (Matthew 13:47).

As the Apostolic movement gains momentum, the practice of networking has begun to flourish again in the Body of Christ.

Church-growth analysts are beginning to identify apostolic networks as a modern movement. World changing leaders and movements are arising to establish progressive structures for families of churches and ministries. The weaknesses of traditional denominationalism are succumbing to the strengths of apostolic networks...An Apostolic network can take many forms. Essentially it is a band of autonomous churches and individual ministries that are voluntarily united in an organized structure...the network becomes a melting pot of strategy, vision, methods, teaching training and programs...An even higher level of networking is on the horizon for the church. Networks forming in the emerging apostolic movement will noticeably benefit the Body of Christ. Consider how these same benefits could increase in quantum force if the various networks could connect with each other in relationships and shared resources. What could be accomplished by networking networks?[103]

Having an apostolic network of networks means nothing if all anybody does is periodically come together for an event. The following are some of the biblical principles needed for an active apostolic network:

1. Your mission and objective must be apostolic and not pastoral in nature.

   The pastoral is primarily inbred for fellowship, while the apostolic is for activation and mission.

   Thus, the apostolic visionary initiator of the network should articulate a compelling vision to motivate action and ownership amongst the participating pastoral and marketplace leaders.

2. The Apostolic Leaders need to have not just unity in meetings but exhibit biblical oneness. Unity is merely temporal, based on a particular event; it does not go deep enough to be described as oneness. Biblical oneness results in creativ-

ity and purpose; it arises out of a true relationship, prayer, and covenant not merely joint activities and ministry.

3. The apostolic leaders need to be transparent with the pastors and leaders in their network. Paul as illustrated in 2 Corinthians 12:1-12, was incredibly transparent. This enabled people to know his heart which in turn built greater trust amongst his spiritual sons and congregations.

4. The apostolic leaders need to have an egalitarian spirit while being able to exert the apostolic government. What I mean by this is to treat everyone like a peer even if you are their spiritual father or if they are under your oversight. By doing this, the apostolic leader will build friendships, not only ministry associates.

5. The apostolic leader should host regional gatherings so that pastors can come together
   In CCC, we host quarterly regional prayer gatherings that build further unity in the city. These gatherings also create a platform for significant corporate intercession and deeper relationships.

6. There can be apostolic mission trips that include pastors and marketplace leaders.
   Taking a week-long trip to accomplish a kingdom purpose can be a significant way of building deep, purposeful relationships amongst those serving together in an apostolic network

7. Include various levels of leadership in annual planning processes.
   By this I am referring to getting as many people involved in the process of planning as possible, using a layered approach of different levels of interaction based on the levels of spiritual authority, maturity and commitment to the vision. Pastors and leaders that are part of the planning

process will have more "buy in" and make the network more cohesive.

8. Be process driven through relationships, not event driven. Doing events together should be viewed merely as a catalyst for leadership to connect informally after said events. Apostolic networks that are merely driven by events will be limited in its capacity to be effective unless there is intentionality related to providing an ecosystem conducive to covenantal building amongst the members.

9. Have annual seasons of prayer with all the key leaders to hear the voice of God.
I have found that there is nothing more powerful related to building purposeful relationships than when leaders pray for one another as well as for their city and region.

10. Activate marketplace leaders who are good at strategic planning and development.
In both CCC and USCAL, I utilize marketplace leaders significantly as part of my inner circle since they are the best at understanding how to go from A to Z related to vision implementation.

11. Activate leaders based on their abilities and passion.
The most frustrating thing a visionary leader can do is to give another leader a role that does not fit their gift mix and passion. There is a reason why God gave the church the fivefold ministry as found in Ephesians 4:11. Never give a pastor the role of an apostle or an evangelist the role of a teacher.

12. Decentralize and distribute labor. The key to creating a movement is the distribution of labor. Hence, the more leaders are mobilized and given a task they can run with, the more movement will take place.

13. Allow the network to highlight and organize around events, outreaches, and ministries that leaders in the

network are already doing. Why recreate the wheel? Find out what is already happening amongst the leaders in the network and have the whole apostolic family connect to it!

14. The apostolic council needs to communicate regularly. In both USCAL and CCC, we regularly receive input from those who serve on the council. In USCAL we have about 70 national council members, scattered among the various regions of the USA, from both the church place and workplace. Prior to the COVID pandemic we met face to face twice annually and have approximately three to four zoom meetings per year. If leaders are not engaged, there will be a tendency to feel like they are merely council members in name only and will quickly lose interest.

15. Each apostolic leader has an autonomous network that affiliates with the network of networks. In CCC, we encourage all our members to develop their own networks related to their spheres of influence, (whether the church or the marketplace). Since we started having a vision for this since our inception in 1999, we have seen many of our leaders develop their own networks, which has morphed CCC into being established as an apostolic family of networks.

16. Do life together. In CCC, we primarily attempt to do life together by meeting together in person, via zoom video, and by staying in touch outside of the context of official gatherings. We have been there for each other in emergencies and have been able, as a coalition, to help build each other up so that our various ministries can be sustained for the long haul. Thus, we have morphed into being a fraternity of brothers, sisters, and sons who are advancing the kingdom together. Conversely, a non-relational network is merely an association of professionals meeting together to compare notes and enlarge their platforms.

17. Do doctrine together (Acts 2 :42) in which all other activities arise. In ICAL and CCC, we have common core teachings and confessions that we gather around, hence, we are confessional movements.

18. Apostolic teams need 4 types of leaders
I have found that for every network there needs to be at least four kinds of significant leaders working together.
    1. visionary or directive
    2. strategic
    3. team builder
    4. operational who builds administrative systems and policies
Lacking one of these is most likely the death knell of the movement.

19. Need to develop apostolic vertical churches with horizontal impact.
By vertical we are speaking about the need for every network to help cultivate the emergence of apostolic centers or churches in each region or community represented by the members. Churches have to be vertical in nature to depict the fact that they have overseers in the church who direct the members. True apostolic churches impact their community and integrate church and marketplace ministry. True apostolic churches consistently nurture leaders to send out to plant other churches or to have horizontal marketplace influence so that the church "gathered" on Sunday becomes the church "scattered" on Monday. In these kinds of churches, the lead pastor eventually emerges into the apostolic function, focuses on the community or church planting, and is able to lead the church via the pastoral elders. Consequently, the apostolic leader develops an extra local ministry but retains local governance and oversight through the elders.

20. Need the apostle/prophetic component to understand the times and the seasons in order to adapt the methodology. Every apostolic leader needs prophetic people around them (sometimes it is their spouse!), to give them spiritual insight, warnings, as well as strategies from the Lord.

Seven Primary Stages Involved with the Launch of Any Viable Movement

The following were seen in the context of one who has launched a national network, several church campuses, a "vertical" apostolic network, and a multi-ethnic multi-denominational social political movement called "City Action Coalition" (that lasted from 2003 to 2016). That being said, from my experience and observation, I have found that there are 7 primary stages related to launching any kind of movement:

1. Conviction

A conviction can be described as a fixed or firm belief in something. In order to have an effective movement, there usually has to be one primary visionary person serving as the catalyst. A person with great vision is necessary to overcome all challenges and making sure there is a significant accomplishment. This visionary's passion ignites a fire so that his or her conviction spreads to others, in the same way fire spreads to other combustible material. The combustible material, in this case, are the strategic people who are recruited by the visionary based on shared convictions.

One of the challenges of the church today in this post-modern culture is that there is so little conviction about truth. This has resulted in an "anything goes" culture, in which we rarely, if ever, aggressively attempt to confront the status quo. For example, liberal mainline denominations are seeing tremendous drops in church attendance because their lack of belief in the Bible as the

Word of God leaves them with little or no conviction. Hence, they have little or no distinction from non-believers.

2. Covenant

By covenant we mean an agreement or contract between two people or between a person with an organization or entity. The early church became the greatest force in world history, taking over the Roman Empire by the third century AD because Jesus began the movement by cutting the covenant with His own blood. He required His followers to take up their own crosses and drink this same cup if they wanted to be His disciples (Luke 14:24-27; Mark 10:38).

A movement will have a hard time getting anywhere if there are no criteria for how a person gets involved. I have found that the "loosey-goosey" groups that have almost no commitment amongst followers flounder as organizations and go nowhere as movements. I am aware of countless apostolic movements from the 1980s and 1990s that no longer exist today because there was no real covenant amongst the leaders. The higher the standard for membership, the more committed the followers will be and the higher-level leaders you will attract.

All ministries should be preceded by a relational covenant. This is needed for it to withstand the challenges to its mission and is necessary if it is to be an agent for transformation. The strongest relationships in the world are those built on covenants between two people joined together by what they perceive as God's will.

3. Courage

Courage to start a major movement comes from the camaraderie born out of like-minded people coming together for a significant purpose. Even the greatest leaders in the world have had moments when they needed their closest associates to encourage them to continue on in the battle; i.e. Jesus needed

James, John, and Peter in the Garden of Gethsemane and Moses needed Aaron and Hur to lift up his hands so that victory over their enemies would be assured. The Holy Spirit wants to breathe courage on powerful assemblies of committed people in the same way He did for the early church (Acts 4:29-31). Anytime a person or organization wants to go against culture (the status quo), and systemic sin (Ephesians 2:1-3), it is going to take great courage, especially since the initial stages of their mission will bring great challenges.

4. Collaboration

By collaboration, I am referring to a point in the mission when gifted, successful people, and influential networks, join together as a coalition. This happens because those involved realize that to successfully bring transformation, they will be more effective in accomplishing their goals if they unite with like-minded movements and leaders than attempting to do it alone. This can only happen when the primary visionaries are secure in their calling and willing to defer to one another according to their leadership capacity, skill, resources, and organizational strengths. Too many times movements have failed because visionaries fighting for a common cause were more concerned with remaining the "top dog" in their organization than winning the battle for transformation. The more secure leaders are in their calling and gifting, the more they tend to collaborate with other strong leaders for the glory of God. The more insecure, the less likely they can collaborate with other strong leaders. I have found that, in order for collaboration to be possible, leaders of networks and movements have to be willing to sacrifice some of their "pet doctrines" and methodologies ((issues related to eschatology, pedo-baptism, women in ministry), for the greater good of fulfilling the Cultural Mandate.

Timothy Keller says, "Some churches identify so strongly with their own theological tradition that they cannot make common cause with other evangelical churches or other institutions to reach a city or work for the common good. They also tend to cling strongly to forms of ministry from the past and are highly structured and institutional."[104]

5. Cohesion

For collaboration to last for the long haul, leaders, their networks, and their followers need to cohere. That is to say, they need to attach themselves closer together in their networks so it looks like one big movement to the enemies of their cause. Collaboration implies a strong sense of independence. For it to work, their unity needs to go deeper as they progress closer towards their goals. A movement among gifted, independent people, and networks, can only proliferate and multiply commensurate to the ability to cohere as interdependent people and entities.

6. Confluence

When various independent streams of people and networks cohere, they begin to flow together in such a way that they actually become a powerful movement (similar to the confluence that occurs when numerous streams come together and become a river). God's power is described as a mighty river proceeding from His throne to the universe (Revelation 22 and Ezekiel 47).

7. Change

Nothing motivates the continual perpetuation of a movement more than creating positive change for people and communities. The more a movement can actually point to real-life success, the easier it will be for them to gain both followers and money to fund their vision. In the beginning stage of a movement, called the idea stage, only a few will invest financially into the organization (usually because they trust in the visionary more than the vision). An organization needs to tout as many success stories as possible in their journey to keep morale high and money pouring in. The bottom line for any movement is to produce lasting change in individuals and beyond. A movement without testimonials to its effectiveness is an organization that only exists to satisfy its leadership.

Networks in the Context of the Pauline Model

Paul started churches in approximately 31 major cities in the Roman Empire.

Some of these churches, like the Ephesian church, served as hubs that became a feeder church out of which other churches were planted; they also served as a resource center for other churches. For instance, from Ephesus the word of the Lord went out to all of Asia Minor and several other churches were started out of this Apostolic church (Revelation 2-3). The churches in Macedonia helped other churches financially (II Corinthians 8-9). From these churches, apostolic teams also emerged and served with Paul. All of the above resulted in Paul creating complex apostolic networks that helped perpetuate the spread of the gospel in Europe and Asia Minor for generations to come. As a result, the church rapidly expanded across Europe and North Africa in the first three centuries of its birth until it slowed down in the West the next 1500 years when it took a hierarchical turn.

The first century Pauline model of church planting created an unprecedented Jesus movement ignited by spontaneous expansion, "St. Paul's theory of evangelizing a province was not to preach in every place in it Himself, but to establish centers of Christian life in two or three important places from which the knowledge might spread into the surrounding country. This is important, not because he preferred to preach in a capital rather than in a provincial town or in a village, but because he intended his congregation to become at once a center of light...all the cities or towns in which he planted churches were centers of Roman administration, of

Greek civilization, of Jewish influence, or of some commercial importance."[105]

Jeff Reed sheds the light on the explosiveness of the early Church and God's divine hand in such an expansion. He writes:

What do I mean by spontaneous expansion? The churches expanded throughout the Roman Empire in a spontaneous fashion, not according to a carefully detailed plan of man, but rather within the strategic intent of apostolic leaders who responded to open doors, under the circumstantial and sometimes interventional direction of the Holy Spirit.

As described in Acts and Paul's letters, the expansion contained the following elements:

1. *The scattering of the Jerusalem church through persecution...*
2. *The strategic intent of Paul as he evangelized strategic cities...*
3. *Individuals and churches spontaneously permeating the surrounding areas, planting new churches*
4. *Other apostolic leaders and leaders contributing to the progress of the gospel in key cities and regions of a Europe*
5. *Paul and eventually other apostolic leaders giving shape to all the churches through the circulation of the body of their letters and Gospels, grounding them in the Kerygma and Didache.[106]*

Reed references the book, *Linked*,[107] to bring understanding to the Apostolic networking that could have occurred in the early beginnings of the 1st-century church. The following is a summary of Reed's points:

The book, *Linked*, described various expressions of connectivity, which eventually evolves into a complex network of networks. He makes a distinction among Nodes, Clusters, hubs, hierarchies and communities, and scale free networks/complex networks.

Nodes (the smallest points of the network).

Clusters, Modules (When Nodes cluster together if they are similar in nature).

Hierarchies and communities (collections of node clusters and modules that in essence multiply, creating a natural, weblike hierarchy).

Scale-Free Networks, Complex Network (Scale free networks are networks with many complex webs, surrounding us, which are far from random. (p. 34,35).

Reed states that in the beginning to understand the incredible network of the early churches we must understand house churches in and around strategic cities...(Antioch, Rome, Ephesus, Corinth).

To summarize some of the findings of Jeff Reed:

The Small World of the churches (Nodes which were house churches averaging between 30-70 people in each church that networked together all over the Roman Empire that shared the common DNA of the Gospel (Kerygma) and the teaching (Didache).

From nodes (churches) to clusters (Small city-based church networks) to hubs/connectors (strategic cities) to complex networks (apostolic leaders-sodality/modality, Jerusalem councils, publishing house, Paul's communication network.

As the churches multiplied, they also began networking together with each other and with strategic city-based network clusters....

From church clusters to strategic church hubs.

Strategic cities became network hubs.

From strategic church hubs to complex apostolic networks.

Hence, we see in Reed's analysis that hubs evolved and were shaped into complex apostolic networks by the Apostle Paul and his team. The result shown by this book is that "the system he (Paul) built held the network together in the correct way for 300 years".[108]

In the following chapter I will share some of the foundational theological constructs that contributed to the contemporary apostolic movement. This is important to understand if we are going to further evolve as a church into the N.T. pattern of the way of Christ and His apostles.

QUESTIONS TO ASK YOURSELF

1. What is a master builder?

2. Why was Paul the apostle considered a master builder?

3. What are the primary differences between master builders and thought leaders?

4. What is the 4 R vision of USCAL?

5. How does this vision statement comport to the way of Christ and His apostles?

6. What are some primary things to consider when planting an apostolic church?

7. What are some primary things to consider when launching a network of churches?

8. What were some of the methods Paul utilized when he planted churches and networks of churches?

9. What are the seven stages involved in the launch of a viable movement?

10. If you were to start a local church or movement of churches -what would be your primary focus in the beginning?

Chapter 6

The Theological Construct and Paradigmatic Patterns of the Global Apostolic Movement Since Its Modern Reemergence in 1948

In this chapter, I will analyze the foundational theological assumptions of the apostolic movement, some foundational biblical writers who frame the movement, and its evolution (since 1948), to the present apostolic theological paradigm.

Some of the basic theological paradigms underpinning various apostolic movements since the mid-20th century[109]

For years, (thanks to scholars like Jeff Reed and Hans Kung), I have been reflecting on what is the core gospel, what is the essentials of Christianity, as well as trying to comprehend what my response is based on the ecumenical perspective of men like Hans Kung. Although I don't agree with Kung regarding his theological ecumenicism, I have been stimulated to ask questions regarding the essence of what I truly believe – to which I am grateful for Kung and other ecumenical scholars.

I have reflected on what Christianity should look like in its purest form, which has led me to attempt to formulate a Christianity based on the first-century apostolic church and apply it to the network of churches I oversee. I have also been stimulated by the question regarding which century reflected true Christianity the most so I can have a model to back up my theological perspectives regarding what the church and Christianity should look like? Another question I have asked is, "what is the true church?"; Is it Roman Catholicism, Eastern Orthodoxy, Protestantism, or fundamental Evangelicalism? In addition, I have sought to understand which expression of Christianity is closest to its purest form?

In reflecting on these, I have concluded that the Evangelical stream, the New Testament Apostolic movement, is Christianity in its purest form. I believe this for a number of reasons, one such reason is that churches and leaders relate on a voluntary covenantal basis and not on a legal hierarchical basis that is often more political than it is spiritual and Christian. This is why the first "R" of the vision statement of USCAL is, "To Restore the Church to the Way of Christ and His Apostles".

Theological Constructs that Have Influenced the New Apostolic Movement

1. The Word of Faith Perspective

Those who have been taught in the tradition of Kenneth Hagin, Kenneth Copeland and others in the Word of Faith movement (which started in the 1950s and gained great popularity in the 1970s), often read everything in the Scriptures with the lens of using their faith to access God's promises and view Christ's finished work on Calvary as the keys to receive divine healing and prosperity. Their focus on the New Testament often causes them to neglect much of the Old Testament except when references are made to passages regarding healing in the Pentateuch (Exodus 23:25, Psalms 103:1-5, and Proverbs 4:22). They read the New Testament to see who they are or what they have "in Christ." Thus, it is an individualistic, rights-centered approach to scripture that is very weak on the corporate nature of vision, purpose, and prosperity. Also, this perspective lacks a biblical worldview when it comes to the application of the Old Testament law of God to civil society. In my opinion, this perspective is also an American cultural construct that has framed their view of the Scriptures and Christianity. They greatly lack a proper view of ecclesiology that is especially found in the New Testament Didache and the epistles of Paul.

They don't necessarily embrace such things as the functional ministry gifts of Jesus (Ephesians 4:11); leading with the consensus of a multiplicity of elders (1 Timothy 3:1-15); the need for interdependent cohesion amongst churches through complex apostolic networks; the making of disciples according to the Pauline pattern of 2 Timothy 2:2; and mutual accountability amongst apostolic leaders (Acts 15). Their lack of understanding related to faith is also evident since faith is used primarily for individual blessing, resulting in their hermeneutic totally missing the corporate essence related to the application of Scripture. Their view of prosperity is disconnected from the church and is totally individualistic, which is totally against the corporate blessing taught by Paul in passages such as Philippians 4:4-19.

In spite of its many weaknesses, this perspective can still be effective when it comes to learning how to believe God for the miraculous!

2. The Liberation Perspective

Liberation theologians and their adherents emphasize the suffering of Christ because they read the scriptures generally through the lens of class warfare, prejudice, and victimology. Thus, the sufferings and cross of Christ (who was crucified by the majority culture), become a model for all suffering, oppressed people who believe Jesus has come primarily to give them economic and political liberty from their oppressors. The challenge regarding this view is its potential to reduce Christology to anthropology and Christianity to a mere geopolitical and economic liberation movement. They have allowed their view of the role of large government (Marxism) to overpower the Scriptures to such an extent it doesn't even remotely represent the "Way of Christ and His Apostles".

That being said, some in the apostolic movement have been influenced by this message when it comes to their perspective regarding the alleviation of poverty, systemic injustice, and social activism. This is especially the case when it comes to some expressions of the church in Latin America and among some in the African American church that has been exposed to Liberation Theology.

3. The Perspective of Self-Empowerment

In the past two decades, we have seen the incredible rise of motivational speakers (i.e. Tony Robbins). Many preachers have used this perspective in their preaching. The result is that many sermons are based on the practical issues of the Bible related to topics such as hard work, faith, focus, understanding a person's unique gifts and calling, and bearers of the image of God to do great works like God. The challenge with this perspective is the lack of balance. Proponents often do not balance their message with other passages related to Jesus' teachings on self-denial, suffering, taking up the cross, and forsaking everything to follow Him. Scripture teaches us that before we can save our lives we have to lose them (Mark 8:35). Also, the emphasis in the Scriptures on long-lasting blessing is tied to personal transformation through holiness, humility and dependence on God and not self-empowerment through confidence in our own natural abilities.

They also miss the corporate nature of both the Scriptures and the application of the teachings of Jesus and the apostles, since it is replete with a sense of the cultural aspect of rugged American individualism. Truly, a Christ-follower can never fulfill his destiny by mere self-empowerment, rather, that follower needs to function in the context of the Body of Christ (1 Corinthians 12:11-26).

4. The Pietistic Perspective

The perspective of the Pietist lends itself to searching the scriptures primarily to bring inner transformation and a personal closeness to Christ. Holiness, walking in the Spirit, hearing the voice of the Lord, and denying oneself are all emphasized. While all these are necessary for the Believer, the weakness of this perspective is that believers can become so contemplative and self-focused that it stops them from being effective. Their focus on their own emotional and spiritual transformation cause them to neglect the proper emphasis Christ gave us when He called us to go to all the world to preach the gospel (Mark 16:15-18) and influence culture (Matthew 5:13-16). Also, the emphasis on participating in a disciple-making church planting movement is lacking. This is because there is no missional focus of the "Way of Christ and His Apostles" (as found in the catechetical missional book we call the book of Acts) because individual transformation is the focus.

Nonetheless, the historical Moravian movement as modeled by Count Zinzendorf in Herhut in the 17th century, is an amazing corporate model of community that gave birth to the modern Protestant missionary movement that emanated out of a 100 year-long prayer meeting. If the contemporary Pietistic, Apostolic and other movements mimicked Herrnhut, then its proponents would more closely reflect the "Way of Christ" and His Apostles.

5. The Great Commission Perspective

This perspective involves an individualist view of the gospel that is all about winning souls and making disciples. Anything done by a church or believer that does not directly lead to converting and maturing people in Christ is jettisoned or viewed as unnecessary and lukewarm. The weakness of this view is its tendency to be one-generational and not practical enough for the everyday lives of growing families. It was generally a construct of Western European

159

fundamentalists in the USA beginning in the late 19th century to the present time. These are the ones who live in the suburbs, in affluent communities, and who did not see the need for a holistic gospel that helped ameliorate the conditions of poverty, lack of quality education and family fragmentation in at-risk inner-city communities.

It is also not always conducive for those who have a long-term goal of producing wealth for the kingdom, and who want to put their children through the best universities for cultural credibility and access. There is also a possible lack of emphasis regarding empowering influential marketplace leaders called to infiltrate the systems of the world (e.g. like the prophet Daniel).

Although it can and should lead to disciple-making, in general, its adherents do not understand the way of Christ and His apostles when it comes to such things as embracing the fivefold functional ministry (Ephesians 4:11), the reign of God, and the corporate nature of evangelism and conversion experiences as illustrated by Paul (2 Corinthians 10:10-15; 1 Thessalonians 1).

6. The Reformed Perspective

Those trained in the Reformed (Calvinist) system of interpretation will read the Bible deductively through the lens of the sovereignty of God, instead of through the big story of God. Although I resonate much with this system, I have seen some that subscribe to this system go to extremes. As a result, they become passive regarding fasting and prayer as it relates to winning souls and extending God's mission and kingdom on earth. Some proponents of this perspective deemphasize human responsibility more than scripture does. The result is, instead of proactively extending the kingdom of God through the kerygma, they passively wait for God to convert people and add them to their congregations (which are generally small, inbred subcultures that center around theological correctness). This is in spite of the fact that the book of Acts is a prescriptive, catechetical missional narrative that makes it clear the church is called to continually extend the way of Christ and His apostles to the ends of the earth.

Also, in general, this sect of the church disregards the gifts of the spirit and embraces only two of the functional ministry gifts (pastor, teacher) because of their Cessationist leanings. However, many of us in the contemporary apostolic movement have been able to glean from reformed theologians. We "eat the meat and spit out the bones." We apply some of their perspectives related to having a system of sound doctrine (the shorter catechism of the Westminster Confession) that aids us in our pursuit of the Way of Christ and His Apostles.

7. The Free Will Perspective

On the opposite extreme from the Reformed perspective is a Free Will (Arminian) perspective. Such a perspective overemphasizes human responsibility to the extent that God's sovereignty is sometimes compromised. This leads to superficially interpreting difficult passages regarding divine calling and election (Romans 8:29; Ephesians 1:4) by replacing predestination with foreknowledge so that God chooses someone based on Him already knowing that person would (of their own free choice) choose Him in the first place. Such an overemphasis on free will leads to process theology and open theism, which teaches that God doesn't really know everything in the future because much of it is unknowable. This extreme emphasis on free will makes it very hard to trust in the relevance of scripture since God is still learning and growing as the future unfolds. Such a view makes it extremely difficult to have a biblical worldview in economics, science, politics, law, ethics, morality, family and sexual orientation because of the inability to have trans-historical universal principles that we can trust. Also, if God is not sovereign then humankind is semi-autonomous.

This view has historically flung open the doors to liberalism. While a small handful of those connected to the apostolic movement espouses some aspects of this view like "Open Theism" (Peter Wagner), they have not successfully infiltrated our movement. Among the many challenges I have with extreme Arminianism, is that it goes against the clear fact that the sovereignty of God was clearly manifested in orchestrating the events for His Kingdom to manifest on earth. One can look at the gospel of Luke, and the Acts narrative, and see that they are replete with instances demonstrating how God was behind many of the events, connections with people, and providential guidance to such a degree that even demonic rulers were confounded by the turn of events as noted in 1 Corinthians 2:8.

8. The Kingdom Perspective

The Kingdom's perspective interprets much of scripture and biblical themes through the lens of the original cultural commission as found in Genesis 1:27-28. The primary theme of the New Testament is not the church, soul-winning or even discipleship, it is the Kingdom of God. The Kingdom of God is the rule of God over all creation. This perspective motivates people to understand the sacred calling they have regarding the stewarding their God-given gifts and abilities to serve with excellence in the marketplace. Discipleship in this perspective does not just involve the teaching of individual sinners but the discipleship of whole nations (people groups and subcultures), in accordance with their interpretation of Matthew 28:19. They believe that the gospel is holistic and should not only redeem sinners but also transform the systems of culture (politics, economics, art, law, ethics, music, family, education, science, etc.).

The challenge for this perspective is the tendency to think we are doing God's kingdom work just by improving the quality of life in our communities, even if we are not winning souls and making disciples. In our catechetical missional narrative (Acts), we find that the making of Spirit-empowered disciples who formed Jesus centered communities was the key in the transformation of communities and regions (Acts19). Hence, Paul never focused on politics and economics; he focused on forming disciple-making communities and movements that transformed their marketplace sphere.

9. *The Individualistic Perspective*

This is a common perspective that can arise out of our national culture (i.e. rugged American individualism as personified in our iconic action heroes like John Wayne and Rambo). The weakness of this perspective is that much of the Bible was written either to the nation of Israel (Old Testament) or the Body of Christ (New Testament). Thus, we cannot fulfill our destiny and accomplish our mission in life merely by ourselves; we need to submit to a local church and function in the corporate context of scripture if we want to reap the fullness of the blessings of the promises of scripture.

It is unfortunate, but many in the global apostolic movement have been so influenced by this perspective that they generally have an individualistic view regarding biblical hermeneutics. It translates into them wanting to build their own kingdom instead of partnering with other apostolic leaders. This hinders them from understanding the corporate essence and nature of the Body of Christ as we see in the "Way of Christ and His Apostles."

10. *The Ecclesial Perspective*

Those with this perspective think that the church is the Kingdom of God. They don't teach that Believers are called to infiltrate and disciple the nations of the world with the gospel. Instead, they believe that we are to focus on building our own subcultures within our congregations. Those with this view have a great understanding of the corporate nature of scripture. However, many in this camp fail to understand how the church should be sent into the world as salt and light. Although they believe the church is to function as heaven on earth, they fail to understand the breadth of the mission of the church which is to bring God's kingdom and will on earth as it is in heaven (Luke 11:2-4). They believe that the Kingdom is only truly manifested to the extent that their local church is healthy. Although I agree with this, I would add that a truly healthy congregation will commit itself to good works that benefit the surrounding community, not merely the particular congregation. (Titus chapters 2-3; Ephesians 2:10; Galatians 6:10).

In conclusion, there are many more perspectives I could have mentioned. For the sake of time, I have only mentioned ten of the main perspectives I have seen influencing the people of God today in the global apostolic church. As stated earlier, these are only based on my observations and, because of this, it is limited by my own perspective and experience. I also realize that this section merely paints pictures with a broad brush and misses the nuances and overlap of many of these perspectives. My prayer is that we will try to be more open as to the interpretive system we bring to the table based on our perspectives. Also, we ask God to help us see what ways we may be limiting our capacity to interpret the Word based on the biblical authors' original intent as inspired by the Holy Spirit.

Theological Constructs of the Contemporary Apostolic Movement

All the charismatically laced theological constructs noted above have contributed in varying degrees to the theological construct of the modern apostolic movement. It was already mentioned in a prior chapter that the roots of the Apostolic Movement is found in the Pentecostal movement of the early 20th Century –hence. By and large, most of those identified in the Apostolic Movement are either Pentecostal or Charismatic in nature or are sympathetic to it.

Influential Apostolic scholars who have influenced the foundational Apostolic theological constructs.

The purpose of this overview is merely to survey seminal foundational writings related to the Apostolic Movement since it began to mature in the late 20th century. Highlighting the following authors is not necessarily an endorsement of all their teachings and practices.

Furthermore, as a general critique of the following authors, I cite (with the exception of Alan Hirsch), these pioneering theologians that emerged since the Restoration movement of the late 1940s. They generally do a marvelous job of laying out the foundation and patterns of understanding the local church and the role of the fivefold ministry gifts of Ephesians 4:11.

However, they indicate in their writings that the five cluster gifts (Ephesians 4:11) are only for some in the Body of Christ, not everyone. Such an understanding stands in opposition to a clear contextual reading of Ephesians 4:7-16. Ephesians 4 clearly indicates that the ministry gifts, which were Jesus' ministry DNA, reside in every member of the Body of Christ.

Hence, these authors are not broad enough regarding to their understanding that every single believer, to one degree or another, has at least one of the fivefold gifts functioning inside of them. These gifts are not relegated to the church place but have room in the workplace.

That is not to say that the church is so flatlined that there are no people with the stewardship to be fivefold ministry, called to be the spiritual leaders in the church like we see in Hebrews 13:7,17. There are obviously people with a special grace like Paul (Titus 1:1) who have received their apostleship for the sake of God's elect.

While some of these scholars seem to lack the panoramic egalitarian view of Ephesians 4:11, some would argue that Alan Hirsch goes too far the other way and flatlines the ministry gifts to the point in which some could argue he believes in a totally decentralized, position-less movement of disciples. They argue that Hirsch's view lacks an understanding of the need for spiritual leadership as exhibited by Paul and his protégés Timothy and Titus (2 Corinthinas13:2; 1 Tim. 1:3-4; 4:11-12; Titus 2:15). That being said, I do not hold this view of Hirsch because of my numerous interactions with him.

Since I want to be fair in my representation of the present apostolic movement, I desire at this point to allow some of the significant contributors to the maturation of the movement to speak for themselves.

Kevin Conner. A summary of his biography indicates that he is recognized internationally as a Teaching-Apostle after many years in both Church and Bible College Ministry. He has written many textbooks used by ministers and students alike throughout the world. Conner was perhaps the most prolific of the early apostolic scholars whose numerous books laid a sound biblical foundation for those involved in Apostolic networks. His most important contribution, in my opinion, to the apostolic movement was his seminal book, *The Church In The New Testament.*[110] This was the primary book that shaped my view (back in the early 1980s) regarding the function and government of the New Testament Church.

In this work, Kevin lays out the pattern for building churches according to the New Testament as well as gives an understanding of the fivefold ministry gifts as taught by the Apostle Paul

(Ephesians 4:11). In addition, he underscores that their primary function is to equip the saints for the work of the ministry.[111]

The Set Man. Conner speaks about the "Set Man" principle which is based on 1 Corinthians 12:28; he observes that Christ has "set first in the Church Apostles". His premise is that the founder of a church should not be automatically called a pastor, but that "set man" overseeing a church is the apostolic elder.[112]

Elders. Kevin teaches that the "Set Man" is also an elder and serves as the "first among equals" in an egalitarian system that is somewhere between the modern Episcopal and Presbyterian view of church government.[113]

Deacons. Conner shows how the original deacons were to function in the "ministry of helps" (Acts 6:1-12) as opposed to the apostolic leaders, whose main call was the ministry of the Word and prayer (Acts 6:3,4)[114]

Church Government. Conner lays out the various expressions of church government common today in the church which include: Presbyterian (Elder ruled), Episcopal (Monarchical rule through the Bishop), Congregational (Congregational vote rules). He shows the contrast between biblical and unbiblical forms of church government.[115]

All of the above insights served to be foundational and gave the burgeoning Apostolic movement in the 1980s a pattern for building local churches and networks.

Ron Cottle. His biography indicates that he has been serving the body of Christ for more than six decades. He has developed more than one hundred advanced courses of Christian development and biblical training and has authored more than four dozen books. Cottle has advanced degrees which include a PH.D. in religion (University of Southern California), an M.Div. (Lutheran Theological Seminary) a Master of Science in Education and a Doctor of Education (U.S.C.)

Dr. Ron Cottle is another one of the premier scholars in the 20th century Apostolic Movement and is also a key leader in the ICAL movement. As a Hebrew and Greek scholar, he is in high demand as both an academic and a teacher. He also led his own network of churches and started an international school that has at least thirty thousand students enrolled at one time.

Since he has published hundreds of articles, dozens of books and video teachings on every subject imaginable for the church, I will give some bullet point excerpts of two of the seminal presentations that he delivered at one of our ICAL gatherings.

- The Old Testament Ekklesia[116]

The Root of the New Testament Writings:

- Old Testament /written in Hebrew / translated in *Koine* Greek through the Septuagint and the N.T. translated from the Septuagint version in *Koine* Greek.

Every great theological concept and idea in the New Testament came from its root in the Old Testament by the way of the LXX (Septuagint).

- The Hebrew word for *Church* In the O.T
  Qahal is the Hebrew word for church in the O.T.
  Ekklesia is the usual Greek translation of Qahal in the Septuagint and New Testament.
  Qahal is used first as a secret assembly (Genesis 49:6.)
  Qahal is any army or its leaders. (Ezek.17:17). Ezekiel 23:45-47 shows that it is gathering to judge or deliberate. 1 Kings 12:3 the *Qahal* is a representative group of leaders that represented the whole people. An assembly representing a larger group. Leviticus 4:13-15 shows the difference between the congregation (*Edah*) who sins and its transgression is hidden from the eyes of the *Qahal* (Governing assembly of leaders).

The New Testament:

- Acts 7:38 - mentions the *Ekklesia* in the wilderness with the angel. By using the term *Ekklesia* it is significant that he used the term *Qahal-Ekklesia* to address the church in the wilderness. By this, he meant the fathers who received the lively oracles to give to us. As successors of Moses, the Sanhedrin acted in Stephen's day to govern Israel.
- Acts 19:39 ...is a perfect description of the *Qahal*, a legal or legislative group representing the whole" (in this case it was the *Ekklesia* assembled with the authority of the local deity as well as that of Rome, hence, it was not fully a secular but a religious gathering.

Conclusion

- The *Ekklesia* in the N.T. is not equated with the congregation as a whole. It is made up of persons from the Body appointed and authorized to represent, govern, and lead the larger people of God.

  Members of the *Qahal-Ekklesia* are members of the Edah (congregation or body) just as a general is a member of the army, but is called out of the ranks to lead, members of the *Qahal-Ekklesia* are legislative leaders with the authority to decide the course of action the whole Body will follow. Members of the *Qahal-Ekklesia* were not elected by the people. While open to any who qualified, members of the *Ekklesia* were appointed by God's delegated authority before them. The *Qahal-Ekklesia* was self-perpetuating.

Ekklesia in the N.T[117]

- In Acts 15:2,6,23, it is the apostles and elders who alone are the representative authority (*Ekklesia-Qahal*) of the whole body of the church. Still, there is no mention of Bishops (Episkopoi) at this stage of development.

- In Acts 15, we see the Jerusalem elders "functioning as the representative authority for the entire Christian community.
- Acts 21:18 Note the separation of James from the rest of the Elders in this passage. They (the elders) gather around James who acts as the undisputed Chief Elder or Overseer-Bishop of the Jerusalem church. James emerges as the presiding Apostle or Bishop-Overseer of the Jerusalem Central Church. Surrounding him is the presbytery (elders) of the church. They are the chief representative officers of the entire church. Acts 14:23; 20:17-38 shows that Paul appointed local elders in each church as Apostolic representatives to the church and as representatives of the church to the Apostles.
- In his address to the Ephesian elders, (Acts20) Paul called on them to shepherd the flock (20:29) in his absence. Paul eventually sent Timothy to take his place as the overseeing Apostle/Bishop (1 Timothy) of the local church in Ephesus, hence, the elders were to carry on the shepherding duties in the absence of an Apostle-Bishop. This indicates that by this time in the major Christian churches, Bishop-Overseers were working with local Elders as first among equals to shepherd the church flock. It also indicates that all these bishops were apostles.
- In summary, in AD 60,61, Elders in the predominantly Gentile churches of these various cities were an *Ekklesia* entrusted with the spiritual oversight of the local church. They were to serve willingly, were in charge of church funds, held disciplinary powers, and were to be godly examples to the other members of the church.
- One final point about elders is revealed in these letters. The Bishop (*Episkopos*) is seen as one of the elders and his functions are the same as theirs.

- The important difference between Bishop and Elders is that Bishop is always singular. Each church has one, while Elders are plural and form a council, committee or board.
- The Bishop is *primus inter pares* (chief among equals) upon the Elder Council (1 Peter 5:1) and as such, he is colleague, representative, and successor of the Apostles.

Implications

What are the implications of these matters for us who are seeing the restoration of the offices of Elder and Bishop and the emergence of the *Ekklesia* in today's New Apostolic Restoration? There are important implications for those of us who wish to see the anointings restored in a biblically correct manner. We must be clear in our understanding of how the Spirit created them in the first century and what they were then if we are to re-create and establish them properly as today's emerging *Ekklesia* in the movement we call the New Apostolic Reformation Church.

Apostolic Architecture[118]

- Matthew 16:18 and 18:17: These were the first two times He used the word (*Ekklesia*) for Church.
- The Foundation (Ephesians 2:19-22) Jesus is the chief cornerstone of the foundation of the church 1 Corinthians 12;28
- 1-APOSTLES -PROTOS - Revelation
- 2-PROPHETS -DEUTEROS -Proclamation (the word deuteros implies that apostles and prophets go together since deuteros means a repeat of something)
- 3-TEACHERS -TRITOS-Explanation
- 4-EVANGELIST -Gather
- 5-PASTOR - Guard

As A Result, On This Foundation
- Gifts of healings - *Charismata Iamaton*
- B-Helps - Lifter uppers
- C- Governments -*Kuberneseis* - Steerers of the Ship (Nautical Team)
- D -Diversities of tongues (implies the gospel is for all people and to reach all people)

David Cartledge. A summary of his bio indicates that he was the President of Southern Cross College of the Assemblies of God in Australia. He has planted churches in Tasmania, New South Wales, and Queensland. He was the State Superintendent of the Queensland Assemblies of God and has been a member of the AOG National Executive for twenty years. He was also a member of Dr. Cho's Church Growth International Board. His classic book, The Apostolic Revolution,[119] made the rounds across the globe and helped explain and facilitate how Evangelical denominations can transition towards the New Testament Apostolic paradigm.

I invited David to N.Y in 2003 where he spoke to almost 200 pastors about the Apostolic revolution. His book and teachings inspired and helped expand the present Apostolic movement across the world, especially in Australia, and North America. Cartledge describes the book as one that, "Reveals the history of a current apostolic revival, and a biblical framework for the recognition and release of apostolic and prophetic ministries in the modern church."[120]

Cartledge observes how the Australian Church has been impacted by the Apostolic teaching, "The Assemblies of God in Australia is a classic example of what can happen to any Christian movement that has the courage to change. This movement made the transition from an ineffective democratic religious system to leadership by God appointed apostolic ministries and the dramatic results are now a matter of record. Since 1977 the Australian

Assemblies have multiplied many times over after forty years in the wilderness."[121]

An important observation about Pentecostals and the Bible is made by Cartledge. To this day there is little debate about the validity or divine inspiration of the Bible at a church level.[122] The style of preaching in Pentecostal churches tends to be based on proof texts and personal perceptions, rather than comprehensive biblical teaching that conforms to consistent interpretive principles...The average Pentecostal accepts without question that the Bible is the final authority for our faith and practice.[123] Cartledge makes more important observations about the Apostolic Movment.

The Impact of Credible Apostolic Leadership on Denominations and Movements

Dr. *David Yonggi Cho* was a major catalyst in igniting the Australian Apostolic revolution. Regarding Cho, Cartledge says, "His ministry at the 1977 conference became one of the major components of redirecting the entire movement (Australian AOG) and enabling it to become united and effective.[124]

Cartledge states that the reason why Dr. Cho had such strong credibility and impact as an Apostle in Australia was because he, like other effective Apostolic leaders, has "demonstrated a capacity to affect other churches from the strong base of credibility they have gained as local church leaders...This was the power of Dr. Cho's impact on the Australian Assemblies of God in 1977."[125]

Apostolic leaders can enable people to see and know what the purposes of God for the church are. The Apostle sees and knows the vision and revelations of God for his sphere of ministry more than others. The Visionary capacity of the apostle, and the ability to discern the direction and agenda of the Lord for His Church, is a key ingredient of both its health and growth. It is this unique and God given ability that is the basis of the Apostle's authority.

His authority is not generated because he has been appointed to a particular position in the church. In fact, it is the reverse. His ministry will make way for him.[126]

Holy Spirit Hermeneutics. Concerning the need for the Holy Spirit in hermeneutics, Cartledge's view was that it is necessary, "The Holy Spirit inspired and experienced interpretation of Scripture must be accepted as valid. People who are able to identify with the attitudes and experiences of the first century Christians because they have experienced the same things are likely to have a better understanding of the early Christians way of life and ministry.[127]

Hermeneutics and Missiology. Cartledge adds that the role of the Holy Spirit in missions is necessary, he states, "it will not be possible to establish a Pentecostal hermeneutic or ethos that does not take into account the missiological activity of the Holy Spirit, through both the first century Christians and the modern Pentecostals."[128]

Hermeneutics and Diversity. "Another factor that should be identified as part of a Pentecostal hermeneutic is the diversity of expressions of the Spirit. While there is also a tendency towards unity, it is always a unity within diversity rather than a sterile uniformity. The modern Pentecostal movement is dramatically diverse, not only nationally, but also denominationally....The first century Christians also had this wide diversity.[129]

Hermeneutics and Apostolic Leadership. In the modern world, most interpretations and religious ideas are propounded by people who are often removed from the realm of leadership. Theologians who dwell in a remote and sterile non-ministry environment frequently take upon themselves the right to define what is genuine and necessary in the church. In the first century, this was the role of the apostolic and prophetic leaders. They claimed that the Holy Spirit enabled them to know what was right and appropriate in directing the church.... The techniques of biblical interpretation developed since the Protestant Reformation are so far from the means used by the first century apostles that a completely opposite result almost always occurs. It should be remembered that no New Testament writer or preacher employed anything like the historic/ grammatical, linguistic or redaction critical methods applied by modern theologians to their first century interpretation, or application of Old Testament Scriptures...There is not a single reference by any New Testament writer to a Hebrew, Aramaic, Chaldean or Ugaritic text, or language root in the Old Testament Scriptures they used and interpreted. Yet this would have been valid considering the length of time since the original writings occurred, and the various translations and sources that existed in their time. There was obviously more than one version of the Old Testament available (the Septuagint version was translated by this time) and yet no writer of the Gospels or Epistles refers even to this.[130]

Hermeneutics and Experience. Modern Pentecostals may be well advised to acknowledge this and seek an understanding of scripture that is based on the early Christians' method. John Christopher Thomas points out the hermeneutic process of apostles in Acts 15 and suggests that they did not discount experience. They took notice of what had been happening through the Spirit's work, they evaluated that, and when it became clear that an idea or a new emphasis was emerging in this way, they appealed to scripture.[131]

Ministries, Manifestations, and Motivations. In this section, Cartledge breaks up the list of spiritual gifts in the Body of Christ into three sections:[132]

- MINISTRIES - Ephesians 4:1-16
- MANIFESTATIONS -1 Cor. 12:4-11
  "The word employed by Paul is phanerosis and means "shining forth" hence it is not a list of nine "gifts" but manifestations.[133]"

- MOTIVATIONS - Romans 12:4-8
  The purpose of the Ministry Gifts[134]
  Cartledge lays out the purpose for the ministry gifts very
  clearly: Below they are listed in bullet points:

"The Ephesians chapter 4 mandate shows the way in which
the Lord achieves His purpose through the ministries of apostles,
prophets, pastors, evangelists and teachers. It is primarily by
bringing them into the unity of the faith (4:13)
  ▷ Maturity (4:13)
  ▷ To release Body Function (4:16)
  ▷ To equip the saints to do the work of the ministry (4:12)
  ▷ To edify the body of Christ (4:12)
  ▷ To reach the stature of the fullness of Christ (4:13)
  ▷ To avoid error (4:14)
  ▷ Speaking the Truth in love (4:15)

Cessationism in the Pentecostal church. In chapter 33 of
Cartledge's book, The Apostolic Revolution, he deals with the
reluctance of historic Pentecostal denominations to recognize the
ministries of Apostles and Prophets.
  He lists two main reasons below:
- "A reluctance to recognise the ministries of apostles and
  prophets in case there is undue elevation of these people.
  Bureaucratic church officials cannot cope with the attrac-
  tion that is generated by these two ministries, because
  they have a desire to conform all ministries to a set type.
  Denominations prefer clones rather than charismatic
  leaders."[135]
- "Apostolic and prophetic ministries carry a greater level of
  authority than the others and this is hard to accommodate
  in a "democratic" system of Church Government.[136]"

- The reason that some of the modern Pentecostal movements adopt a cessationism attitude to apostolic and prophetic ministries is that these gifted ministries operate at a supernatural level more than others. They do not easily fit within the constraints of a hierarchical or democratic denominational system...Denominational administrators and managers will always be nervous of the authority generated by the ministry of the apostles. It is not derived from denominational headquarters and cannot be controlled by either the hierarchy or the systems they create... Administrators frequently rule the church and confine all spiritual activity to a level they can control.[137]

On the use of titles.[138] Cartledge has the same position that most of us in the USCAL have, an aversion to the use of the term "Apostle" in front of our names. We are more interested in function than the use of the term to identify an official office. With regards to this, Cartledge states,

> *Almost all Australian apostolic ministries are quite emphatic that they will not use the title apostle...The terms "apostle" and "prophet" were not titles in Bible times. However, it is abundantly clear that none of the terms for ministry gifts were used as titles in the early church. They were simply designations of function and descriptions of their responsibilities in the church. Paul never refers to himself as 'The Apostle Paul' but only says 'Paul, an Apostle'...The original apostles did not experience any depreciation of their authority by not having a titular designation. Their gift made way for them.*[139]

Alan Hirsch. Alan Hirsch is considered by many to be the father of the modern missional church movement and is the founder of numerous missional collectives. He is on the leading edge of those in scholarship helping to restore the way of Christ and His Apostles back to the Body of Christ. The following are some key excerpts from one of his seminal books, The Permanent Revolution.

Hirsch's missional philosophy. Clearly one of the biggest issues in the church today is the discussion about what it means to be missional. We believe that how we deal with this will determine the future viability of the church in the West. But we fear that so many of these vital conversations are doomed to frustration because the people in them are unwilling or unable to reconfigure ministry to suit the missional context. Although many buy into the concept, they are unwilling to recalibrate the ecclesiology. Christendom church has been run on a largely shepherd-teacher model, and because it has had a privileged position in society, it has been inclined to dispense with the more missional or evangelistic ministry types (apostle, prophet, and evangelist). These inherited forms of church are not equipped for the missional challenge because they refuse to recalibrate their ministry along the lines suggested in Ephesians 4. We believe that in order to be a genuinely missional church, we must have a missional ministry to go with it, and that means putting this issue of the apostle, prophet, and evangelist roles back.[140]

Hirsh's definition of the Apostle, Prophet, Evangelist, Shepherd, Teacher (APEST) is as follows:

- The **apostle** is tasked with the overall vigor, as well as extension of Christianity as a whole, primarily through direct mission and church planting. As the name itself suggests, it is the quintessentially missional ministry, as "sentness" (Latin *missio*) is written into it (*apostello* sent one).
- The **prophet** is called to maintain faithfulness to God among the people of God. Essentially prophets are guardians of the covenant relationship.

- The **evangelist** is the recruiter to the cause, the naturally infectious person who is able to enlist people into the movement by transmit- ting the gospel.
- The **shepherd** (pastor) is called to nurture spiritual development, maintain communal health, and engender loving community among the people of God.
- The **teacher** mediates wisdom and understanding. This philosophical type brings comprehensive understanding of the revelation bequeathed to the church.[141]

Hirsch's view is that the JESUS' DNA is manifested in APEST which, in turn, is ingrained in all humanity. He states, "Apostles in the generic sense are those sent to pioneer something new, for example, teachers who are called in to turn failing schools around, along with people who start movements of sorts, architect systems, or start entrepreneurial business ventures. Can we see non-Christian people who fit this category? Definitely.

- Prophets tend to be visionaries, but in a very different sense; they often have a keen interest in issues of justice, environmental responsibility, or the creative arts. Are there such people outside the church? Of course.
- Evangelists are particularly gifted at enthusing others about what they stand for, selling the significance of their work, company, or product outside the group itself. These are easy to spot. The United States is full of them.
- Pastors are those with a special concern for seeing and affirming what is human within structures. They might not be the most appropriate people to put together a policy for addressing drug abuse, but if they are not part of delivering the policy, the addicts are in trouble. Are there people who create community and bring healing to others in the non-Christian world? Indeed.

- Teachers are those who are effective trainers and inspirers of learning. They are philosophers, thinkers, people who understand ideas and how they shape human life. Do such non-Christians exist? No brainer."[142]

Regarding the necessity of restoring APEST back to the church, Hirsch points to Ephesians 4 and states the following:

"[I]f we take the text plainly (inductively) and without prior theological prejudice (deductively), it is not hard to discern that we cannot be a healthy movement without the necessary APEST ministry. Verse 13 explicitly says as much, but the logic of the entire text aims at this. So, for instance, we can ask whether there is any doubt about the universal significance of verses 1 to 6 for any church in any time and place. We seriously doubt that anyone reading this book would suggest that they do not still have abiding authority over us. They were clearly not intended just for the Ephesian Christians. So if both sections on either side of verses 7 to 11 are true and binding on the church for all time, then by what form of theological trickery have we come to believe that verses 7 to 11 would be any less abiding and universal, especially when grammatically and thematically they are placed at the heart of the same piece of scripture? As far as we can discern, it is simply not possible to be the church that Jesus intended if three (APE) of the five constitutional ministries are removed. According to the explicit teaching of Ephesians 4:1–16, it cannot be done. But in fact it has been done, and the tragic consequences are dramatically demonstrated in and through the history of the Christian church through the past seventeen centuries."[143]

Hirsch agrees that the key to a movement is its ability to unleash the APEST in all believers. He states: "On the importance of restoring the Apostolic function, we believe that out of all the APEST ministries, the apostolic is the most generative and catalytic of them all, and because of this, it carries the most

180

promise in helping to reverse the decline of the church. If this is correct, then the apostolic both initiates and maintains the permanent revolution at the root of the constant reformation of the church. This is also the reason that we believe that the apostolic is the key to unlocking Ephesians 4 and therefore all other New Testament forms of ministry. It is not that prophets, evangelists, pastors, and teachers cannot function independently from the apostolic; rather, as far as we can discern, they are designed to function interdependently with it and each other. It is through their relationship with the apostolic calling that they will come into the fullness of their own role and purpose in Jesus's church. Activating the diversity within APEST necessitates the activation of an equal or greater force that can hold them together in dynamic tension. Apostles are so critical to this inherent dilemma because they are the ones most naturally prone to cultivate a compelling missional focus around which those potentially polarizing forces within APEST can gather. Without the unifying force of a common mission, the diversity within APEST will drift toward fragmentation. By initiating missional ventures, the apostolic provides the cohesive framework in which the other ministries can focus their seemingly disparate interests in collaborative ways. In essence, the apostle is the one who is most likely to facilitate the emergence of communitas, a particular kind of community that is shaped and formed around a challenge or compelling task. Like all other catalysts, the apostolic vocation initiates a reaction that changes a system."[144]

The Apostle Paul as the prototype. Hirsch writes: "[M]uch of our understanding of the church's ministry stems from [Paul]. Clearly there are other apostles, and therefore other models of apostleship, but the quantity of Paul's writings and our focused exposure to his ministry through scripture have made his apostleship stand out as the norm throughout history. Paul can be used as a legitimate prototype if we extrapolate some generic descriptions from his apostolic vocation. We can do this by looking at the various terms he uses to describe his role; 1 and 2 Corinthians serve us well in this regard... Ironically, it was because some were questioning the legitimacy of Paul's apostleship that he was forced to map out his role through metaphors and analogies. A brief glance at these two letters reveals at least five insightful metaphors for the apostolic role:

- *Planter*. A basic feature of apostolic ministry is seeding the gospel and the genetic codes of ecclesia into unbroken soil. It is catalytic in this respect, bringing soil and seed together, yet the source of life and growth is contained within the gospel and God's activity. This is perhaps one of Paul's most organic metaphors for apostolic ministry (1 Corinthians 3:6–8). All contemporary apostolic ministry shares in this planting function.

- *Architect*. Our translations use the word "master builder," but the exact wording in Greek is archetekton—arche meaning origin or first, and *tekton* meaning craftsman or planner, which offer the idea of primary designer or blueprint crafter. The word is loaded with notions of design, innovation, and strategic craftsmanship. Yet unlike modern architects who rarely visit job sites, the cultural understanding of the architect in Paul's day was of one who not only designed the building but directed the building process (1 Corinthians 3:10). Apostolic ministry is on-site work, not just ivory tower ideation.

- *Foundation layer*. Paul qualifies the constructive metaphor of architect by limiting it to the initial phases of building. Architects may envision the entire project from start to finish and sketch plans accordingly, but the apostle's primary work includes laying solid foundations as well. Paul makes it clear that the community must build on these foundations as well. If the foundations are weak, the community will not stand (1 Corinthians 3:10–15).

- ***Father***. Paul sees himself as a father to his churches because he was the catalyst who brought them into existence by the gospel. As such, Paul occupies a unique role within those communities. As their spiritual father, he retains the right to step in and intervene in communal affairs when he perceives they have deviated from the essential truths of the gospel (1 Corinthians 4:14–21). Paul also uses this father metaphor in 2 Corinthians to explain his interests in guarding his daughter's virginity in order to present her as a chaste, pure bride to her bridegroom; here the notion of purity and integrity comes to the fore...

- Ambassador. As in our day, the decisions that the ambassador makes legally bind the person or country that they represent. There is real representative authority in the role. The apostle is one who is fully empowered to represent the missional interests of the missio Dei. He is an emissary of the King. This kingdom agency infuses all the functions of the apostolic ministry (2 Corinthians 5:16–21)."[145]

On Apostolic networks: Cultivating Translocal, Fully Networked Movements Through Vision, Purpose, and the Management of Meaning:[146] "The functions of seeding and guarding the genetic codes of ecclesia in effect produce a burgeoning multicultural, multidimensional movement networked across a wide cultural landscape. But how does leadership maintain a sense of meaningful unity in a movement that is spreading rapidly into so many different realms? Apart from the necessary work of the Holy Spirit in maintaining identity and cohesion, the answer reaches back into the nature of the gospel codes themselves, as well as the management of the meaning inherent in the gospel itself. This is where theological identity, meaning, and purpose blend to create a common identity with a unique sense of destiny and calling.

Much apostolic work, both then and now, has been focused on these very issues...We belong together; we have a common root and destiny and a mission that only we can fulfill because of what Jesus has done in and for us. This forms the basis of our fellowship and provides the very fabric of movement. The apostle both mediates this knowledge and draws on it to keep the movement going.

"A sense of common meaning and purpose both initiates movements and keeps burgeoning networks together. This is especially the case in relation to Jesus movements in history and is clearly evident in the movement we can observe in the New Testament itself. In the early church, there was no central body issuing orders and delegating responsibilities. Ecclesia in the scriptures is clearly a more liquid, more movement phenomenon, one that is more like a distributed network. Networked movements have the advantage of being able to reproduce easily and can spread very fast but leading them requires significantly different gifts and skills from the centralized bishop or CEO type of leadership that we have become so accustomed to.

"The most authentic forms of apostolic ministry forgo the hierarchical, top-down, transactional forms of leadership and power and draw mostly on what can be called inspirational, or moral, authority...Built on vision, meaning, and purpose, inspirational authority is able to motivate and sustain networks without the promise of remuneration that the transactional forms of leadership are built on. In effect, apostolic ministry therefore creates the web of meaning that holds the networked movement together. It does this by reawakening the people to the gospel and embed- ding it into the organizational framework in ways that are meaningful. It is because of this apostolic meaning web that the movement maintains itself over the long haul.

"This distinctly apostolic, decentralized, networked approach, where order and chaos are held together in dynamic tension, is critical to all people movements because it is the only way a trans local movement can hold together. Each individual, church, or agency relates to the apostolic leader only because it is meaningful for them to do so (by virtue of the gospel itself) and not because they have to. It is because the gospel is implanted, and the Holy Spirit is present in every Christian community, that apostolic leadership can maintain the network and develop the movement network....So to sum up to this point, we can say that the apostolic ministry is basically a stewarding function that is responsible for the extension of the gospel's cause."[147]

On the need for apostolic leaders to maintain generational movement: "Some will question whether it is truly possible to experience a permanent revolution. The routinization of charisma, the process of institutionalization, reification, and a host of other factors all conspire to work against such durability. Entropy and dissipation are part of the physical and social fabric of reality, yet the very nature of the church's mission calls for continuous movement; it requires the ever-expanding saturation of cultural and geographical spheres with the gospel until the task is done or our Master returns. We suggest that the concept of perpetual advance and renewal is directly linked to the presence and activity of the apostolic ministry; they are the permanent revolutionaries who maintain the permanent revolution. As long as Wesley was alive and active, the movement continued to grow. The same is true for people as diverse as Aimee Semple McPherson and John Wimber. The loss of the apostolic influence opens the door to encroaching decline."[148]

Creating Movements, Not Just Churches: "If you want to end with a movement, you need to start with a movemental idea and approach. This seems obvious, but all denominations started as dynamic movement, but because they were not attentive to the shifting issues of organization, they likely ended up in another place altogether. So plant movements, not churches. This is a big part of why it is important to begin with the end in mind: if you want a movement, you must think of ecclesia beyond the idea of a single local church before you begin. Once again, as every seed has the full potential for a tree and the tree the full potential of the forest, so too every church (indeed every believer) has the full potential of a movement in it. This is implied in the powerful slogan of an underground Chinese church movement: 'Every believer is a church planter, and every church is a church-planting church.' Every believer has ecclesia (church) in him or her, and every ecclesia is responsible for the reproduction of others; in other words, they all make a movement.

"This approach is also useful in getting beyond distorted, highly institutionalized ideas of the church in order to focus on planting movements instead of planting churches. The distinctly apostolic form of thinking behind this is to think movements and not churches."[149]

My critique

Alan Hirsch is my friend and perhaps the greatest scholar as it relates to understanding the missional nature of the apostolic. The only concern some have had with his writings is that he focuses so much on the decentralization of the church-related to movement and mission (like the underground church in China). Some also say he flatlines the APEST gifts of Ephesians 4:11. By pointing out that said gifts are inherent in every believer, some would say that Hirsch is promoting what can work only in an egalitarian house church movement that doesn't recognize leadership positions in the church.

Knowing Hirsch as a friend, (I have had him as a guest in my conference and video conferences with some of the leaders I work with), Alan believes that the APEST function can be adopted in various movements that have divergent structures and wineskins. That being said, it is important to clarify the fact that in the New Testament Didache, it was clear that there were spiritual leaders the church was called to obey and submit to (Titus 2:15; Hebrews 13:7,17). Hence, related to APEST, it is clear that Christ designated people to function in these ministry gifts according to the measure of the gift of His grace (Ephesians 4;7). Thus, some have a measure of the anointing and gifting of the fivefold which is commensurate to what is needed to lead in the church that is distinct from the members of the Church who aren't called to lead. Hence, even though all partake of APEST in some measure, not all have the God-given capacity to be an overseer in the Body of Christ.

Peter Wagner. As a notable professor of missions and church growth at Fuller Seminary, Peter Wagner made headlines when he transitioned from being a cessationist to partnering with John Wimber as they hosted a class on "Signs and Wonders." He and Wimber launched what they called the "3rd Wave". The 3rd Wave was descriptive of what Evangelicals who embraced the manifestations of the Spirit but (unlike classical Pentecostals) did not believe the Baptism of the Holy Spirit necessitated the need to speak in tongues.

From there he began hosting conferences and writing about such topics as "High level spiritual warfare." In the mid-1990s, he discovered the modern Apostolic movement, and hosted a significant conference in 1995 on "Post-denominationalism." Eventually, he began working with high-level apostolic leaders and networks. Apostle John Kelly, founder of ICAL, after two years, handed the new organization over to Wagner.

The following excerpts are taken from Wagner's important book, *Apostles Today*. It gives us a snapshot of how this significant missiologist framed the modern global apostolic movement.

In *Apostles Today*, Peter Wagner maintains that being an apostle is a spiritual gift. Apostles are chosen by God and thus have a solid foundation of spiritual authority as well as a given ministry assignment. Their holiness of character also attracts a following. If there is no following, that person is not an apostle. Apostles also can receive prophetic revelation from the Holy Spirit specifically for churches. [150]

Wagner also agrees with Vinson Synan that apostles are not self-appointed. God decides who is an apostle, and such is recognized by others in the Body of Christ including pastors, evangelists, teachers, and prophets.[151] An apostle also has an apostolic sphere or territory and is not an apostle appointed with authority over the whole Church. [152]

Finally, in his landmark book, Wagner defines the roles of *horizonal apostles* and *vertical apostles.* [153] Vertical apostles give spiritual covering to those under them while a horizonal apostle essentially connects, networks, and serves church leaders. [154]

ICAL STATEMENT ON APOSTLES[155]

"An apostle is a Christian leader gifted, taught, commissioned, and sent by God with the authority to establish the foundational government of the Church within an assigned sphere and/or spheres of ministry by hearing what the Spirit is saying to the churches and by setting things in order accordingly for the expansion of the kingdom of God."

Gifts and Ministries

Apostles, by definition, have been given the spiritual gift of the apostle by the grace of God. This gift is listed among many others in 1 Corinthians 12. The same chapter, however, indicates that not all of those with the same gift have the same ministry, and not all those with the same ministry have the same activity (see 1 Cor. 12:4-6).

Many apostles minister primarily in the nuclear church, which traditionally takes the shape of congregations of believers that meet on Sundays or groupings of such congregations, while others minister primarily in the extended church, which is the church in the workplace. These would be termed "nuclear church" apostles, rather than "extended church," or "workplace," apostles. Some are territorial apostles to whom God has given authority covering a certain geographical area such as a neighborhood...Others are horizontal apostles, who have a ministry of convening and connecting peers such as other apostles or pastors or prophets, etc.

Gifts and Offices

The gift of apostle, as in the case of all spiritual gifts, is given to believers by God as He pleases (1 Cor. 12:11,18). Spiritual gifts are given only by the grace of God. However, an office, such as the office of apostle, is not given by grace alone but is given as a result of works that have demonstrated faithfulness in the stewardship of the gift. If God has chosen to give a man or woman the gift of apostle, the fruit of that gift will be evident to others, and in due time the Body of Christ will confer the office of the apostle on that person. This act is most often termed "commissioning," and it is performed by peer-level apostles, as well as prophets, representing the church, and by laying on hands. The title "apostle" is ordinarily used only by those who have been duly commissioned into the office; although in some situations this principle has not yet been formalized.

Extraordinary character. Apostles fulfill the leadership requirements outlined in 1 Timothy 3:1-7. They take seriously the warning of James 3:1 that they will be judged with a stricter judgment than most other believers. They are holy (1 Pet. 1:15).

Humility. Jesus said that only those who humble themselves will be exalted. Since apostles are exalted by God (1 Cor. 12:28), they must be humble in order to qualify.

Leadership. Not all leaders are apostles, but all apostles are leaders. Apostles must have followers to verify their leadership role.

Authority. The characteristic that most distinguishes apostles from other members of the Body of Christ is the authority inherent with the gift of apostle. They gain that authority through fatherhood, not through arrogance or imposition.

Integrity. Apostles are expected to display the integrity that will cause them to be "blameless" (1 Tim. 3:2), and to "have a good testimony among those who are outside" (v. 7).

Wisdom. True apostleship does not come without maturity, and maturity brings wisdom. Apostles have the God-given ability to see the big picture and to help others find their place in God's plan.

They receive revelation. Apostles hear what the Spirit is saying to the churches. Some of this revelation comes directly to them, some of it is received together with prophets and some through proper relationships with prophets.

They cast vision. Their vision is based on the revelation they receive.

They birth. Apostles are self-starters who begin new things.

They impart. God uses apostles to activate His blessings in others (Rom. 1:11).

They build. Apostles strategize and find ways to carry a project along its intended course, including any funding required.

They govern. Apostles are skilled in setting things in order. Along with prophets, they lay the biblical foundation of the Kingdom (Eph. 2:20).

They teach. Early believers "continued steadfastly in the apostles' teaching (Acts 2:42).

They send. Apostles send out those who are equipped to fulfill their role in expanding the kingdom of God.

They finish. Apostles are able to bring a project or a season of God to its desired conclusion. They are uneasy until the project is done. They seldom burn out.

They war. Apostles are the generals in the army of God. (This Excerpt was from *Apostles Today* by C. Peter Wagner).

My critique

Although God used Peter Wagner to highlight the burgeoning global apostolic movement, there were many things taught and practiced by Peter and within the ICAL movement that demonstrated the need for more clarity and maturity in the movement.

Many of these concerns have already been mentioned in my section related to the NAR Movement, so it is not necessary to critique this any further.

Jonathan David. Jonathan David's partial biography reads, "Dr. Jonathan David is the founder and senior pastor of Full Gospel Center Muar, a thriving territorial church in Jahor, Malaysia. He is also the presiding Apostle of the International Strategic Alliance of Apostolic Churches, a network of governing churches and ministers across the nations. He has been recognized by apostles and prophets around the world for his contribution to God's present move through this popular book 'Apostolic Strategies Affecting Nations.'"[156]

Since David wrote the above-mentioned book in the late 1990s from a non-western cultural context, his book was also foundational to the burgeoning apostolic movement in Asia as well as Africa and beyond. I will give some snapshots of this massive, classic book of approximately 500 pages. One of the reasons for choosing this book is because I wanted to make sure I highlighted some apostolic writing that did not emanate from the USA to demonstrate that this Apostolic Movement is not particular to only North America but is a global phenomenon. It's the reason why I also highlighted David Cartledge and Alan Hirsch (although

Hirsch lives in the USA much of the time, he is an Australian by birth).

Understanding An Apostle's Ministry. [157] "Every believer in our congregation needs to fully understand the importance of the call, the anointing and the function of the apostolic ministry that God is restoring today. The restoration of this ministry gift in the context of the last day church, helps us redefine all the other five-fold ministry gifts that have already been restored. The distinctiveness of the apostolic ministry separates it from all other ministry gifts." [158]

Paradigms and Perspectives of Apostles (pages 369-374). David gives a broad base regarding the perspective and paradigms of Apostles. He states, "Apostles think according to the written word of God, that is to say, that they are first and foremost teachers and preachers of the Scriptures Apostles think in terms of permanence, that is to say, they always build with an eternal perspective for an enduring work that will last the test of time." [159]

David states, "Paul did not concentrate on having too many big meetings but concentrated on building with the future in mind. He trained many disciples and raised up strong support teams within each church." [160]

Hence, to summarize this thought, an Apostle thinks extensively. That is to say, like Paul, they address every major area and issue of life. An Apostle thinks architecturally. This means they are builders (not mere blessers), who place people properly in the community.

Apostolic Signs. David identifies 6 identifiable signs of an apostle

1. The call and commissioning of an Apostle:
   David states that a true apostle has had a genuine encounter with God that is very personal and supernatural. In other words, it has to be God-ordained and not emanat-

ing from Man. Concerning their character, they have to be Christlike; they not only mimic the works of Christ but also the Character of Christ. They have the Apostolic Grace to suffer for the kingdom. Jonathan uses the experiences of the Apostle Paul as shown in 2 Corinthians 11-12 to give his criteria for authentic apostolic grace.

2. They have access to apostolic revelation in his generation: David states "The access to the apostolic revelation is the sign of an apostle. An Apostle is given this unusual access to revelation flow by God, without which no apostolic ministry can be authenticated[53]".
Apostolic influence over people, cities and demons:
Here he uses the experiences of Paul as shown in Acts 19. Here we see Paul planted the Ephesian church that in turn affected the whole region by uprooting Satanic entities, shifting the economy and exerting governmental authority over a city.

3. Apostolic Impartation: David states, "One of the distinctive signs in the apostle is his ability to attract sons he can reproduce himself in through apostolic impartation."[161]
He further states how true apostles are able to grow people into their full potential in Christ, due to the grace given to them because of their apostolic call.

4. Apostolic Grace as Wise Master Builders: David states that Paul had the grace to bring order, structure, and procedures to the church. In addition, he had the grace to provide revelatory teachings that became the plumb line for doctrinal purity and discerning of false doctrines.

5. Apostolic Foundations. David deals with the fact that apostles are able to lay foundations for governing churches to arise (1 Cor. 3:10-12). He goes on to explain that, although Jesus is the firm foundation and chief Cornerstone of the church, the apostles and prophets in the New Testament

placed the foundation of Christ into the heart of believers. David further on talks about the need for apostles and prophets of today's church to lay down the apostolic foundations of biblical truth for the churches (Acts 2:42).

6. Spiritual Fathering.[162] David goes into the various aspects of the call of Apostles to father men and women in the faith. He said this results in the Apostolic leader being an extension of God the Father to them which motivates them to reach their full potential. This eventuates in equipping successors to perpetuate the apostle's ministry.

7. Boundaries and Spheres. Basing his teaching on Romans 15:18-21, and 2 Corinthians 10:13-18, David calls on contemporary apostles to replicate the New Testament Pauline apostolic pattern. This involves working within and continually expanding their spheres of authority by being able to adapt to new cultures and environments. The measure of the rule Paul had (2 Cor. 10:13-15) is described as a field of operation with clearly defined boundaries.

    Apostolic divergence.[163] Jonathan states that each apostle differs from another apostle like the stars differ from one another (1 Cor. 15:41). They differ according to their calling, as demonstrated in the way Peter was called to the Jews and Paul to the Gentiles. They also differ according to the measure of the grace upon their life, the depth of the relationship they have with the Holy Spirit, the depth of their revelation and word content, their maturity of character, as well as in their life and level of holiness.

    Apostolic Networking[164]

    "The ...distinctive feature of an apostolic ministry is its ability to draw groups of churches to be networked together for the purpose of gospel saturation...An apostolic network is the extension of an apostolic team...The apostolic networks are built upon and held together by covenant relationships, purpose, apostolic truth, supernatural experiences together, an Apostolic father, with minimal organization but with distinct working strategies."[165]

Apostolic networks should network with other apostolic networks.[166]

True apostles have the ability to merge different streams together that are under other apostles so that it becomes a mighty river of God. True apostles should not only have a burden for their own network but for the Body of Christ. Networks cross-pollinating with other networks can easily formulate strategies to reach nations. It can also bring wholeness to the Body of Christ and also releases a greater place of accountability for the apostles who need to be accountable to other apostolic peers.

In conclusion, since this book was written in the late 1990s, it's concepts regarding the Kingdom of God, societal transformation, and workplace apostolic leadership are not fully developed. However, it is amazing how all these concepts are in nascent form, which paved the way for other apostolic leaders to build upon and delve deeper.

My first book, *Ruling in the Gates*,[167] was written in 1998. Its focus was more on the call of the church to go from preaching an individual gospel of salvation to the full-orbed gospel of the Kingdom. Although I wrote it in 1998, I could not find a publisher who would retain me until five years later. I reason that perhaps this was the case because the concepts were deemed too radical at the time (I believe they were prophetic but not radical). That being said, David's book is much more robust than most books written on the apostolic within the Charismatic world. It has proved to be a very helpful resource for many apostolic leaders around the world for almost three decades!

In Conclusion

Before I wrap up this section, honorable mention has to go to Dr. Bruce Cook who completed an ambitious 5 part book series called, "Aligning with the Apostolic, An Anthology of Apostleship."[168]

It is a compilation of work from over 70 apostolic leaders (of whom I am one), representing the church place and the workplace.[169] It's interesting that this book series brings together apostolic/charismatic scholar types of individuals within the apostolic movement.[170]

Although they all have global influence, they are rather unknown among the typical Evangelical world of academia. Since this is a relatively recent work, it more accurately reflects the evolution and expansion of thinking regarding the apostolic in Charismatic apostolic circles, especially as it pertains to embracing the idea of "marketplace apostles" as opposed to only identifying apostles in the "church place."

Without going into vast details, one of the quotes in the preface to the first book will give a snapshot of the perspective of Dr. Cook and many of the other authors, "I contend and will present the case here that rather than there being only thousands or tens of thousands of apostles and apostolic leaders on the earth today, as some believe, there are far more likely to be millions of them in existence currently, largely unknown except perhaps locally and to the Holy Spirit, including some who are unaware and even a few who are unwilling. Most of these are found in the workplace rather than behind a pulpit, where risk and reward is an ever present reality and a daily discipline, and where they have been positioned and trained to solve complex problems , make executive decisions, lead multicultural and mult-disciplinary teams, research underlying trends and conditions, assess threats and opportunities, establish and implement protocols, produce new products and services, and measure outcomes, change or enforce organizational culture, discover and harness new technologies." (pages xliii, xliv)[171]

As you can see from reading the above quote, Bruce's view on the apostolic has expanded way beyond the framework of the ecclesial wineskin of the apostolic movement prevalent from the late 1940s to the mid 1990s. To give the reader of this work an idea of the unusual scope and distinct characteristic of this book series, some of the chapters in this book series include topics such as:

"Origins of the Patriarchs and Judaism are found in the Marketplace" (Volume 1, chapter six)

"Origins of the church and Christianity are found in the marketplace" (Volume 1, chapter seven)

"Apostolic reformers in the marketplace...." (Volume I, chapter seven)

"Apostolic leaders in government" (Volume two, chapter ten)

"Apostles and the Kingdom" (Volume two, chapter twelve)

"Apostles as Ambassadors" (Volume two, chapter fourteen)

"Turning the world upside down: The social call of the apostolic" (Volume two, chapter twenty-three)

"Apostolic-Prophetic Intercession" (Volume three, chapter twenty-four)

"Apostles to the boardroom" (Volume three, chapter twenty-nine)

"Society of leaders" (ibid, chapter thirty-seven)

"Spiritual Fathers and Sons in the Marketplace" (Volume four, chapter forty-five)

"Apostolic Mothers" (Volume four, chapter forty-six)

"Apostolic Teams" (Volume four, chapter forty-eight)

"Marketplace Apostles: Raising Up Territorial Leaders (Volume four, chapter fifty-five)

"Apostolic Imagination: A Preferred Future for Apostolic Marketplace Initiatives" (Volume four, chapter fifty-six)

"The Five R's for the Apostle in Business" (Volume four, chapter fifty-nine)

"Apostles of the Business as Mission Movement" (Volume five, chapter sixty-four)

"Apostles as Co-Creators: Imitating the works of the Father" (Volume five, chapter sixty-six)

"Apostolic Wisdom to Redeem the Culture" (Volume five, chapter seventy-three)

"Healing Rooms Ministries: An Apostolic Birthing of a Worldwide Vision" (Volume five, chapter seventy-seven).

An Apostolic Glossary

Finally, another helpful element of this book series is the effort Cook puts towards bringing clarity to the present terms and nomenclature used in various Apostolic expressions

He gives definition to terms such as:

Ambassadorial Apostle, Apostolic Agriculture, Apostolic Alignment, Apostolic Center, Apostolic Council, Apostolic Covering, Apostolic Culture, Apostolic Delegation, Apostolic Embassy, Apostolic Estate, Apostolic DNA, Apostolic Foundations, Apostolic Function, Apostolic Gift, Apostolic Government, Apostolic Industry, Apostolic Intercession, Apostolic Mantle, Apostolic Mission, Apostolic Movement, Apostolic Network, Apostolic Office, Apostolic Order, Apostolic Protocol, Apostolic Succession, Apostolic Tribe, Ecclesiastical Apostle, Bilateral Apostle, Apostolic Worship, Convening Apostle, Horizontal Apostle, Marketplace Apostle, Fivefold, Multilateral Apostles, Presiding Apostle, Territorial Apostle, Trilateral Apostle, Vertical Apostle, Workplace Apostle, etc.

Because the forward of the book was written by Dr. C. Peter Wagner, it gains instant credibility among those associated with the NAR. Since Cook, as the chief editor and major contributor of the content is himself a marketplace leader, there are non-typical annunciations related to the role of the apostolic, which may challenge the thinking of classical ecclesial apostolic thinking. Be that as it may, regardless of your view on ecclesiology and the nature of the Apostolic, Cook has truly done an outstanding and excellent job of connecting with many major apostolic network leaders who represent various realms of society. Cook's book, in my opinion, is a major contributor to this genre of literature.

Summary

The above-mentioned authors and books are by no means the only ones I can cite. They are just a mere cross-section of some of the major books and authors who have done a superb job of producing works that reflect the movement from the past to the present, along with various developments in different expressions of the church that have embraced a particular view of the Apostolate.

Of course, the primary apostolic writer/practitioner that has shaped my theological understanding of the way of Christ and His apostles is Jeff Reed. His writings are way too numerous to cite or summarize here; suffice it to say that a person can go online to BILD.org<http://BILD.org> and see the vast material he has written which greatly contributes to this conversation-especially note his book containing "The paradigm papers", the encyclicals, the Acts course leadership series and the Pauline epistles leadership series.

In the next chapter I will give an honest assessment of some of the theological and methodological challenges of the contemporary apostolic movement. My objective is not to be a mere critic but to motivate people who identify with these expressions of Christianity to align more accurately with the way of Christ and His apostles.

QUESTIONS TO ASK YOURSELF

1. What are some of the theological constructs that have influenced the new apostolic movement?

2. Which of these theological constructs do you identify with?

3. Who are some of the apostolic scholars who have influenced the contemporary apostolic movement?

4. What are some of their strengths and weaknesses?

5. Have you ever checked out the vast material related to the way of Christ and His apostles as found in BILD.org<http://BILD.org> ?

Chapter 7

Theological and Cultural Challenges in the Present-day Apostolic Movement

In this chapter, we will analyze some of the theological/cultural trends and challenges of the contemporary apostolic movement.

1. Theological Challenges with the advent of workplace apostles in the Marketplace:

I am choosing this topic first when discussing some of the primary theological challenges in the contemporary apostolic movement since it seems to have the most potential to wrest the movement from a biblical understanding of ecclesiology.

I am all for an understanding of APEST (apostle, prophet, evangelist, shepherd, teacher) that transcends merely the church place into the marketplace because the kingdom of God has implications for all of life and not just church life. When I teach on the kingdom of God, I have noticed that it sometimes brings a level of discomfort to some church place leaders. Often this happens because such leaders only prioritize Sunday services and speak only of "full-time church ministry."

In the same manner, I've seen some angst with the workplace (marketplace) leaders, especially if they are disconnected from a local church context. This is usually because they define the church as being a couple of people gathering in the Name of Jesus. Sometimes, such a definition may include a group of friends hanging out in a pub, or a weekly office meeting micro church gathering. Of course, one of the challenges of the micro church or extended church concept in which workplace leaders replace the traditional church (since they reason that Jesus is in the midst of any size group), is that this is still an immature or minimalist expression of the church. The Acts and epistles depict the church functioning as a full-blown family of families, from the cradle to the grave.

It goes without saying that the gospel should be planted in cities and communities not just buildings on Sundays. Usually, it takes shape in its nascent form as a micro-entity, but ultimately it should eventuate in growing into a family (similar to a husband and wife who eventually have children). Based on my experience and observation, marketplace leaders disconnected from the church, are usually not properly grounded in their marriages and families. I've seen far too many are who are unaccountable to other more spiritually mature leaders. Often, the reason why some marketplace leaders disconnect from the local church is because of a lack of apostolicity in their local regional church leadership. When the local churches' pastoral paradigm is bereft of the apostolic kingdom paradigm, it often causes frustration with the apostolic/prophetic type workplace leader in congregations because such churches are limited in their overall vision, which causes boredom with the high-level workplace leaders. Often, the workplace leader has a higher "lid" of leadership than the lead pastor.[172]

An example of this may mean that a workplace leader may be an 8 on a scale of 1-10 in leadership abilities, while the lead pastor may be only a 6 in leadership on that scale. This means the #8 workplace leader have greater leadership capacity and responsibility. Often this translates into the marketplace leader looking elsewhere for guidance and oftentimes forsaking his church; instead, he will look for peers in the marketplace for mutual edification. In situations like these, I sometimes advise high-level marketplace leaders to align personally with an apostolic leader outside of their region, only if they cannot find a local pastor who is apostolic and is able to understand them. At the same time, I advise them to continue to attend a local pastorally led church with their family for the sake of ministering to all the family's needs.

Unfortunately, because of some of the above-mentioned challenges among Christian businessmen/marketplace leaders, some erroneous views have been articulated by workplace movement leaders with regard to relationships with the local church. These marketplace movement leaders' teachings have either dismissed the proper role and function of the local church with regards to the marketplace or replaced it with a "mobile church" mentality. This "mobile church" mentality posits that a "church" or "congregation" exists "whenever two or three are gathered in His name." What such teaching does is it legitimizes the "church gatherings" that occur in the marketplace leaders' offices, para-church ministry, or association meetings. This is not good, as they are disconnected from the typical local church congregations.

Furthermore, since these marketplace movement leaders teach that there are five-fold ministers in business, politics, the arts, etc., they teach that the marketplace leaders are equal to ecclesial apostles and prophets. Such a view then dismisses the need to submit to and function in the context of a local congregation.

Some may argue that marketplace ministers have even more authority in the kingdom of God than church leaders. They base this understanding of the separation of the Believer into two camps. These two camps are the priest and the king:

a. Priests: those operating primarily as fivefold ministers in the ecclesial realm such as apostles, prophets, pastors, evangelists, teachers, and intercessors.
b. Kings: Christians functioning in the marketplace such as business people, political leaders, educational leaders, etc.

This view falsely dichotomizes saints. Scripture teaches us that all saints serve as both kings and priests (Revelation 1:6; Romans 5:17; 1 Peter 2:9). All believers are royalty and are part of the priesthood. Obviously, kings have more authority in a kingdom than a priest, thus, those who hold this view subtly believe that marketplace ministers have more prominence than the clergy and full-time church ministers. This view is indicative of missiology divorced from a proper view of ecclesiology. The fact is that a kingdom has various jurisdictions. When it is taught that some saints are in the ecclesial realm and others in the marketplace realm, the implication is that the latter is not part of the Church. A proper understanding of jurisdictions should help bring clarity in regard to this issue.

The Seven Mountains teaching, popular teaching in some evangelical circles, deals with the realms of society not the jurisdictions of the Kingdom. Religion is one of the mountains we need to influence for the Kingdom. Thus, the true church is not in the Religion Mountain because the Church overarches all Mountains. The Church is God's hierarchy of the Kingdom (Isaiah 2:2).

Because I believe Scripture teaches that the Church is the pillar and ground of the truth, the hope of the world, and the entity in which the purposes of God will be fulfilled (1 Timothy 3:15; Ephesians 3:8-11), I am concerned that anything less than a proper ecclesiology will spell disaster for the fledgling marketplace movement.

To be fair, I believe many pastors have frustrated marketplace leaders within their churches because the nature and function of the church has been changed. Jesus' intention is that the Church is supposed to come together to represent His rule on earth. The Greek use of the term Church is *Ekklesia* and indicates the coming together of citizens to enact public policy for things concerning their city/state. Instead, of the Church coming together to exert His rule, it has become a coming together merely to assemble for worship, prayer and preaching (this interpretation is based on the underlying Greek word translated to synagogue-Hebrews 10:25).

The following points should bring clarity:

There are five different jurisdictions (governments).

The fact is, when we say government, we only think of civic

government. This shows how we have been brainwashed into thinking the secular government should rule over every aspect of our lives.

1. *Self-Government.* This includes individual responsibility as shown in the following passages: Jeremiah 31:29-30; Ezekiel 18:20; John 3:16; Acts 17:30-31. This biblical view is contrasted from the worldview of modernists. These modernists downplay individual responsibility. Instead, they emphasize genetic determinism, environmental determinism, psychological determinism, etc., which are all related to forces outside of the individual. They believe that these shape individuals and causes individuals to make certain choices and behave in a certain manner.

2. *Family Government.* Biblical passages illustrating family government include: Genesis 2:24; Numbers 1:52; Joshua 7:13-14, 16-18; Acts 16:31; Matthew 28:19 (in which heads of households are baptized first); Ephesians 5:22-25; 6:1-4; Acts 5 (Ananias and Sapphira).

3. *Church Government.* Passages alluding to this subject include Leviticus 13-15; Matthew 16:18-19; Matthew 18:15-17; Ephesians 4:10-1. The Priests in the Old Testament had to judge in matters of health, money, land, etc. which would be how we use the term kings today in the apostolic movement. Additionally in 1 Corinthians 6, one of the church's responsibilities was to self-adjudicate.

4. *Business.* Some passages alluding to this include James 5:4; Isaiah 65:21-23; 1 Kings 4:25.
   This has to do with a God-given right to form voluntary associations for the sake of commerce and sustenance.

5. *Civic Government.* Passages on this subject include Proverbs 8:15-16, 20; Romans 13:1-7 (according to this passage in Romans, the primary role of civic government is to keep order and promote freedom, justice, and peace);

In addition, 1 Timothy 2:1-5 Paul states that the purpose of those in civil government is to keep the peace so that the gospel can go forth without hindrance.

Unbiblical Overlap

None of these five governments should overreach or lord over one or all of the other four governments. An example of this is seen in today's socialist concept of Statism that insists on taking responsibility for every aspect of a citizen's life including their health, wellbeing, the care, and education of their children, as well as their social identity.

Examples of violations of the five jurisdictions in society include:

- A violation of self-government is when the state makes a law that forbids Christians from praying or reading their bible in a public school or praying in a graduation ceremony.

- A violation of the biblical view of family government is when the state infringes on private family wealth by imposing an inheritance tax/marriage tax; passes welfare laws that penalize marriage; has a progressive income tax (1 Samuel 8:11 18); removes children from their family because they are homeschooled (as we have seen in Germany).

Examples of state infringing upon business include overreach in environmental laws; excessive zoning laws and fees for work permits; excessive taxing; excessive use of antitrust laws (Microsoft breakup).

- A violation of the Church government: the popular 501(c)3 puts churches under the jurisdiction of the state which prohibits churches from promoting political views (based on the unconstitutional "Johnson Amendment" which was passed in 1954); Churches have been threatened with losing their tax-exempt status if they do not conform to certain state policies and laws.

Biblical Overlap

- Self-Government: When a person breaks the law by stealing someone else's property, or by committing a homicide, they lose their right to self-govern and the civic government rightfully incarcerates them.
- Family Government: It is perfectly in line with Scripture that if parents can't take care of or manage their children (neglect, abuse, school truancy, or juvenile criminal activity) that the Bureau of Child Welfare can take the necessary measures to ensure the safety of the child.
- Business: The government should close down sweatshops or businesses that discriminate based on race or because of tax evasion or safety violations.
- Church: The civil government can intervene in cases where there is sexual or mental abuse, financial fraud, etc.

That being said, the ecclesial realm (the Body of Christ which is made up of believing individual Christ-followers, not the institutional church), is the lead agent in the kingdom and influences all the other realms as salt and light. Jesus called His church the light and salt of the earth (Matthew 5:13-14), that would storm the gates of hell, (Matthew 16:18) and disciple the nations of the earth (Matthew 28:19-20). Furthermore, the ecclesial realm equips the saints to fill the earth and influence every realm and jurisdiction of the earth, as we see in the New Testament Didache. Ephesians 4:10-12 teaches that ecclesial fivefold ministry prepares saints to "fill all things", which has to do with mature saints standing in the gap and bringing systemic change in every realm of the created order. This obligates the church to train leaders for various realms; the Church as the *Ekklesia* should permeate every aspect of society with the gospel and Lordship of Christ.

The Role of The Marketplace Leader in the Context of Apest

It is my understanding related to the context of Ephesians 4:7-11 that marketplace people may function as apostles and prophets in their respective realms, but are not necessarily ecclesiastical apostles, even though they are in the church. I have also observed that a few leaders have hyphenated callings.

Thus, someone can be a marketplace apostle called to oversee a congregation or be an ecclesial apostle called to lead in the marketplace. So it is not a cookie-cutter as it depends on the individual's call; however, most people excel in either one or the other.

From my experience, I have observed that when those called to oversee a congregation attempt to do something outside of their God-given grace, such as venturing into the marketplace and launching a business, often disaster occurs that can hurt both the church and the business.

The Challenge of Walking Out the APEST Gifts in Biblical Unity and Order

An egalitarian vision related to Ephesians 4:11 can divide the church if some marketplace leaders consider themselves as equal to ecclesial apostles and prophets and create mobile churches in their own businesses or associations. Consequently, their theology allows them to tithe to themselves and/or to their own business or ministry. What also complicates this is the fact that, in some cases, marketplace ministers may indeed have more anointing, maturity, and authority in the kingdom of God than some who call themselves apostles and prophets in the ecclesial realm. It also cannot be overemphasized that a person gifted to be an apostle in one nation/region, may not be equal to apostles in another nation or region. For example, the deacons in the book of Acts had more authority than most of our present-day apostles, prophets, and evangelists (Acts 6-8).

Consequently, even though a marketplace leader may be apostolic, there is no clear scriptural or historical precedent to give them the title of apostle. While they may function apostolically, they are not equal to ecclesiastical apostles in the kingdom mandate to disciple the nations. An exception to this is if they have an anointing like Daniel or Nehemiah, who were called to both realms. However, it's still difficult to make this comparison (Daniel and Nehemiah), with the present Church because the nation of Israel was in captivity during Daniel and Nehemiah's ministries. In the nation of Israel's exilic context, the body of believers was fragmented: prophets and priests had to work secular jobs to satisfy their captors and the whole situation wasn't as cohesive with regards to function as when Israel lived in their own land.

There are no scriptural examples or precedent for the "mobile church" concept.

In the New Testament *Didache*, even though Paul always traveled with an apostolic team to various churches, they never called themselves a mobile church (Acts 19:22; 20:4,7).

Biblically, a church is not just a place where two or more believers are present but is an extended family (Ephesians 3:15). It is made up of believers who are sent out with a mission and a cradle-to-the-grave ministry; they are recognized and released by the leadership of their mother church, network, or denomination. Other characteristics are modeled both by Scripture and church history. I believe that a hermeneutical community is necessary as it relates to the need for biblical interpretation; this ensures that we don't go off on tangents with subjective, individualistic interpretations. The Acts 15 Jerusalem council exemplifies how the early church elders functioned as a hermeneutical community.

To summarize, these are some of the biblical characteristics that describe the nature of the church:

- The cradle-to-grave ministry made up of an extended family of families.
- Called out assemblies of believers that are sent out and recognized by a mother church through the laying on of hands of a presbytery of fivefold ministers and elders.
- Sent to a specific geographic area that can extend to the ends of the earth (Acts 1:8).
- Has a leadership team of elders and deacons, with some elders functioning in one or more of the fivefold ministries.
- A community of believers that administers the sacraments of the Lord's Supper, baptism, marriage and performs funerals.

Without this understanding, we will be forced to recognize various non-Churches as Churches, like Christian clubs in high schools and colleges; two believers listening to a television preacher every Sunday in their house; two people gathering for bible/prayer during their lunch break. Recognizing these, as Churches would water down what a church is, making present congregational Church meetings irrelevant. That being said, I do believe it is clear that marketplace leaders need ecclesial leaders that function as apostles that they can relate to and learn from.

The "law of the lid"[173] teaches that leaders need to submit to or work with other leaders with a leadership level either equal to or greater than their own. Thus, when a marketplace apostle or prophet is in a local church in which the overseer is a pastor and not an apostle, the pastor will generally not know how to relate to and lead prominent marketplace ministers. As I already mentioned, in situations like these, marketplace apostles and prophets should join apostolic churches that have a vision big enough to celebrate, recognize, and bless marketplace leaders in their congregations. One marketplace billionaire I know said that if he were to tithe to his local church, he would destroy it because they would not know what to do with the money.

To summarize some poignant conclusions from above: All believers function as both kings and priests (Romans 5:17; Revelation 1:6; 1 Peter 2:9. To separate this is dangerous and without biblical warrant; both ecclesial and marketplace ministers serve in distinct jurisdictions and as such, both should function together as part of the body of Christ in the multi-jurisdictional kingdom of God.

The challenge of adopting nuances of the prevailing cultural values of a nation that are anti- biblical.

The apostolic movement is not exempt from making the same mistakes the rest of the Body of Christ makes. It must not succumb to imposing upon the Scriptures or church practice/leadership style, an interpretation that emanates from the surrounding culture. Instead, it must see through the lens of Scripture as the movement gains momentum. This is a great challenge as it relates to truly advancing the agenda of the Kingdom of God instead of perpetuating the agenda of a leader who may have certain cultural blind spots.

Challenges in Latin America

For example, in Latin America, I have observed within some Apostolic leaders what I term, "The Conquistador Spirit." This displays itself when an apostolic leader uses the message of the Apostolic/The kingdom of God, to build his own kingdom, as in the case of the Roman Catholic Pope. This is historically in line with the Conquistadors from Spain and Portugal who conquered

211

and ruled with an iron fist what is known presently as the nations in South and Central America. Often their conquering was done in the service of the Roman Catholic Pope, which resulted in forced conversions to the Christian faith. Since Latin America is a continent that has a Catholic paradigm, this view of ruling in the name of a Church of God can be easily accepted. This is because imbedded in the culture are strong "Alpha Male" type leaders who mimic this cultural construct, as opposed to the meek lowly servant approach of the Lord Jesus Christ and His Apostles.[174]

Consequently, I have seen very strong autocratic leadership exhibited among many Latin American Apostolic leaders who often rule like a Spanish or Portuguese General instead of an empowering Servant Leader, who pulls opinions from the bottom up while teaching their people the skill of critical thinking. This autocratic style of leadership tends to create followers rather than self-empowered leaders. Another unfortunate consequence of this kind of spirit among Apostolic leaders is the tendency to become extremely territorial and competitive with other Apostolic type leaders. This makes any attempt at uniting the Apostolic church in a nation or region very difficult, since many of the leaders of the largest and most influential churches and movements may not want to surrender any of their authority over to other leaders.

Thankfully, some significant developments with regards to Apostolic unity have started taking place within Latin America. Conferences like CoiCom, led by Arnold Enns, is an annual conference of apostolic leaders and pastors. It brings together several thousand in various nations of Latin America for the purpose of education and edification. I have had the privilege of preaching in at least three of these conventions in nations like Honduras and the Dominican Republic. There is another significant movement afoot in Columbia, with apostolic leaders like Hector Pardo. Within the past decade, he has been bringing together some of the top church places and workplace leaders for the purpose of societal transformation. I have also heard of great movements of unity among Apostolic leaders in the Evangelical church in certain parts of Argentina which are being led by a great servant leader, Gustavo Lara. Apostle Gustavo galvanized over 60 movement leaders of networks with over 1000 churches from all over Latin America.

These gatherings are held annually in Panama City, Panama as well as in Buenos Aires, Argentina and other parts of Latin America. In September 2019, I was privileged to speak at their Buenos Aires meetings to approximately 500 leaders. My friend, Yasser Rivas, who leads a megachurch in Santiago, Dominican Republic, also has tremendous influence. He convenes hundreds of leaders from all over the Spanish speaking world. I once spoke at a stadium event he convened in Santiago that had approximately 7000 people with hundreds of pastors in attendance. More can be mentioned about what God is doing in Latin America; there are definite signs of hope as more and more apostolic leaders are embracing the biblical pattern of the "Way of Christ and His Apostles".

Challenges in the Continent of Africa

In my travels and interactions with key African Apostolic leaders in ICAL, they tell me that the biggest challenge they have with regards to uniting the Body of Christ in their regions is "the tribal territorial spirit". Of course, this refers to the tribalism embedded in their culture as is evident when a strong tribal leader claims a certain territory for him and his tribe, over and against other tribal leaders and their tribes. Unfortunately, this permeates the Church, resulting in extreme autocratic leadership among many Apostolic leaders who have not yet discerned the difference between the lens of worldly cultural leadership and the "Way of Jesus and His Apostles".

Another huge challenge in Africa is "syncretism". Numerous conversations with African Apostolic leaders have revealed that it is common to mix tribal African cultural/religious practices with Christianity. Unfortunately, the practice of polygamy, magic, forms of witchcraft, ancestor worship and Judaism are sometimes found in rural biblically illiterate churches and movements.[175] Another huge challenge in the Apostolic Church of Africa is the embrace of the so-called "Prosperity Gospel" which many of their leaders copied from televangelists from the USA. The focus on wealth creation, equating financial prosperity with great faith, as well as viewing wealth as a blessing from God, has made many African preachers rich while their congregations remain relatively poor. However, some signs of hope are evident.

One of my Apostolic leader friends, Bishop Arnold Muwange of Kampala, Uganda, gathers thousands of pastors together twice a year to feed them both the Word of God and literally feeds them meat from a cow he slaughters just for this event. My local church was honored to partner with Bishop Muwange to help build an extension of an orphanage, "Kampala Children's Home." This orphanage provides education for three hundred children and houses approximately 150 orphans. Other African pastors, like Apostle Joseph Adefarasin of Lagos Nigeria, lead a large network of 500 pastors that reaches beyond Lagos to the city of Abujah. In 2014, I taught in both cities of Nigeria in 2014 to approximately 700 pastors and leaders from the church place and marketplace.

Apostle Joseph Adefarasin is one of the humblest, Kingdom-focused leaders I have ever met. His approach to leadership is a great model for the entire continent of Africa. Additionally, Apostles Thamo Naidoo and Sagie Govendar are two incredible servant leaders in South Africa. Naidoo conducts "Apostolic tables" in North America, Europe, Africa and Latin America where apostolic leaders and pastors are inculcated with a pure New Testament pattern of the "Way of Christ and His Apostles".

In 2015, I spoke for him in Johannesburg, to over three thousand leaders from all over the continent of Africa.

Dr. Govendar, who is a medical doctor, convenes 500 pastors twice per week in the city of Durban. It is the greatest example of "one church /one city" I have ever witnessed in my life.

His church never grows beyond 100 people because he is constantly sending out leaders to plant other churches in his city and nation.

Before we leave this section, I also want to bring to the reader's attention the excellent encyclical Jeff Reed recently published called, "Global Pentecostalism and the Spirit".[176] In this significant work, Jeff brings out the concern he has for the future of global Pentecostalism in developing countries. His concern is based upon the fact that they greatly lack the biblical training necessary to make mature disciples, which has also led to syncretism and even heretical doctrines in some cases. Reed tries to answer the questions of why these massive Pentecostal movements in developing countries have failed to bring societal transformation and why is there such a high attrition rate? Reed states, "I believe most of these Global Pentecostal networks have a very significant misunderstanding of how the Spirit works to stabilize and mature their movements. They know how the Spirit works to birth their movements, like Pentecost, but not how to stabilize and mature their networks and movements."[177]

Reeds' understanding of the power of the Spirit that Jesus promised in Acts 1:8, challenges the typical charismatic view of the nature of that power. While most Pentecostal and Charismatic believers equate Acts 1:8 with the "sign gifts" of the Spirit, Jeff adds his understanding as he recalls the teachings of Jesus in His final discourse as it related to the nature and purpose of the coming of the Spirit. He states that in John chapters 14-16, the Holy Spirit comes primarily as the Spirit of "Truth". This means that the Holy Spirit is meant to teach us all things, alerting us regarding things to come, as well as functioning as our advocate and counselor. We see this aspect of the Holy Spirit profoundly illustrated in the Acts narrative:

1. The Spirit brought a "one mindedness" right after He fell upon the church on the day of Pentecost. Acts 2:42–47 states,

   "[T]hey continued steadfastly in the apostles' doctrine and fellowship, in the breaking of bread, and in prayers. Then fear came upon every soul, and many wonders and signs were done through the apostles. Now all who believed were together and had all things in common, and sold their possessions and goods, and divided them among all, as anyone had need. So, continuing daily with one accord in the temple, and breaking bread from house to house, they ate their food with gladness and simplicity of heart, praising God and having favor with all the people. And the Lord added to the church daily those who were being saved." NKJV

2. The Spirit brought wisdom and boldness of speech despite Peter and the apostles lack of traditional Jewish training: Acts 4:13: "Now when they saw the boldness of Peter and John, and perceived that they were uneducated and untrained men, they marveled. And they realized that they had been with Jesus." Hence, because they walked with Jesus and were empowered by His spirit this produced boldness because of the wisdom inside of them. NKJV

3. The Spirit of God granted wisdom to Peter and the apostles to know how to deal with ethnic inequality which resulted in inequitable distribution of food. In Acts 6 we see the challenge of provision when the Grecian widows were being overlooked in the daily distribution of food: Acts 6:1–7 reads, "Now in those days, when the number of the disciples was multiplying, there arose a complaint against the Hebrews by the Hellenists, because their

widows were neglected in the daily distribution. Then the twelve summoned the multitude of the disciples and said, 'It is not desirable that we should leave the word of God and serve tables. Therefore, brethren, seek out from among you seven men of good reputation, full of the Holy Spirit and wisdom, whom we may appoint over this business; but we will give ourselves continually to prayer and to the ministry of the word.' And the saying pleased the whole multitude. And they chose Stephen, a man full of faith and the Holy Spirit, and Philip, Prochorus, Nicanor, Timon, Parmenas, and Nicolas, a proselyte from Antioch, whom they set before the apostles; and when they had prayed, they laid hands on them."

What was the result of this act of Spirit led wisdom? Acts 6:7 says, "Then the word of God spread, and the number of the disciples multiplied greatly in Jerusalem, and a great many of the priests were obedient to the faith." NKJV

4. The Spirit of God fell on Stephan and granted him wisdom as he was filled with the Holy Spirit. Acts 6:8–11 says, "Stephen, full of faith and power, did great wonders and signs among the people. Then there arose some from what is called the Synagogue of the Freedmen (Cyrenians, Alexandrians, and those from Cilicia and Asia), disputing with Stephen. And they were not able to resist the wisdom and the Spirit by which he spoke." This amazing passage connects faith, power and wisdom together as a mark of being Spirit-filled. NKJV

5. The Spirit of Wisdom was demonstrated through the Antioch elders as they heard from the Holy Spirit to release Paul and Barnabus as apostles to the Gentile world. Acts 13:1–4 states, "Now in the church that was at Antioch there were certain prophets and teachers: Barnabas, Simeon who was called Niger, Lucius of Cyrene, Manaen

who had been brought up with Herod the tetrarch, and Saul. As they ministered to the Lord and fasted, the Holy Spirit said, "Now separate to Me Barnabas and Saul for the work to which I have called them." Then, having fasted and prayed and laid hands on them, they sent them away." Consequently, when the leaders of the early church created space for God to speak to them through fasting, worship and prayer, the strategy for the first missionary movement was downloaded to them. NKJV

6. The Holy Spirit revealed His will concerning the Gentile world. The First General Council of Apostles was held regarding the future of the gospel for non-Jewish believers. Acts 15 shows how the apostles and elders spent a considerable time in dialogue so they could discern the mind of God through the Spirit regarding the issue of Gentile conversions. They ended this important Council by saying, "[I]t seemed good to us and to the Holy Spirit." NKJV

7. The Spirit's guidance of Paul through his missionary endeavors:
Acts 16:6–10 reads, "Now when they had gone through Phrygia and the region of Galatia, they were forbidden by the Holy Spirit to preach the word in Asia. After they had come to Mysia, they tried to go into Bithynia, but the Spirit did not permit them. So passing by Mysia, they came down to Troas. And a vision appeared to Paul in the night. A man of Macedonia stood and pleaded with him, saying, 'Come over to Macedonia and help us.' Now after he had seen the vision, immediately we sought to go to Macedonia, concluding that the Lord had called us to preach the gospel to them." NKJV

8. The Holy Spirit, or Spirit of Jesus, led Paul on his missionary journeys and forbade him from going into certain parts of the world. The fact that the Holy Spirit is here is

called "The Spirit of Jesus" further illustrates the fact that the Holy Spirit came to empower the church to continue to do the works of Christ by making disciples and planting gospel movements all over the world (Acts 1:1). Acts 16:6-9 shows that the Spirit of God would not allow Paul to prematurely preach in the province of Asia but instead directed him to preach in Western Europe. Eventually Paul planted a burgeoning church planting movement in Asia Minor in the city of Ephesus (Acts 19). In closing, Reed believes that one of the reasons why the contemporary Global Apostolic church is in trouble is due to the lack of understanding of the role of the Holy Spirit in offering strategy; The Apostolic Church must understand the Holy Spirit as the "strategic" Spirit if it is to grow properly and exponentially. NKJV

Apostolic Challenges in the USA

There are many challenges with Apostolic leadership in North America, especially when measured against the New Testament pattern of the "Way of Christ and His Apostles".

I will mention just a few that I deal with all on a recurring basis:

1. The far right nationalistic spirit or far left leaning apostolic leaders espousing the apostolic kingdom message. People who fall into this category tend to mix their faith with the Conservative Republican Party or left-leaning Democratic party. This violates the concern of Jesus when He warned the disciples about the "leaven of Herod" (Mark 8:15). The challenge with this position is that sometimes Apostolic leaders can be exuberant over a political victory while at the same time neglecting to fulfill the Great Commission. Often, the churches they participate in are not reproducing disciples, planting churches or extending the mission

219

of Jesus in accordance with the Acts narrative of Luke. Consequently, when we wrap Christianity in the flag of any nation, we tend to equate said nation with the Kingdom of God while at the same time alienating unchurched and churched people who may not agree with our political ideology. This was not the focus, nor the way of Christ as demonstrated in the Gospels.

When Jesus told Pilate "His kingdom is not of this world" (John 18:36,37), He was making a clear distinction between the Kingdom of God and the nations of this world. The Apostle Peter even states that the church is actually a "holy nation" set apart for God (1 Peter 2:8,9). Although I believe the church should speak prophetically to nations and culture, I also do not believe that the focus or loyalty to a nation should transcend the focus towards edifying the Body of Christ. I have seen this nationalistic spirit cause the Body of Christ in the USA to ignore the global expression of the Church as well as the needs of the greater Body of Christ. Many, if not most, Apostolic leaders in the USA have no clue what is happening in the other continents of the world.

One of the reasons for this is that the majority of American citizens are well provided for and also because the US is so big, we tend to only care about what goes on in our nation. This is why groups like ICAL are so important for church leaders in the USA as they help bring understanding to the global context of the apostolic movement. In contrast to the US, when I travel abroad to China, Malaysia, the Middle East, Eastern and Western Europe, Australia, New Zealand, Latin America, and even Canada, most people are more informed about the major political and economic issues they face as a nation. In addition to this, most people in other parts of the world, especially Europe, speak more than one language, including English. At the same time, most living in the USA (unless they are recent immigrants), only speak English. This aids in the lack of global understanding most Americans have. This ignorance has also spilled over into much of the Apostolic movement.

2. Another challenge for the North American apostolic movement is the "CEO corporate" leadership culture, with an emphasis on church growth. This has resulted in Apostolic leaders mimicking the leadership principles of men like Tony Robbins, Steve Jobs, Jack Welch, etc., The problem with this is that much of the principles of leadership are caricatures of the American cultural dream more than a Christo Centric model.

   This has led to churches treating their congregation like a business instead of the New Testament model of the family (1Timothy 5:1-2). It objectifies people, as people are used just to further the vision and mission of the church, instead of being seen as a valuable image-bearer of Christ. It also focuses more on programs that would attract and keep people in their Church, rather than focusing on doing life with people with the goal of maturing them into Christ Followers.

3. Another theological and cultural challenge with some in the American expression of the Apostolic movement is the American view of happiness and success. This is prevalent in the churches (including the Apostolic movements), emanating from the "prosperity and self-fulfillment" genre replicated across the world. The US is a big exporter through its high-profile preachers across the globe.

4. Another challenge that I see is that many conservative American Evangelical Christians in the USA (including the Apostolic) put a priority on protecting Freedom of Speech and Religion (I agree that the First Amendment of

the U.S. Constitution should be upheld), while at the same time objecting to the immigration of Muslims and Latinos (I am against illegal immigration but will welcome and aid any illegal that comes to our church). Churches often object to immigration out of fear of losing safety and comfort. In my opinion, we should welcome immigrants from Muslim nations so we can love them and share the gospel with them. We have seen many Muslims come to Christ in our community through children's outreaches, which have been able to provide aid to their families.

In conclusion, all of the above challenges are counter to the "Way of Christ and His Apostles". USCAL and ICAL are working towards remedying much of this.

How Culture Has Influenced Evangelical Church Theology and Practice

It is my intention here to show the relationship between theological formation in the church and its particular culture and contemporary movements. By culture, we mean the language, arts, habits, values, currency, and aspirations of a people group, a community, city or nation. As a new Christian, I thought the church just preached by and large what was plainly taught in scripture, however, in 1995, through my reading of church history, I was shocked to see how much the Church veered away from the scriptural model. During that time, I started to discover how much theologians and Evangelical Christian leaders in America abandoned societal reformation. One of the reasons for this was their eschatological views were changed from more of a postmillennial to a hyper dispensational premillennial view. Such a view emphasized the imminent return of Christ and the rapture.[178]

To simplify what happened, preachers like Charles Finney preached and worked for societal reform (abolition, temperance, and women's suffrage). He and others like him had an understanding that doing so was part of the expression of the kingdom of God on the earth as it is in heaven (Luke 11:2). After the horrors of the civil war, when eight hundred thousand men were killed, the church got discouraged by the state of affairs, lost hope in bringing the kingdom of God on earth in America, which made them open to the hyper premillennial view, which emphasized the imminent return of Christ and the rapture. This shift in theology coincides with the civil war. Therefore, it wasn't primarily the study of the bible, but the state of society and culture that influenced the belief system of the church. This paved the way for the present dispensational nature of much of Evangelicalism for the past 135 years.

Unfortunately, this teaching led to the church abandoning culture. Although church attendance in America is at an all-time high, morality, and culture is at an all-time low. This dispensational thinking has separated the cross from culture, the creator from redeemer, and has resulted in a false dichotomy between the spiritual and material world; as a result, most of the Church tries to only win souls for heaven while leaving the stewardship of the earth to the secularists. This teaching is also responsible for peripheral movements and teachings like the one of the late Harold Camping espoused. On family radio, he espoused that the world would end and Christ will return on May 21st, 2011. When Camping and others like him were exposed as false teachers, due to their eschatological summations, their excuse was that they made a simple mistake in their calculations and instead proposed another date.

Doing Theology in culture

Of course, the Church is called to incarnate the teachings of scripture through its participation in culture. Biblical application is a combination of theological exegesis and cultural engagement, but the primary doctrines and truth of scripture are universal in nature and should not shift with a changing culture. For example, the Deity of Christ, salvation by the vicarious death, burial and resurrection of Christ, heaven for the believers, condemnation for the damned, and even the gender roles of the family (Ephesians 5:22-33), are grounded in the created order, not in culture. For example, according to 1 Corinthians 10:8, the husband, as the head of the family, is grounded in the created order, not culture. In spite of this, today more and more evangelical leaders are calling for an egalitarian view in the family and church as it relates to spiritual headship. This is driven more by culture than the bible. Some argue that Paul's epistles are not relevant today because he was a sexist who spoke from the context of a patriarchal culture. This is a charge he refutes in 1 Corinthians 10:8 and 1 Timothy 2:12-14. Galatians 3:28 presents an egalitarian view as it pertains to male and female, and their legal standing in Christ, while exegetically it does nothing to override the other passages regarding male headship in the home and Church. To be fair, Ephesians 5:22 frames the family text by stating that we should submit to one another and verse 25 talks about husbands loving their wives as Christ loved the church -which has to do more with demonstrating spiritual leadership by being the first to forgive and leading by example-not touting headship and ordering a spouse to submit.

However, it must be emphasized that women's leadership in the home and church is absolutely biblical and necessary to reflect God's image (Genesis 1:27) and to express His Dominion (Genesis 1:28). Another error that has invaded the Church in various forms is due in part to process. Process theology is a form of cosmic evolution and is the kissing cousin of Open Theism that teaches that God doesn't even know some aspects of the "unknowable" future. Inherent in this teaching is that the gospel and biblical teaching are always evolving with the progress of culture. It falsely reasons that God is always learning with the unfolding of time.

Although we need to stick to the core message of scripture in spite of our cultural context, we also have to relate the gospel to our particular culture in order for the people to understand and receive it. Much of the time people are not rejecting the core gospel but the cultural accouterments we attach to the gospel. For example, a historian friend of mine said that some of the reasons Christianity lost North Africa to Islam are because Western culture, language, values, and methods were forced upon the churches. When Islam came, Islam adopted its message and method to the African culture, which made it more amenable for new converts. Legalism is another hindrance to the gospel. It is usually concentrated especially among the ethic Pentecostal groups. Some of their rules require women not wear pants, earrings, make up, and no cutting of their hair. Such prohibitions have hindered these groups from passing down the faith to the next generation, especially because young people do not connect these rules and regulations with authentic Christianity, as well as the fact that they do not want to be ostracized by their peers for their weird dress code and austere lifestyle.

We must distinguish between certain aspects of a culture that are not harmful to biblical beliefs, but that can assimilate into the Christian faith. Cultural aspects like food, modest dress, language, monetary currency, and mode of work can easily be assimilated with a gospel presentation without compromising the message. However, other aspects of a culture may be a challenge to biblical norms and values. For example, tribal people in Papua New Guinea were shocked to find out that Christian missionaries taught against cannibalism. These indigenous people thought it was much better for their family members to eat the bodies of their loved ones who died than to bury them and allow worms to eat them. Also, people in India who practice the ancient ritual of Sati (where a wife is burned alive next to her dead husband's body), think this practice demonstrates a woman's devotion to her husband more than anything.

Presently, the Church in parts of Africa is grappling with

the issue of polygamy with members of their congregation. The challenge is that some believe that it's more ungodly to separate a woman and her children from the husband and father. To do so would mean they would be on their own without any support. The woman got married in good faith to her husband. If she was forced to divorce her husband, she would have no other way to make a living and would have to be forced into prostitution. Some Africans reason they have a more of a biblical culture because they at least honor lifelong covenants and partnerships, while we in the West think nothing of breaking the marriage covenant through a divorce, thus destroying families, and often end up remarrying. I Timothy 3:2 makes it clear that the standard for an elder of a church should be that they are the husband of one wife. This shows that the biblical standard changed from the Old Testament, in which the Kings and patriarchs often had polygamous relationships. Is monogamy the standard that should be enforced for everybody who attends the church or just those who aspire to eldership?

It takes much biblical and cultural exegesis, as well as prayer, to know how to proceed in situations that are particular to nations such as Africa. The easy thing to do would be for the church to allow a form of syncretism in which there is a combination of Christianity, tribal religions and cultural traditions. This is akin to what has been reported in the Catholic Church in Haiti. There, some of the native people attend the Catholic Mass while continuing to practice voodoo. Also in some Latino cultures, they practice both Roman Catholicism and the magic arts, such as Santeria. It is clear that God is against any form of syncretism. He said that He will have no other gods besides Him! (2 Kings 17:32-45; 1 Corinthians 10:20-22). We cannot worship the Lord and serve idols or demons!

In America, syncretism plays itself out in another way. We

see it in the political arena. For example, when the minority communities equate the Christian-led civil rights movement with the Democrat party and when the Christian right marries its faith to a nationalistic dedication to America and the Republican party, it becomes a form of syncretism. During WW1 the churches in Europe were so caught up in nationalism that they all sided against one another based on who their nation was at war against. We also saw many German churches join the national socialistic party of Adolf Hitler even though he was advocating the genocide of non Arian people.

In 2008, and 2012 presidential elections in the USA, Barak Obama received almost 90 percent of the Black vote. He even received votes from among many black Evangelical conservative leaders, even though they knew Obama was a left-leaning progressive who espoused values contrary to their historic Christian faith. What was the reason for this position? It was not based on the standards laid out in the bible but what was dictated by culture. As if often the case, culture trumps vision, mission and unfortunately even the anointing. Jesus even said that the traditions of men nullify the word of God (Mark 7:13).

In conclusion, if the church is going to be an effective witness for Christ, we have to exalt the universal truth of Scripture and exalt Christ as Lord of all, even over our ethnic and national culture. It is very difficult to take ourselves out of our culture to critique it, some say it is like trying to push a bus while you are sitting in it. The reality is that our minds, values, and language have been shaped by our culture. This often creates the lens by which we read and interpret scripture. We must trust in the teaching of the Holy Spirit to transform our hearts and minds, which will then give us God's perspective on public policy and theology. This prevents us from being captivated and led by the sinful and selfish torrents of culture and humanity, instead of being led by the One who made us and saved us to be His witnesses to the world. We may not be able to separate religion from culture or culture from religion, but we can separate ourselves to God in holiness. We must be His mouthpiece to the nations of the world, just as He called the prophet Jeremiah to accurately deliver what He had seen from God (Jeremiah 1).

Finally, we have to trust that the gates of hell will not overcome the church (the gates of hell are the pinnacle and power base of a society that control ungodly systems in politics, economics, law). We must follow the Scriptures and the leading of the Lord. Jesus gives light to every man coming into the world, is the true Light that transcends culture; He is the One who created humanity that helps frame the culture (John 1:9-10).

Some General Theological Trends in the Evangelical Church

I have observed that the Evangelical church has been in flux the past several decades, going from one extreme to the next, and in some cases losing its center. Thus, it is really hard to define what an Evangelical is today except for the very ambiguous definition of a person who believes the Bible is the word of God and who believes that salvation occurs through the vicarious death and resurrection of Jesus Christ. Truly, the Evangelical church is at a crossroads. We must choose if we will follow a more culturally amenable position or a more orthodox, biblically sound approach to faith and culture.

The following are some trends and developments, some good and some bad, that will enable us to see where the church is heading in the near future. Truly, the Evangelical church is in the midst of a seismic shift.

Note: The following is based on my personal opinion that stems from having multiple discourses with multi-denominational leaders and theologians, my doctoral studies, and personal observations. Some of the following have also been a framework for a few lectures I gave regarding this subject. I think it is appropriate to include in this book due to the fact the global apostolic movement is also a part of the overarching global Evangelical movement.

1. The continued development and ascendancy of complex apostolic networks with regards to mission, evangelism, and church partnerships.

   Complex apostolic church networks, as reminiscent of the first-century church movement, will continue to develop and explode, especially in the Global South, Latin America, and Asia. These networks are also growing (more slowly), in North America and Canada. These are non-denominational networks or alliances of churches that often include denominational churches that partner for evangelism, community development, prayer, and rallies. Strong apostolic leaders, head up most of the great movements in the global South, Asia, India, and Latin America. They often have regional influence and are able to garner support even among mainline Protestant communities and leaders, for specific Christian causes.[179]

   Of course, I am in favor of this methodological development since it is modeled after the "Way of Christ and His Apostles".

2. The continued development, acceptance, and growth of postmodern churches and theology.

   A growing movement today, amongst young Evangelical leaders, is what some use to classify as the emergent church movement. This is a loosely connected movement among independent pastors and leaders who espouse a postmodern methodology (and in some cases theology), in order to reach our present postmodern generation. Postmodernism is a revolt against dead, empirical modernism, which first affected secular universities. In the past decade, it has infiltrated Evangelical universities and students. As a result, there are now many leaders and movements focusing their church mission with a postmodern mindset (the emergent church movement). While Christian postmodern proponents do not teach there are no universal truths they do argue there is no way to empirically prove a universal truth. They are against the modern empirical realist approach to verifying the truth. They believe the Evangelical church has been held captive the past 200 years to a propositional view of truth. Such view espouses the correspondence view of truth (or realism), in which the defense of Scripture is based on it being the most objectively rational view of life, in the same way, the scientists approach the verification of truth. Postmodernism says this is foreign to the way the early church functioned. They say it is more akin to the Gnostics, who believed that only the mentally "enlightened", that had the true biblical worldview and knowledge of Jesus, were saved.

These postmodernists especially take umbrage with what they call the "Enlightenment trap" that Evangelicals have fallen into as it regards to the defense of the Bible's "inerrancy." They say the early Church knew no such thing as inerrancy, as they never tried to scientifically, forensically, and empirically, defend the faith or the inspiration and authority of Scripture. Even prominent past leaders like Anglican Bishop Lesslie Newbigin, taught that biblical inerrancy is not the way we should approach Scripture. God chose faith and Scripture to come through human beings who were part of the faith community. He continues to spread His truth through error-prone human beings, who are also limited in their speech and understanding, based on their cultures, education, and upbringing.

Postmoderns also claim many Evangelicals are trying to act

more like secular philosophers than preachers. Tertullian condemned this practice when he sneered, "What does Athens have to do with Jerusalem?"[180] The conversions of the masses are subjective, never objective. Faith is spread by the moving of the Holy Spirit on the hearts of people, not by apologetically proving Jesus was the Messiah with the use of linguistics, archeology, or science. Postmoderns say the elements of the Christian faith include things that are not rational, but based on subjective belief, such as the raising of the dead, the witness of the Holy Spirit in men's hearts, the gifts and anointing of the Holy Spirit, and even conversion experiences like that of Paul the Apostle on the road to Damascus (which was not a rational but a supernatural conversion experience). Whether you agree with the Postmoderns or not, they are becoming more of a force to be reckoned with. Many of them even believe the church will eventually do away with theology as we now know it.[181]

3. Charismatics will become more Evangelical and Evangelicals more Charismatic.

There is now more acceptance across the Body of Christ regarding the Pentecostal gifts of the Spirit such as speaking in tongues. This is mostly because those who embrace Pentecostalism, something theologians and missiologists cannot deny, are involved in the overwhelming majority of the explosive global growth of Christianity.[182]

Another reason is because of the culture wars, persecution and the general hardship of being a believer in the world. The church is uniting primarily over the Great Commission and Cultural Commission. As a result, they are refraining from making a major issue of non-essentials regarding redemption, such as speaking in tongues, and whether the baptism of the Spirit is distinct from the initial salvation experience. With exceptions such as John MacArthur and people like the late Harold Camping, fewer Evangelical leaders are speaking out against Pentecostalism.

On the other hand, many people saved in charismatic, Pentecostal-type churches (especially among the educated family oriented middle-class and professionals) eventually seek the safety and stability of a biblically sound Church. These people are even willing to jettison the public charismatic manifestations of the Spirit in congregational assemblies, for a more non-charismatic Evangelical church, if they feel the Evangelical church has more to offer their growing family needs. Many get sick and tired of the over-emphasis of the gifts in some charismatic churches without a corresponding emphasis on sound doctrine, leadership accountability, financial transparency, and proper biblical protocols.

4. The continued growth, development, and acceptance of local church-based theological education
   In June 2010, the Antioch School in Ames, Iowa[183] became the first decentralized, local church-based theological program, to gain accreditation recognized by the U.S. Department of Education. They now have literally millions of students using their curriculum internationally. This breakthrough signaled a growing trend in which more pastors worldwide will attempt to educate their emerging leaders theologically within the context of their local churches. Shipping their best and brightest leaders out to seminary, into an atmosphere bereft of the local church covering and accountability is being recognized as less than ideal. In seminaries, students are graded merely on academic intellectual prowess instead of other areas like character and emotional intelligence, because such areas manifest itself best in a community of faith, where spiritual authority and

biblical values exist.

5. There will be a continued and expanding controversy regarding the doctrine of universalism.

   Pastor Rob Bell's book, *Love Wins*,[184] encapsulates the feeling among many Evangelicals who are grappling with the idea that God sends all unbelievers to hell for eternity. Many believe this is only a fundamentalist belief that is was not taught by the early Church Fathers. For example, the great church father Origen, supposedly embraced "ultimate reconciliation", in which even the devil will ultimately be saved. This is something other scholars refute because Origen's writings were discursive, ambiguous and confusing in many instances. In addition, other notable Catholic theologians in the 20th century such as Hans Kung, Hans von Baltashar, and even popular Anglican missiologist, Leslie Newbegin, seem to espouse some form of either ultimate reconciliation or universalism.

   This present move towards universalism, in my opinion, is being driven by:

   a. Evangelicals who desire to take away the offense of the cross; they try to avoid ridicule with cultural leaders, as they attempt to go mainstream in their community and society.

   b. The leakage of liberal theology into Christian colleges.

   c. The lack of biblical knowledge and literacy among many pastors.

   d. The lack of biblical worldview training and discipleship among church attendees.

6. "Evangelicals who are hungry for cultural acceptance will embrace alternate forms of human sexuality, family and gender in their theology."

   As more Evangelicals come out of dysfunctional homes

affected by divorce, abandonment, and neglect, these views will be harder to fight off among our young people. In addition, fluid forms of human sexuality and family are now becoming more acceptable and imbedded in both American and international law and culture. It has seeped into our public schools, media, music and Hollywood and is espoused by cultural icons. This is making our upcoming generations more unlikely to label these lifestyles as taboo. Unfortunately, by and large, many Evangelical churches do not know how to minister to those struggling with these issues. Often, they look the other way or even silently accept it, especially if it is practiced among those talented members who participate in their church choirs, music, and theatre. As more Evangelicals lose their center and become liberal, the Word of God will be reinterpreted as something that came through the lens of culture. Thus, some of the passages against alternative forms of human sexuality and passages advocating binary gender are being viewed as the result of the "homophobic patriarchal non-progressive" culture of biblical times that is not culturally or biblically relevant today.

Many Evangelical leaders and organizations more pragmatically grounded, than theologically grounded, will begin to accede to "unbiblical theological views regarding human sexuality and identity "as a way of becoming more culturally acceptable for the sake of the gospel.

7. More Evangelicals will coin the phrase "biblical world-view".

Although I am excited to hear more pastors using the phrase "biblical worldview", my excitement is beginning to wane because contemporary Evangelical pastors do not mean the same thing about this subject as someone like Abraham Kuyper, Francis Schaeffer, Charles Colson,

Cornelius Van Til or others.[185] When I hear pastors and leaders describe what they mean by "biblical worldview," I find many are describing a general belief in the inspiration of Scripture and systematic doctrines of the faith. Biblical worldview has more to do with a world and life view, which is seen through a lens through which Christianity encompasses every realm of life, including economics, politics, law, justice, education, philosophy, history etc. It is not relegated to only spiritual things, like salvation and the Church. The problem is, the more a term is used, the more people fake that they understand it, and the more the term is watered down.

8. The house church movement will continue to multiply in response to the superficial corporate life of larger, more institutional church models.

From the writings of church history and the New Testament, we believe the Church of the first century mainly met in homes. Due to persecution, they could not meet in synagogues or build cathedrals until after the Edict of Milan was issued in AD 313. The average size of these house congregations was no more than 50-70 people. Coincidently, this is the average size congregation of churches in North America today, even though our churches mostly meet in storefronts or old church buildings, not homes. Many have found that megachurches, which are often driven by large programs, do not meet their needs for community and connection. As a result, they long for something more authentic. Although I understand and appreciate this movement, I also think it is not the size of a church that matters, but the structure of a church.

For example, you can have a megachurch of over 700,000 (like the church in Seoul, Korea previously led by David Yonggi Cho), with a strong sense of community. Such a church usually depends on multiplying small groups that disciple the people as opposed to just the Sunday services. One of the challenges of house churches is that it can have a hard time ever exerting any substantial community or cultural influence. This is because today's societal leaders (including both political and ecclesial) mainly give more respect to leaders of congregations larger than the typical house or storefront congregation. They also view house churches with suspicion, often thinking such churches are self-ordained, not accountable and therefore illegitimate. Francis Chan is perhaps the most visible advocate of a House Church construct in Christianity today. He is famous for walking away from a 10,000-member mega-church that he founded in Los Angeles because he didn't think he was making disciples according to the New Testament pattern.

I recently spoke at Jesus Life International, a house church movement led by my friend Brian Echevarriaa. This movement is producing hundreds of disciples with a goal of eventually making one million disciples. They are able to counter a perceived lack of community and cultural influence (because they lack official church buildings), because they focus on having strong marriages, families and marketplace influence. They do this by creating community platforms with entrepreneurship, business ownership and having leaders in key positions in culture. Truly, what Brian and Jesus Life International are doing is more closely aligned with "The Way Of Christ and His Apostles" than most of the traditional church models I have observed around the world. Their focus is on being a disciple-making movement.

9. Ecumenism will become the norm as the culture wars

heat up.

When I first came to Christ, it was taboo to speak about Evangelicals working closely with Roman Catholics and Anglicans. Now there is a growing movement of this type of collaborative work, especially because of the cultural wars regarding same-sex marriage, abortion, and the general persecution of the church by media elites and public officials. This only furthers the need for more cross-denominational partnerships.

Although I do not see a total unifying of the church anytime soon, I would not be surprised if in the next 100-200 years, denominational distinctions are functionally useless because of greater communication and partnerships that have been evolving over time. "Evangelicals and Catholics Together", initiated by Charles Colson and Richard John Neuhaus in 1994, and the ecumenical magazine "First Things", also initiated by Neuhaus, are some profound examples of how the church is unifying.

Also, as a result of Vatican II and the charismatic renewal movement of the 1960s and 1970s, Rome has come closer to the Protestant Reformation ideas such as justification by faith, making the Bible available to the people, and presenting the mass in the vernacular of the people. The Catholics are also working more with conservative Protestants and Evangelicals fighting the culture wars, aiding the poor, and social justice. Protestants are starting to prove their faith by their works (like the Catholics in some sense) and have begun to appreciate some of the contributions of the Catholics as well. Although we are still very far apart in essentials, such as celibacy among the priesthood, Mariology, prayers for the dead, purgatory, papal infallibility, and other important areas of disagreement, we are making progress towards unity.

10. There will be stronger, more conservative Evangelical movements based on integrity, accountability and biblical discipleship to counter superficial, nominal American Evangelical and mainline Christianity.

Finally, I see a growing hunger among young Evangelicals (and also a remnant of top leaders) for authentic, accountable relationships and community, as we follow the "Ways of Jesus and the apostles". This is a result of a greater passion to serve God and a reaction against the superficial, therapeutic "self-help" gospel taught among many popular pastors and leaders. It is also a reaction against the lack of integrity among many high-profile Evangelical leaders who have been publicly humiliated in numerous scandals. Many churches are also incorporating a greater level of serious discipleship in their Sunday preaching and programs (for example, Bill Hybels famously admitted in the early 2000s, that his seeker-sensitive church approach failed to make disciples). Others are moving away from a seeker-sensitive, watered-down gospel approach with regards to their Sunday sermons. Many others are also embracing the spiritual disciplines of the early medieval church as a means to give God space to transform us to Christlikeness so we can walk in emotional health and maturity.[186]

11. More independent Evangelical/Charismatic church members will embrace liturgical/historical church models and even mainline denominations.

I have seen a growing trend among congregants, and even pastors, who are embracing a more historical, liturgical approach to ordination, and how we do church, as an attempt to connect and relate to the historic Christian faith. Some like Francis Beckwith, Frankie Schaeffer, and Hank Hannegraaf, have even gone back to either Catholicism or the Orthodox Church. Many independent Evangelicals are embracing the spiritual disciplines of the monastic movement from the Early and Middle Age Church. Some have even become Charismatic Episcopalians or have joined the newly formed North American Anglican Communion. This is a smaller trend than the growing development of complex Apostolic Networks. But it is still a Movement since there will always be an extreme reaction among some who are leery of the independent, disconnected Evangelical church models, that are islands unto themselves. Furthermore, the more one studies history, the more many of the differences that made us denominate, become relativized. Through the lens of church history, we see the common thread of Christian orthodoxy throughout the various denominational streams which have stuck to the essentials of the faith and not gone the way of compromise, like the liberal Protestant Denominations.[187]

12. It will become more normal for pastors, leaders, and churches to embrace a holistic Kingdom approach as taught in the Cultural Commission of Genesis 1:28. More Evangelical pastors are embracing the holistic call to be salt and light to their communities (Matthew 5:13-16). They are aware that the gospel must be relevant by meeting the practical needs of our communities, so that by word and deed, we are proclaiming the gospel and being faithful witnesses of Jesus Christ to the world. Those churches that focus solely on good Sunday preaching and good choirs, will become the new dinosaurs of the twenty-first century. These holistic churches embrace the full import of Isaiah 61:1-4, which involves not only saving individual souls, but restoring whole cities with the power of the gospel of the Kingdom of God.[188]

13. Hyper-dispensational theology is being jettisoned.

When I first came to Christ in the 1970's, everyone was purchasing Hal Lindsey's dispensational, best-selling books like *The Late, Great Planet Earth.*[189] Most pastors were fixated on the last days, the rapture, the identity of the antichrist, and the battle of Armageddon. The only difference in theology/eschatology for most believers was whether a person was pre, mid or post-tribulation, not whether or not they espoused a dispensational view. In the past three decades, there has been a huge shift (especially in theological seminaries and colleges), among future Evangelical thinkers, theologians and pastors, away from focusing on last days teachings regarding the rapture, the identity of the anti-Christ and the imminent return of Christ, toward the teaching that the primary call of the Church is to manifest God's kingdom on earth as it is in heaven.

Most of the dispensational preaching today is coming from older, popular pastors. But the new crop of influential pastors under 40, reflect this emphasis toward a more classical pre-millennial view or a post-millennial or amillennial view of Scripture. What all these views have in common is the call of the church to manifest the Kingdom of God on the earth in practical ways that impact communities, instead of passively waiting for the rapture and splitting hairs over when God's Kingdom will come. Most, like the late Charles Colson and others, do not publicly mention their views on eschatology as much as emphasizing our Cultural Commission. Others, involved in what they call "reconstruction", emphasize the post-millennial theology of the Puritans who founded this nation. Still, others do not know exactly what they believe; they just know it is important to attempt to transform their communities with the holistic approach of the gospel.

14. Higher criticism of the Bible and systematic theology will

lose more prominence among scholars; views on biblical inerrancy will continue to regress. There is a growing trend among top biblical scholars in liberal circles to focus their research on determining the original intent and meaning of the authors of Scripture. They agree the Scriptures are the books that the people of God have received by faith. No amount of argumentation as to their historicity or canonicity would be fruitful at this point, since it is impossible to either prove or disprove the Scriptures with the data we presently possess.

More conservative scholars (whom I agree with) believe there is enough extra-biblical source material to back up the historicity of the Scriptures (for example, writings in non-biblical books, archeological findings, the oral and written histories of the early church fathers, etc.).

Other scholars like NT Wright, believe that the gospels have within itself enough source material without extra biblical writings, to be esteemed as valid in the same way other sources of literature (the writings of Virgil, Pliny and Cicero wrote about the Rome of their day) are used as a resource for understanding history. Wright, better than most, is able to deconstruct the erroneous views of those who are proponents of the so-called historical Jesus movement and it's offspring like the Jesus seminar.[190]

Liberal scholars take a more reductionist approach from a starting point of skepticism in which they attempt to reconstruct the biblical story based on scientific empirical data that cannot be proven because of its basis in subjective conjecture (for example, the Jesus Seminar). However, more writings from liberal scholars dealing with the culture and history of biblical times are being used in conservative schools because this kind of research is extremely helpful! Regarding how we approach theology:

Systematic theology is losing steam because it usually only includes about 20-30 topics of the Bible, based on what each writer deems important.

Biblical theology is gaining more popularity because this discipline takes the approach of studying the Bible as it was written (instead of topically and thematically), which enables each subject or topic to unfold as we inductively study each book in both the New and Old Testaments, as God's word originally intended. (This is, in contrast, to artificially lifting passages out of various books of the Bible and systematizing Scripture thematically.)

Regarding biblical inerrancy, we mean the conservative view that the scriptures in the original autographs were divinely inspired by God and without error. This view is constantly under attack and being constantly revisited and modified. We see this especially with regards to those who have revolted against the rigid fundamentalist approach, that they say has replaced the Pope with the Bible, resulting in a sort of Biblicist idolatry. Younger Evangelicals who want to be more culturally acceptable and open to the latest findings in science, and who have been influenced by postmodernism, will have more of an open view of the scriptures. Although they believe the scriptures are inspired by God, they leave room for human error (not only in translation and transmission but in the original writings), do not take the Bible seriously in areas relating to anything outside of salvation and redemption (they say it has scientific errors), and take more of a conceptual view of Scripture in which the basic narrative is true and inspired. However, they say we cannot believe that every word of the Bible is divinely inspired. In summary, in their view, the Bible not only has some elements of human error and mythology, but it has to be taken in its historical-grammatical context which, in their minds, means that some views related to moral issues today are anachronistic (e.g. homosexuality and same-sex marriage). They believe the scriptural passages dealing with these so-called sins, are merely reflections of the cultural times they were written, not universal applicable principles related to all believers in every age.

In this area, I would counter that the Ten Commandments and the moral law of God are rooted in the nature and character of God. Thus fornication and all sexual sin outside of traditional marriage are always wrong in the eyes of God because God's nature never changes (Hebrews 13:8).[191]

15. The Celtic model of evangelism will become more prominent.

The prevalent model for spreading the gospel will be reversed.

The traditional model is presentation of the gospel; people accepting Jesus as Lord; new believers embraced by the church community.

This will be reversed toward the Celtic model:[192] embrace the community; presenting the gospel within the community; people receiving Christ as Lord and joining the church.

I believe that the church is going from church-centric to community-centric (Kingdom-centric). This transition is resulting in the following:

a. It releases the saints to serve God by serving their communities

b. It is giving churches favor with God and man

c. The church's main cause becomes the community

d. Churches are equipping people for life, not just

church life

e. Churches will enhance their kingdom influence by working with community spheres of influence

f. Today's influencers in the church will become tomorrow's influencers in the community

g. Common grace issues become common ground for the church to connect with key community leaders and initiatives

h. Senior pastors become chaplains/statesmen to whole communities instead of only their own flocks

i. Churches become "cities on a hill" and the "light of the world"

j. Soul-winning that reflects the Daniel/Joseph model

k. Churches penetrating and transforming culture before emphasizing politics

l. Churches viewing their communities (or cities) as gifts to them, not only vice versa

16. More Evangelical scholars are embracing theistic evolution and denying the existence of Adam and Eve as the first parents of the human race.[193]

This is because Evangelical intellectuals want cultural affirmation, which comes by embracing mainstream science and the status quo. This leads to the question: Who should guide theology, Christians who are scientists or theologians? Ultimately these should not contradict but complement each other; however, science does not always catch up to divine revelation. Today's theory may be jettisoned in 10 years. Hence the church must be careful when allowing science to take the lead in biblical interpretation. The leading Evangelical group espousing this view is BioLogos.[194] Its founder, Francis Collins, is a prominent scientist with much cultural clout. Many of the leading Evangelical scholars such as Tim Keller, N.T. Wright, Os Guinness, Peter

Enns and Alister McGrath have been to BioLogos' private gatherings and have all seemed to have come out in favor of some form of theistic evolution.

Currently, Tim Keller, who believes that the Genesis creation account is poetic and not to be taken literally, is trying to hold onto some form of belief in a historic Adam, whereas Francis Collins and others in the group, do not hold to Adam and Eve as historical. If there is no historical Adam, then Jesus is not the Last Adam, and it stands to reason if there was no Adam, there was no fall since Adam was never the federal head of the human race. Hence, the gospel is not true and the book of Romans is not true. This leads to doubting the veracity of the scriptures.

Some are concerned that such a group is opening a door to process theology. Unfortunately, its end result is that culture ends up dictating scriptural interpretation. This is because, according to process theology, even God is growing in the evolutionary process. This could lead to embracing unbiblical views related to marriage, gender, human sexuality, and universalism. My friend, historian Glenn Sunshine, recently made the following comments to me with regards to this issue:

Darwinism, the idea that species arise as a result of natural selection, operating in a framework of random mutations with no outside direction, is untenable for a theist. Either God is sovereign, or He isn't. Theistic evolution or evolutionary front loading might be possibilities, I suppose, but both presuppose God as an intelligent actor involved in the process. In other words, minimally we should support the idea of intelligent design. Given that evolutionists can't even describe evolutionary development without resorting to the language of design, we need to push the point that it cannot be proven that the myriad of examples of apparent design do not represent actual design—that's a philosophical, precommitment on the part of the evolutionist, not a scientific argument.

In fact, I would suggest that the overwhelming evidence of apparent design makes actual design overwhelmingly probable. Given that Darwinism can't explain punctuated equilibrium, which is at the very least what the fossil record suggests, and which is the most popular theory (I believe), I think we can make a good scientific argument for special creation of species. The theological sticking points are the Adam-Christ typology and the related problem of original sin.

While there have been some interesting approaches to these, I don't find any of them particularly convincing. Everyone agrees that Paul believed Adam was a historical figure and that informed his exegesis; if he was wrong, what does that mean for the typology? And what does that suggest about inspiration, that God inspired arguments that the human author thought were true but which were actually false? The exegetical problems look insurmountable to me. The same applies to Jesus' references to Adam and Noah: was He ignorant or lying?[195]

17. Antinomianism (free grace) churches and preaching will continue to proliferate.

There are more and more preachers putting down the institutional church. They are preaching against tithing, standards of holiness (which they call legalism), traditions of the church, the historic creeds, and even the Old Testament moral law. There is even now a TV channel devoted to grace, which some critics say is unbalanced. This is nothing new, as the church throughout history, has dealt with various forms of antinomianism (that which is against law) and Gnosticism (the flesh or the material world isn't important, God only cares about spiritual things).

Many preachers have resorted to preaching free grace because such preaching leads to a greater following. When there are little to no standards required for the Believer, and all that is preached is the love and grace of God (versus Paul the apostle who preached the whole counsel of God Acts 20:27), people are more prone to come to church. We have seen the church go from the positive thinking gospel in the 1970s to the prosperity gospel in the 1980's to the therapeutic gospel in the 1990's and 2000's. Free grace preaching is a synthesis of all of the above. What is obviously missing in all of this is an emphasis on pure biblical preaching. Anyone can examine the New Testament to see that Jesus and the apostles not only preached the love of God but also the wrath of God against all ungodliness and deception (Matthew 5:27-30; Romans 1:18-32; Ephesians 5:1-7). The Word of God warns us against this sort of thing in Jude 4, in which the grace of God is used as a license for sexual immorality and licentiousness. However, Scripture teaches us that the grace of God has appeared to lead us into renouncing fleshly desires and to live godly lives (Titus 2:11-12).[26]

18. There will be a greater understanding of the role of the *Ekklesia*.

More and more pastors are preaching about the fact that the word Jesus used to describe His followers (Matthew 16:18) was the Greek word *ekklesia*. This was a political word, not a religious word. It was used to describe Greek citizens who came together to enact public policy; it also referred to the Roman Senate who was called the *ekklesia* when assembled. In Acts 19:32,39 the word assembly is the Greek the word *ekklesia*, thus denoting a non christian assembly.[196]

Thus, Jesus was calling His disciples to come together as people who were called to steward the earth. God is calling his people to participate with Christ in the renewal of all things in the created order, to represent His kingdom, and to announce His reign over every realm of the earth. This will empower the church to become servant leaders in every realm of life and get their focus off of just looking for the next life, or just being an ineffective leader in full-time church ministry. This will release every serious Christian to be a minister of God in the marketplace, revolutionizing the way we view and do church! If the church gets this right and if the Body of Christ embraces this view, (in the same way both non-denominational and denominational churches have embraced the Charismatic Movement), then in one generation the nations of the world will be greatly impacted politically and economically. We will have a great movement of Christ-followers who use the Bible as their blueprint to influence nations (Matthew 28:19).

In summary, the Church was to set up an *ekklesia* in each city which consisted of the fivefold ministry, elders and the mature believers. I believe an extension of the local church can include setting up *ekklesia* in each realm of society made up of committed and submitted disciples, who are positioned to take the lead in the marketplace, for the Kingdom of God.[197]

19. There will be more pastors and scholars connecting the gospels to the epistles

Our present dialectical local church milieu features more and more postmodern fragmentation, free grace preaching, and a revolt against all traditions, as well as a revolt against the local church. As a result, we will find, concurrent with these divergent movements, a move back (especially in developing countries) towards a missiology with a strong ecclesiology (i.e. doing mission in and through the local church context).

This is very important because in the past few centuries many parachurch organizations have espoused a model of discipleship based on individual mentoring because they say it mirrors the method Jesus used with His disciples. However, they failed to realize that the methodology of Jesus and the gospels was not an end in themselves. Jesus and His disciples were always looking ahead to the formation of the Church. Thus, we should not separate the Jesus method of discipleship from involvement in a local congregation. Jesus did not operate in a vacuum because the epistles and the gospels were not disconnected from one another in purpose and essence. In fact, most of the gospels (possibly with the exception of Mark), were written after the epistles. Thus, the gospels were furnished primarily to give the local church historical context and development of the core gospel message, which they called the kerygma. An understanding of this concept can revolutionize the way we evangelize and do missions and will force many parachurch organizations to work with the local church as part of its core missiological approach. Also, many marketplace and trans-local leaders may jettison their views on the so-called "mobile church" concept (in which any group of 2-3 people meeting is viewed as a church), thus putting pressure on all of them as individuals to be submitted to spiritual authority that's anchored in their home church.[198]

20. There will be a revival of united prayer amongst pastors in global urban cities.

As the economies, policies and governments of the developed world continue to unravel, because of secularism and unsustainable entitlement programs, it will result in more and more unemployment and despair in urban centers.

I believe the Spirit of God will deal with the church to become the shining light in the midst of all this chaos. This will result in a greater dependency on united, concerted prayer amongst pastors in every challenged city. If this prayer is combined with fasting, unity among leaders and churches, and sustained over the long haul, these prayer initiatives could result in some of the greatest moves of awakening and revival we have ever seen! From my study of church history, it seems that the hearts of people are open the most when they are either under judgment or in the midst of societal and moral chaos.

When people stop depending on their civil government for salvation, they become the most desperate for God to move. Thus, very rarely, if ever, do we see mass revival when nations and people groups are prosperous, living in ease and trusting their civil leaders more than they trust God. Although I want to see a heaven-sent awakening that will turn America back to God, it may well be that God will allow further decay, unemployment, and chaos in our nation, (even the saints suffer when their cities suffer-Jeremiah 29:7). The hope is that the Church will get desperate and seek His face like never before.

21. We are entering more into the "Age of the Spirit".
This is a phrase reiterated by liberal theologian Harvey Cox,[199] in which he cites an obvious trend in the global church. He sees people of faith moving away from a dependence on a Christianity that is merely full of rituals, creeds and liturgies, into more of a way of life based on a moving of the Holy Spirit. This movement is one that is uniting

and inspiring the lives of believers everywhere. In the Book of Acts believers were first defined as followers of the "life" or the "way", which denotes an organic way of life rather than adherence to form and ritual (Acts 5:20, 9:2).

Even in denominational churches, the Charismatic Movement has brought millions into this move. This has caused the church hierarchy to cast a suspicious eye on this movement, since it moves congregations away from depending on professional denominational clerics towards hearing God for themselves, through His Spirit. Furthermore, everyone who knows what is happening with regards to the present explosive expansion of Christianity knows that global evangelism and church growth is being accomplished primarily by those who espouse a Pentecostal experience. Hence, many are predicting that the church is moving from the age of belief (defined by creeds, ritual, and confessions), to an age of the Spirit (towards faith, power and a life in the Spirit). This trend also fits the first point of this paper, because it corresponds to the rise of complex apostolic networks, which is being fueled by the global Pentecostal movement. It is going back to the simpler first century Church methodology, based on the way of Jesus and the apostles.

22. A Revival of Pelagianism as Neo-Pelagianism continues to infiltrate churches.

    Neo-Pelagianism is based on the teachings of the monk Pelagius who lived in the 5th century. He fought with St. Augustine regarding the nature of man, predestination and original sin. Matt Slick writes,

    Pelagianism teaches that man's nature is basically good. Thus, it denies original sin, the doctrine that we have inherited a sinful nature from Adam. He said that Adam only hurt himself when he fell and all of his descendants were not affected by Adam's sin. Pelagius taught that a person is born with the same purity and moral abilities as Adam was when God first made him. He taught that people could choose God by the exercise of their free will and rational thought. God's grace, then, is merely an aid to help individuals come to Him.[200]

The biggest challenge with this view is that, essentially, one could come to the conclusion that it is theoretically possible that a person could live a perfect life without Christ. Thus, we don't need Jesus as Savior as much as we need to receive Him as Lord. Semi-Pelagianism and full-blown Pelagianism are basically reactions to hyper-Calvinism. They are espoused by many adherents of world missions, revival, and evangelism, which emphasize human responsibility to such an extent that it often compromises God's sovereignty. It is not practical and does not take into account the present and theological reality of the moral depravity of the human race.

Many councils throughout church history, including the following, have condemned Pelagius:

- Councils of Carthage (412, 416 and 418)
- Council of Ephesus (431)
- Council of Orange (529)
- Council of Trent (1546) (Roman Catholic)
- Second Helvetic Confession (1561/66) 8-9 (Swiss-German Reformed)
- Augsburg Confession (1530) Art. 9, 18 (Lutheran)
- Gallican Confession (1559) Art. 10 (French Reformed)
- Belgic Confession (1561) Art. 15 (Lowlands, French/Dutch/German Reformed)
- The Anglican Articles (1571), 9. (English)

- Canons of Dort (1618-9), 3/4.2 (Dutch/German/ French Reformed).[201]

23. A Continual Shift Away from Enlightenment Presuppositions towards postmodern understanding of Scripture and truth.

The collapse of the modern era, based on the failure of modernity to demonstrate historical progress towards a human flourishing, has resulted in a massive deconstruction of defining the world by empirical truth. It has also led to reductionism when it comes to all forms of literature, including the Bible. This has opened the doors to an alternative current towards mysticism and postmodernism. This is because people continually attempt to find an overarching construct that will enable them to have an anchor or a handle on what they perceive to be a reality. Because of the preponderance of postmodernity presently in culture, as well as it's seeping into biblical literature, theology, and the church, the following are some of my thoughts related to the postmodern challenge to the concept of theological truth.

24. The Post Enlightenment Post-Modern challenge to the concept of Theological truth.

One of the things all apostolic leaders, scholars and Christ followers will have to continually grapple within the contemporary culture is the challenge of postmodernity to the concept of absolute (biblical) truth. The fact is that Jesus declared Himself to be "the Truth" (John 14:6). The Post-Modern trend towards the deconstruction of all language, concepts, categories and truth (it asserts that all propositions of truth are human constructs), leads to moral relativity and devaluation of the authority of Scripture. With the advent of the primacy of postmodernism in the university curricula, there has been a growing loss of meaning and purpose among generations of students. By post-modernism, I am referring to the assertion that there is no meta-narrative or absolute truth that we can hang our hats on. Of course, this is nothing new, as we see in the gospel of John when Jesus told Pontius Pilate that He came to bear witness of the truth and Pilate responded by asking, "What is truth" (John 18:38)?

The preponderance of postmodernism has resulted in a de-valuation of religious narrative, truth, morals, and boundaries; along with a deconstruction of language, structure, and categories (such as male and female). It has left in its wake a rise of suicide, depression, and hopelessness (all the fruit of its nihilistic philosophy). By Nihilism, I am referring to the rejection of all religious and moral principles, often in the belief that life is meaningless. Thus, Nihilism involves stripping humanity of the grand narrative of Christianity and all the other major religions. Nihilism also maintains that nothing in the world has a real existence that can also lead to a post-structural order of extreme anti-establishment, anarchy, and rebellion against all institutional authority. This is why Buddhism and the Eastern New Age philosophies are popularized on college campuses. One of their primary mantras is "maya", which asserts that all distinctions, in reality, are a delusion.

Consequently, students who are fed and embrace any form of Nihilism are often filled with negativity, cynicism, pessimism and can become anti-social and suicidal (Friedrich Nietzsche, the major proponent of nihilism, eventually died in an insane asylum). Of course, doubting the essence and reality of the concept of absolute truth have been going on for millennia, which is the result of the fall of humanity away from God into original sin (Genesis 3). The "fall" not only separated humankind from God, resulting in spiritual and physical death (Romans 5:12-19) but also darkened (and limited) our rational understanding (Ephesians 4:17-19; 2 Corinthians 4:4). Hence, when Jesus claimed to be the "Truth", He was revolutionary. He countered the negative (rational) effects of the fall in more ways than one. His resurrection power enables the eyes of the believing heart to be opened so that they can "know" (Ephesians 1:18) and so man's minds can be transformed (Romans 12:1,2) to once again love and serve God and humanity with all of our heart, mind, soul, and strength (see Matthew 22:37-40). Unfortunately, the embrace of postmodernism has been catastrophic in the following ways:

- It robs people of faith and hope. The Grand Narrative of Christianity simplifies life, gives believers a handle on reality, and enables them to rest in the fact that their creator designed them for an eternal purpose. Conversely, as was already stated above, the contemporary popularization of postmodernism and its concomitant expressions of Nihilism have resulted in a dire increase in youth suicides and depression.[202]

- It dehumanizes humanity. If there is no grand narrative, there is no creator; if there is no creator, there is no distinction between human and animal/ living and non-living/male and female/good and evil. All of the above takes away from the sanctity of human life in which its devaluation leads to an increase in murder, abortion, maltreatment of people including abuse, violence, and objectification.

- It removes all boundaries and distinctions. If there is no God and no transcendent purpose, then there is no concept of good versus evil. This then leads to a world of subjective truth based on the opinions and constructs of those in power. This can eventually lead to totalitarian governments who usurp the rights of individual human freedom (such as is encased in the US Constitutional amendments). Hence, the power and success of American exceptionalism is based on our unique philosophy of governance, in which the foundation of our Constitution is the Declaration of Independence. It declares that we have unalienable rights given to us by God, not men or earthly elites.[203]

As postmodernism trends, more and more believers are shifting away from using human reason as the final arbiter of truth as it relates to defending the faith. Ultimately, we cannot empirically prove either Christianity or atheism; all humans can only grasp truth to the point of probabilities since all reasoning is subjective and circular. The general idea is that, if we can defend the faith, depending upon human reasoning, then someone else can change our minds based on the latest scientific discoveries.

Even if we successfully talk someone into becoming a Christian using apologetics, when we base it on the human reason, we share the same ungodly assumptions that glorify human reason as the highest arbiter of truth. The result of this has been a move away from rationalism into postmodernism, mysticism, and fideism (faith having no reason behind it). A better approach, according to many who espouse postmodernism, (for example, Soren Kierkegaard), would be to take the biblical position of assuming the existence of God the way the Old Testament prophets and New Testament apostles did. In addition, it's important to speak with prophetic authority, as one who has encountered and knows God when it comes to relating to unbelievers.[204]

In conclusion, related to the continuing relevance of the global apostolic movement and evangelicalism, and based on the previous theological and conceptual presuppositions already mentioned, we in the Charismatic Apostolic church need to think differently regarding the following:

1. We cannot merely depend upon revival. First, it is a mistake

to believe that the culture will shift because of a church revival or a societal awakening. Often, we as believers think the key to societal transformation is to convert masses of people. The truth is that everyone is led by the decisions of approximately 3-5% of people who make up the cultural elite in society. Thus, the only way to effect cultural change is to convert the elite who formulate culture within the various spheres of society.

2. Second, it is a mistake to think that political victories will bring transformation. For example, abortion was legalized in 1973, yet the fight still rages on. Same Sex marriage has been legalized but the culture wars over it will never stop. Homosexuality has been normalized by art, media, and entertainment, yet many in America still reject it

   The truth is that politics is only one expression of societal power. We need to influence the other mind-molding sectors of society if we are going to dictate the direction of culture. For example, we need to influence the Ivy League universities, once again, especially Harvard, Yale, and Princeton, in order to change public policy, education, science, views on economics, etc. We need to influence major news outlets like the New York Times, CNN, MTV, etc., and not only write for Christian newspapers and appear only on Christian television stations like TBN.

   Hence, we need to train the disciples of Jesus to exert leadership, not only in the Church but in the marketplace. We need Christians to become professors, board members and chief executives of leading elite entities. Having famous athletes and entertainers getting saved and giving testimonies is not nearly enough. We need revivals and multigenerational strategies to place our leading thinkers and practitioners in the highest levels of highbrow culture, (like the way God did with Daniel and the three Hebrew youths in

Babylon), if we are going to see societal change (Daniel1).

3. We need to differentiate between the *Ekklessia* and the synagogue

    We need to not just merely assemble together, which is to synagogue (*episynagoge*) together, as found in Hebrews 10:25. This is a common function and conceptual view of most church leaders. Instead, we need to be the Ekklessia. In its classical and biblical usage, *ekkelsia* means to come together as stewards- the way parliament or congress has representative leadership (Acts 19).

4. Fourth, we need to nurture and/or convert those who are part of the emerging "creative class".

    Those in this category comprise between 12-30% of the population. They have by far the most wealth producers and will drive the economy for generations to come.[205]
    Those in the creative class used to be considered mavericks and non-conformists but are now part of the mainstream. They are part of a movement that has radically shifted the future of business and culture.

Some of the characteristics of this new creative class-driven economy are:

1. Businesses are moving towards creative urban centers such as New York City, Seattle, and San Francisco. Thus, geography is essential because it is moving from corporate-driven to people-driven; companies are moving to where the most creative people live, not just where there are tax incentives and highways.

2. Typical hierarchical structures are fast becoming a thing of the past. New companies accommodate creative people who like to be self-managed, set their own hours, and are free to think, create, and dress informally. Autonomy, diversity, and self-identity are valued more than conformity, conservatism, and groupthink. These people like to play at

work and work at play; the lines between work and leisure are becoming fuzzier.

3. Top-down autocratic leadership, which expects people to just follow orders and not think on their own, is no longer effective. Companies are now encouraging creative people to join their ranks who are semi-autonomous and self-managed with leverage to set their own hours. A person being loyal to one community and one company for the rest of his or her life is a thing of the past. People are now moving from company to company every several years based on new opportunities to accommodate their interests, increased skills, need to meet new friends, creativity, and desire for change and advancement. (Because of the information age we are in, there are now also virtual communities with much information changing and being exchanged every day. This is making it harder to have cohesive communities and set societal norms which result in fragmentation and postmodernism.)

4. Diversity is in; conservative values are respected but are not the norm. Only 23% of the families in the United States are nuclear families. Alternate family structures are now becoming the norm.

How should the church respond to these shifts in culture?

The church should build authentic communities to model the city of God before we attempt to transform the city of man. We have to honor family and have kingdom unity with churches in our regions before we can transform the pagan systems and cultures around us.

World-changers need to experience creativity, leadership, covenant, unity, purpose and kingdom power in the church community, so they can be adequately discipled to recreate these things in the secular arenas to which they are called. Senior leaders need to transition away from top-down autocratic leadership style approaches if they want to attract the creative class to their church.

We need to start investing a good portion of our monies towards educating. It is vital that we cultivate the most creative people in our churches and encourage them to be leaders in every sphere of society, starting with the Ivy League schools.

Consequently, we need a multi-generational approach. We need to recapture the classical meaning of *Ekklessia* as used in Athens and in Acts 19 when it referred to assembling together for leadership or stewardship. The church needs to learn how to avoid the extremes of the Christian Right, Christian Left, and the Pietists who altogether avoid cultural engagement. The Christian Right thinks the answer is only political. This approach clothes the gospel of Christ with a particular political party and pits us against people in the world who we are trying to save. This results in us trying to exert power and control people through legal means and changing laws. I believe the laws of a state should be based on the Ten Commandments, and that the law is a schoolmaster that brings conviction of sin (and is an emblem of what a particular society values).

However, the law, in and of itself, is a very weak line of defense because of the vicissitudes of democratic elections. This approach also smacks of Constantinianism. Although Christianity became the favored religion of the Roman Empire in the 4th century, this resulted in weakening the church from within, because unconverted pagans joined the Christian community without abandoning their lifestyles and core beliefs. The Christian Left only accommodates the gospel to the prevailing culture, which results in losing the biblical distinctions of salt and light. A church that recognizes unbiblical forms of marriage and family more than the 10 Commandments has already lost it's soul and reason for existing as a Christian community. The Pietists or Anabaptists take the approach that the Church should only build alternative subcultures that don't engage or affirm the prevailing culture.

The Kingdom's alternative is to take the approach of the Celtic Church in the 6th to 8th centuries. They incorporated the Anabaptist strategy of building an alternative community that was a model for the pagan communities they lived among. However, they also recognized God's favor upon His created order (God blessed His creation and called it good), which many theologians refer to as common grace. Thus, their communities of faith embraced the non-believing communities, loved them, and won them to Christ by demonstrating the gospel in everyday life. This is more in line with the way of Christ and His apostles than the contemporary church models we see today. These models are only focused on building their church community, or go to the other extreme, focusing only on politics and their community. As a result, they neglect the essence and uniqueness of the Body of Christ. This then causes them to assimilate into the world, instead of transforming the world.

I believe that the Church is called to build what James Davison Hunter, in his book, To Change the World, [206] describes as communities of faith. These faith communities both affirm the good in their surrounding societal structures (hospitals, art, police, transportation, commerce, music, science, education, etc.), while also demonstrating the antithesis against that which is sinful and corrupt. They don't necessarily do this only in word but how they live their lives as Christ followers. Davidson calls this approach as having a "faithful presence". He bases it on what God prophesied to the Jewish exiles in Babylon and Persia in Jeremiah 29:4-7.

In conclusion, there are many other theological challenges I could have illustrated in this chapter, however, I have only highlighted some of the salient issues I am dealing with in my own context as a leader of apostolic networks.

In the next chapter I will show how the global apostolic church can be an instrument of community and societal transformation for the good of all people. Hence, a church and or movement that aligns with the way of Christ and His apostles will also cause systemic quality of life change to their surrounding community.

QUESTIONS TO ASK YOURSELF:

1. What are some theological challenges related to the advent of workplace apostles?

2. What erroneous views do some marketplace movements have related to the church?

3. Is there a biblical separation between kings and priests in the New Testament?

4. What are the five jurisdictions of God in the Scriptures?

5. What is the role of a marketplace leader in the context of APEST?

6. Does the mobile church concept comport with the New Testament pattern of church?

7. How has culture negatively impacted the church?

8. What are some theological trends in the evangelical church?

9. Why has postmodernism been a catastrophe in modern culture?

10. What should the approach of the apostolic church be related to advancing the gospel in other lands?

Chapter 8

The Progress of the Gospel in the Global Apostolic Church

In this chapter, we will analyze how the Apostolic Church has gone from bringing internal transformation within the confines of the Church walls to being externally focused, thus bringing cultural transformation. It has gone from preaching an individualistic gospel to preaching the gospel of the Kingdom. According to Philip Jenkins, the churches in developing nations, such as Latin America, have always been involved in some form of social transformation and politics, because of being informed by Liberation theology (which is a Marxist expression of liberation that engages the churches to liberate the oppressed through political and social means).

Towards a Holistic View of Kingdom Engagement

The shift away from Greek Dualism (a form of Gnosticism) that compartmentalizes reality and separates the realms of the Spirit (as the highest noblest realm) from the evil (temporal realm), is a considerable development in the Apostolic movement today.

In 1998, I wrote a book entitled, *Ruling in the Gates*.[207] In it, I predicted this apostolic shift. I was told by various leaders that this teaching influenced them when they either read my manuscript or heard me teach on it. People like Peter Wagner and Ed Silvoso were some of the leaders who were influenced by this teaching. About this Apostolic shift, Dr. C. Peter Wagner said, "My mind had been programmed to distinguish between:

- *Spiritual vs. worldly*
- *Sacred vs. secular*
- *Church vs. world*
- *Clergy vs. laity*

263

What I had not realized at that time, was that the Bible was not written from a Greek worldview but a Hebrew one. While Greek thinking tends to compartmentalize and stratify all of life, Hebrew thinking tends to integrate and connect all of life. Greeks see very little relationship between cosmic forces and daily life. Hebrews think that cosmic forces and daily life are constantly interacting. While traditional Christians believe the Hebrew oriented Bible, the philosophical educational influences of the Greeks tend to separate the secular and sacred. When we do this, work falls into the "secular" category, while Christian ministry falls into the "sacred." For Hebrews, on the other hand, both work and ministry honor God. Interestingly enough, the Hebrew word for worship, *avodah*, is also translated as "work" in the Bible. Imagine the concept of work being a form of worship?"[208]

Understanding the fivefold ministry in Ephesians 4:11 as including the extended Church (not just the nuclear Church) is something Alan Hirsch has articulated in his significant book, The Forgotten Ways.[209] Alan posits that the at least one of the graces of the fivefold ministry (he uses the acronym "APEST"), is in every believer since it emanates from the very DNA of Jesus

Regarding the possibility of an APEST expression in the workplace, Peter Wagner states, "Our Greek mind-set has caused us to fall into the trap of what Ed Silvoso, author of Anointed for Business[210] calls 'four lethal misbeliefs' as it concerns church ministry and business: There is a God-ordained division between clergy and laity. The Church is called to operate primarily inside a building referred to as a temple. People involved in business cannot be as spiritual as those serving in traditional Church ministry. The primary role of marketplace Christians is to make money to support the vision of those 'in the ministry.' 5 As we renew our minds concerning God's love for the workplace, we will distance ourselves further and further from such traditional ideas."[211]

Apostolic Movements Embracing Societal Transformation

Since 1998, I have preached and written extensively on this subject. I have written several books, such as Ruling in the Gates,[212] Kingdom Revolution,[213] Kingdom Awakening,[214] Walk in Generational Blessing,[215] Understanding the Wineskin of the Kingdom,[216] 25 Truths you Never Heard in Church,[217] and The Divided Gospel.[218] Due to my high visible leadership role in the ICAL Movement, much of my teachings and books, since the early 2000s, have ricocheted across the globe. As a result, these have impacted and have helped to shape the Apostolic movements. These have specifically impacted their theology and practice. Consequently, Dr. Peter Wagner read my manuscript in 1998, and after it was published, he became the chief herald of my book. He highlighted it in his numerous seminars. He expressed how he thought that I was functioning as a forerunner and pioneer in our burgeoning Apostolic Movement.

In light of the impact that my book had on Wagner, it might have contributed to Wagner's vast pivot towards social transformation. Peter Wagner observed that in the '80s, charismatics generally believed that fulfilling the Great Commission was measured by souls saved and increasing church plants. Then moving into the '90s. concepts about expanding God's Kingdom expanded beyond the four walls of the church. Church leaders began to talk about "city reaching" and "city taking."

George Otis Jr.'s video *Transformations* defined "social transformation" both within the Church and society as including such elements as transformation spiritually, ecclesiastically, economically, within the family, educationally, in arts and media, politically, and in cultural and community organization and institutions.[219]

Some Challenges with the Shift towards Cultural Engagement

As one of the leaders in the Body of Christ who promotes the Kingdom of God and the Church's call to transform contemporary culture, I have had to navigate through many theological and psychological pitfalls. Many of these could have derailed me, causing me to fall short of fulfilling my purpose in Christ. The following are some of these challenges:

First, it is easy to fall into the trap of taking an all-or-nothing approach, in which nothing we do for God really matters or satisfies us if it does not ultimately result in seeing society changed. With this mindset, we forget that people have to live for eternity, that this present world is temporary, and that the angels in heaven rejoice when one person repents (Luke 15:10). Even though God's ultimate goal for the gospel is for heaven and earth to be united under Christ (Ephesians 1:9-11), heaven also values the salvation of converted individuals. True systemic change must first prioritize reconciling individuals back to God.

Second, our goal to influence top-tier cultural leaders can tempt us to become elitists who only value spending time with people with high power and influence. Jesus never stopped little (powerless) children from coming to Him. Plus, He always made time for folks with little societal influence, like women of ill repute, lepers, blind people, and widows.

Third, we can fall into the deception of valuing mere political, economical, and quality of life progress in communities more than building healthy local churches, which Paul alone identifies as the ground and pillar of truth (1 Timothy 3:15). We can only build healthy communities in the world if we first build strong churches that model how the city of God should function. Leaders who come out of dysfunctional churches and families will never know how to build functional systems in their surrounding communities. Also, Jesus has a unique place in His heart for the Church. Paul mentions that Jesus loves and gave Himself up for the Church so that she may be presented to Him in all her glory, without spot or blemish (Ephesians 5:25-27). Furthermore, during the high priestly prayer of Jesus, He did not pray for the world but for the Church. This establishes the fact that the Church is unique in and of itself, whether or not we are successful in positively transforming communities (John 17:9).

Fourth, pastors and leaders who attempt to change their surrounding culture before they have successfully built a New Testament church will have unnecessary stress because inevitably, such goals are often unattainable. This would be like putting the cart before the horse. Culture is changed out of the overflow of the life of the Spirit that takes place in the context of powerful local churches. Such churches build strong character and encourage creativity amongst their members.

Fifth, we can be tempted to equate political victories with the Kingdom of God being established on earth. Jesus called us to disciple whole nations in Matthew 28:19, which means we should have great influence politically. However, at the same time, the Bible also teaches us that Christ is already reigning over the universe from heaven, whether humankind recognizes that reign and submits to it or not! Mere humans cannot crown Jesus as King; He is already King of Kings. He is already seated at the right hand of the Father (Ephesians 1:17-23; 2:4-6) as the King of Kings and Lord of Lords (Revelation 19:16).

Also, as already noted in this book, the common understanding of the word "nation" as a geo/political construct is less than 500 years old (since 1648) and is not what Jesus was referring to in Mt. 28:19. Nation has to do with tribes, ethnicities, people groups, and subcultures. Hence, if every disciple influenced the subculture they are assigned to, then we will eventually see community transformation. (Of course Matthew 28:20 illustrates that making disciples involves water baptism as well as instruction in the word- hence, the way people groups are discipled is through ethnic individuals joining the ecclesia through the rite of water baptism followed by a process of catechesis . Thus- discipling nations cannot be separated from individuals joining the local church) Thus, to make the call of the Church correspond totally to Christianizing America or any other geo/political nation is to deconstruct the uniqueness of the Church as the Body of Christ and collapse it down to being no different from any other (secular) political and social machine.

Furthermore, even if the Church fails to rescue a nation morally and it collapses under the weight of its sin, it does not necessarily mean that the Church failed in the missional mandate. For example, after the Roman Empire fell, Jesus was still reigning through the Church, which converted all the Barbarian tribes, civilized them, and built what became the modern European states. Furthermore, if the USA ever ceases to exist as a great world power, the Church of the living God will continue to exert its influence, and, as representatives of the only true King of the universe, the Church will disciple the next great world power that arises. God's Kingdom is not determined by the political vicissitudes of elections and destinies of nations. The Church is the only nation (1 Peter 2:9) that is guaranteed to survive (Matthew 16:18) until the consummation at the end of the age when Jesus comes back to judge the world in righteousness.

Sixth, we experience undue stress when we think we are ultimately responsible for building the Kingdom instead of Christ. This can cause us to go out of our lane or specific assignment from God when we become involved in feverish activity since we have placed the world on our shoulders, thinking we can build the Kingdom. However, the same Jesus who said that He would build His Church (Matthew 16:18) is the one who gives the increase to the fruit of our labor in the Kingdom (1 Corinthians 3:7) and is the same one who has the government of the Kingdom on His shoulders (Isaiah 9:6-7). Jesus said to come to Him so our burden would be light, and we would find rest for our souls (Matthew 11:28-29).

Seventh, some marketplace leaders think they can replace their connection to a local congregation with the *ekklesia* (ruling body), which they attempt to set up in their realm of influence (in business, politics, education, etc.). With the renewed emphasis on reaching all of the mountains of society, and with the correct teaching that recognizes marketplace leaders as ministers of the Kingdom, marketplace leaders can easily forget that the primary responsibility for preparing marketplace leaders to transform and lead culture is upon the five-old ministries in the context of the local church environment (Ephesians 4:11-12).

The Church is clearly called in essence to be a "family of families," called to walk according to the "Ways of Christ and His Apostles." Thus, marketplace leaders who are detached from the local Church will not have the proper support system they and their families need to endure through the grid of life. My experience is, marketplace leaders not operating out of a strong local church usually fall short of experiencing lifelong success in their vocational calling.

In conclusion, even though the past several decades have seen a welcome embrace of an understanding of the gospel of the Kingdom, there will be some overreach in certain areas. There is sloppiness with regards to hermeneutics, extreme views not rooted in Scripture, attempts to manifest God's Kingdom without the local Church, and an extreme focus on (American) nationalism (where the Church is infected with the leaven of Herod, often equated with conservative politics as much as it is with the Lord Jesus). As a result, one cannot have a proper missional view without a proper ecclesial view, as is being argued in this book, and made clear in the Gospels, as well as the book of Acts.

In the next chapter I will deal with the challenge apostolic practitioners have related to being theologically substantive. I will also talk about the need to nurture practitioner/scholars to lead churches and movements.

QUESTIONS TO ASK YOURSELF

1. What does it mean to have a holistic view regarding kingdom engagement?

2. What has been the result of apostolic movements who connect the gospel to societal transformation?

3. What are some of the challenges that churches have who are engaged with culture. ?

4. What are some ways we can avoid making these same mistakes?

5. Have you been preaching a gospel of individual salvation or a holistic gospel of the kingdom ?

Chapter 9

The Theological Challenges of the Present-Day Apostolic Leader

In this chapter, we will analyze the challenges the present-day apostolic leader has with being theologically substantive. Typically, many apostolic leaders are pragmatic practitioners who rely on spiritual gifting and intuitive leadership but are weak when it comes to serious ordered learning and theological reflection.

Practitioner or Scholar?

"By and large, pastors (and by implication we can also include apostolic leaders) aren't viewed as theologians, but as practitioners. As such, pastors who desire to do robust theological work for the good of the church find they're often misunderstood by both the academy and their congregations. And the result? Frustration and, not infrequently, isolation."[220]

One of the greatest challenges to apostolic practitioners, based on my observation, is that the majority of them are task driven "doers" who rarely possess the internal proclivity to spend time in reflective study, "Too many pastors have exchanged their vocational birthright for a bowl of lentil stew (Gen.25:29-34; Heb.12:16) management skills, strategic plans, leadership courses, therapeutic techniques, and so forth."[221] This is because they have lots of management and or shepherding responsibilities due to the fact they are overseeing a network of churches, in addition to an influential church or ministry.

The very nature of the "apostle" has to do with an action word, "sent"; they are sent to accomplish the mission. This is why the first historical narrative of the early church was called "The Book of Acts" (or action) rather than the "Book of Truth" or "The Book of Theology".

Many of the legitimate apostolic leaders I know according to the DiSC personality types[222] are rated as people who place "emphasis on accomplishing results."[223] They do not have a lot of patience for mere talk due to the fact that they are action-oriented. Unfortunately, many of them lack the theological depth of a "Teacher-Thinker"; hence, they are not very familiar with a lot of the theological nomenclature and jargon in the academic/scholarly world. A Christianity Today article several years ago even asserted that it is impossible to be both an effective pastor and scholar at the same time.[224] Of course, there are exceptions to the broad observation above; with some legitimate apostolic types also having a scholarly bent and depth. Many apostolic-scholarly leaders like myself constantly wrestle with the two worlds. We are constantly striving for a balance between being a theologian and being a practitioner.

If the Apostolic movement is to continue to exert authority through its various networks, it's imperative that its leaders become more informed. Having at least a decent level of theological training as it relates to current theological debates, church history, will better equip them so that they can adequately nurture true disciples. It also helps give discerning churches the necessary tools to teach a biblical world and life view to its members.

Models of the Apostolic-Scholar in Scripture

While Apostolic scholars today are few and far between, when we examine both the Scriptures study Church history, it's obvious that they existed.

Jesus. We see from that from childhood, Jesus prioritized sitting and dialoguing with the Rabbis. His intent was to understand the Tanakh (Luke 2:46,47). The Tanakh is an acronym of the first Hebrew letter of each of the Masoretic Text's three traditional subdivisions: Torah ("Teaching", also known as the Five Books of Moses), Nevi'im ("Prophets") and Ketuvim ("Writings").[225] His knowledge of the Scriptures, even at a young age, amazed the Rabbis (Luke 2:47). Jesus of course not only mastered the Word as a child, but He was also and is the embodiment of the Logos or Word of God (John 1:1). In His human form, He was "[T]he Word [who] became flesh and dwelt among us" (John 1:14). So here we have the best convergence between Word and being and or Word and physicality, which can represent our life and actions in this material world.

Jesus treated the Scriptures in the same way many conservative scholars today understand the original autographs to be, it was the infallible inerrant Word of God. He was immersed in and utilized the Scriptures in His walk with the Father. The Word was used to fulfill His assignment was evident in the way He quoted the Scriptures as He battled against the Devil in the wilderness (Matthew 4). Furthermore, when He inaugurated His ministry, He started by reading from the Prophet Isaiah (Luke 4:18,19 which was a quote from Isaiah 61:1-2). Jesus chided His disciples who did not believe the Scriptures (Luke 24:25)

Finally, before He ascended into heaven, He opened up the minds of His followers so that they could understand the Scriptures (Luke 24:27, 44, 45).

Paul the apostle. One has the impression from reading the Acts narrative that Paul was constantly on the go with very little time for study and reflection. However, we have to realize that there were seasons in his life in which he spent much time alone with God in prayer, study and reflection.

His letter to the church in Galatia seems to indicate that he spent three years alone in the Arabian desert, unpacking the implications of the Gospel towards the Gentiles in the formative years of his newfound faith (Galatians 1:15-2:2).

Evidently, Paul gave God adequate space for Him to "reveal His Son in him" before he would be sent out by the Holy Spirit as an

Apostle (Acts 13:1, 2). That Paul had a high view of the bible, along with a mastery of the Scriptures, is evident by reading his sermons in Acts (which demonstrate his immersion into the meta narrative of the bible). It is also evident in his letters to the churches as they are laden with Old Testament scripture and Old Testament types, shadows and metaphors. Furthermore, Paul applauded Timothy for knowing the Scriptures that were able to give him the wisdom needed for salvation, in addition to being profitable in his ministry for teaching, reproof, correction and training in righteousness (2 Tim.3:15,16).

Paul took advantage of every circumstance and integrated his passion to seek God with his everyday life experience (such a model is more practical for leaders on the go as they aren't relegated to merely carving out an hour per day to pray). For example, when Paul was thrown in prison, he worshipped and sang hymns (Acts 16), when he was awaiting trial in Rome, he asked Timothy to bring him parchments, presumably, so he could study (2 Timothy 4:13). When he was on a ship bound for Rome, he spent adequate time in prayer and reflection as is implied when he spoke to the crew about the divine instructions he received from an Angel that appeared to him (Acts 27:23).

Also, many of the Epistles he wrote were done while he was in prison (Philippians 1:7). Some come to the conclusion that perhaps God allowed Paul to be secluded for long periods of time for deeper prayer, study and writing so he could apostolically feed the church through his inspired writings, that even the other Apostles considered Scripture (2 Peter 3:15,16). Of course, God also sovereignly intervened in Paul's life and took him up to the third heaven to give him direct revelation (2 Corinthians 12).

Moses. Perhaps there was no one in the bible busier than Moses. After all, he was responsible to shepherd approximately three million people in the desert! Just looking at his schedule can wear one out as he was busy judging people from morning until evening (Exodus 18). At one point he was so burdened down with the problems of the people that he wished he could die (Numbers 11). With all of the above, it is easy to forget that God prepared Moses for this calling by having him secluded in the wilderness of Midian for 40 years. Furthermore, even in the midst of his busy schedule, he regularly took time out daily to spend with the Lord and learn of His ways (Numbers 33:7-11). Of course, on two separate occasions, he also spent forty days and forty nights alone with God without food or water (Numbers 34). Moses was so taken up with being with God that knowing Him and seeing His glory was the greatest desire of His life (Exodus 33:12-23). At the end of his life, his epitaph was, "Since that time no prophet has risen in Israel like Moses, whom the Lord knew face to face" (Deut.34:10).[226]

Models of the Pastor-Scholar in Church History

"[T]he pastoral office was once compatible with robust theological scholarship. Irenaeus, Athanasius, Basil, Gregory of Nyssa, Gregory of Nazianzus, Augustine, Gregory the Great, Anselm, Calvin, Edwards, Wesley, etc., all demonstrate the historic and native relationship between theological leadership and the pastoral vocation. But we lost sight of this heritage. Our collective living memory no longer extends back to the majority narrative of the church with respect to the pastor theologian. What was once normative, theologians as pastors is now novel."[227]

Abraham Kuyper (1837-1920).[228] Kuyper became one of my primary models for ministry (in the mid-1990s) because he, like me, was torn between a desire to do scholarly study along with a desire to impact his surrounding culture. Consequently, he was indeed an incredible model of an Apostolic-Scholar with vast accomplishments.

Some of his notable accomplishments are:
- He was Prime Minister of the Netherlands between 1901-1905
- He was an influential neo-Calvinist theologian and a journalist
- He established the Reformed Churches in the Netherlands
- He founded a newspaper
- He founded the Free University of Amsterdam
- He founded a political party called the Anti-Revolutionary Party

All of the above is why one biographer of Kuyper called him "God's Renaissance Man"[229]

Augustine (354-430),[230] Saint Augustine was the most influential theologian in Christianity (outside of the Apostle Paul), a claim made by both Roman Catholics and Protestants alike. He helped shape Western Civilization with his writings more than any other person in the past 1500 years.

His vast writings include his famous works The City of God (which influenced Western culture and the church more than any other book in the middle ages with the exception of the bible). In addition, his book, Confessions, opened up a genre of writing which involved self-disclosure, awareness and an understanding of sin and psychology; this created ripples through the ages. Other major works, not including his massive outlay of personal letters replete with Scriptural and philosophical truth are, On Christian Doctrine, and Handbook on Faith, Hope and Love. What people often fail to realize is that Augustine did all his writing in the midst of a demanding administrative schedule as the Bishop of Hippo. It was during a time where he was involved with fighting heresies, such as Pelegianism and Arianism. In addition, he was also dealing with a multitude of challenges in the church and culture due to the looming collapse of the Roman Empire (which became more salient as he passed into the next world). Together with Gregory the Great, Ambrose, and Jerome, Augustine was one of the original four doctors of the church.[231]

Martin Luther.[232] If there ever was an Apostle in church history it was Martin Luther. Not only did he prophetically challenge the powerful Roman Catholic Church, but also he left in its wake the Protestant Reformation. This resulted in the denominational movement of the past five hundred years (unfortunately resulting in over 30 thousand denominations and expressions of the Protestant Christian Church). Luther was a theologian and activist whose teaching and writing catalyzed a seismic shift in ecclesiology and soteriology through the Protestant Reformation. This Reformation brought about some of the following changes:

- A new understanding of God; not a God abstractly in himself but a God who is quite concretely gracious to us.
- A new understanding of human beings. Human beings in faith and at the same time righteous and sinful.
- A new understanding of the church; not as a bureaucratic apparatus of power and finance but renewed as the community of believers on the basis of the priesthood of all believers.
- A new understanding of the sacraments not as rituals but as promises of Christ and signs of faith.
- A new understanding and appreciation for Scripture as the highest level of authority in the church over and against the church councils and canons.[233]

John Wesley (1703-1791)[234] John Wesley was an Oxford scholar, who had a vast understanding of the Western European classics as well as a pure devotion to the bible. He was an Apostolic-Scholar who engaged in debates regarding the doctrine of predestination. Such debates occurred between him and his Calvinist friend and fellow evangelist, George Whitfield. John (his brother, Charles) and Whitfield were used in catalyzing the First Great Awakening in the United States and England. He was not only a great preacher, teacher, and scholar, but he also founded an Apostolic movement that became the Methodist Church.

Contemporary Examples of Pastor/ Scholars

Today's pastors should be able to informatively speak in such a manner that will address the various arenas like the academy, the church, and broader society.

According to Vanhoozer, Strachan, "Pastor-theologians need to be trilingual, able to speak the language of all three social locations"[235] N.T. Wright is one of the most esteemed New Testament Scholars in the world today. He graduated from Oxford University with a D.Phil. in New Testament and was a teacher of New Testament at McGill University and later on returned to Oxford to teach the New Testament.[236] In 1994 he left the Academy, held various ecclesial posts including the prestigious post as the Bishop of Durham. However, after almost two decades of church-based ministry, Wright went back to the academy because evidently it was too difficult to balance the workload of ecclesial and academia.

Other prominent contemporary pastors also esteemed as scholars who communicate to all three public locations include: Timothy Keller, John Piper, J. Ligon Duncan, John Scott, Dr. Martyn Lloyd-Jones, W.A. Criswell, John MacArthur, Tony Evans (the first African American to publish a study Bible), etc.

In the book, *The Pastor Theologian*,[237] the authors describe three types of pastor theologians:

1. The local church theologian (one who simplifies theology and church history and preaches it to his congregation is a way that is practical and applicable).

2. The popular theologian is a pastor who writes theologically to a broader audience of laity and other pastors.

3. The ecclesial theologian is one who not only preaches in their local church but also writes (to influence) other theologians and scholars. You often see their work in various peer-review journals, books, Christian publications, etc. Generally, in light of the above three categories, we see more of the first two. Ecclesial theologians are the most underrepresented in the church today. Those with the theological skills usually go to the academy rather than the pastorate, often leaving a dearth of pastoral, practical scholarship in the local churches.[238]

There needs to be a more intentional approach between the local church leadership and the academy to work together and bridge the gap so that the old tradition of robust theology can return back to the congregations.

As such, I applaud the attempts being made toward that end. "The Center for Pastor Theologians"[239] is led by my friend Mark Chironna (working on behalf of the Charismatic Church). His "Issachar Initiative"[240] brings scholars and pastors together. Such work should give us hope as it is necessary for the advancement of the Church.

Last but not least, perhaps the most proficient apostolic practitioner /scholar I know is my dear friend Jeff Reed. His vast church-based networks that orbit around the teachings of the way of Christ and His apostles make him a modern-day master builder in the genre of Paul the apostle. (Go to BILD.org<http://BILD.org> to understand what I am referring to.

The Importance of Being a Practitioner-Scholar

Related to the subject at hand, Scripture does not divide practice from knowledge or truth. Consequently, "high D" apostolic leaders have a certain advantage over scholars and academic types who are not involved in the context of growing and nurturing others in the context of a local church or faith community. There are certain biblical truths that cannot be fully understood without actually doing the work of the ministry.

Also, to know God is an experience, not just an intellectual construct. For example, when Moses asked God to show him His ways, he was asking God not to show him a mere theological truth but to grant him an understanding of what makes God tick; He wanted to know God's motives, characteristics, attributes of Mercy, Righteousness, and Justice. Additionally, God was able to reveal Himself deeply to Moses in the context of him leading the people of Israel on a challenging journey in the wilderness. Hence, Moses was able to know God's ways by witnessing God's actions, activities, and power in delivering and guiding His people from slavery to freedom (Moses was not some hermit-isolated from people and problems in the mountains seeking God).

God spoke through the prophet Jeremiah and told the people not to boast of mere strength, wisdom, and riches, but that those who boast should only boast in their knowledge of Him (Jeremiah 9:23, 24).

When Paul said that he wanted to "know Him" (Phil.3:8-10) the Greek word for *know* is "gnosis." It is derived from *ginosko*, which means, to experientially know. It is a functional knowing, a working knowledge gleaned from firsthand, personal experience. It connects theory to application, which is gained by a direct relationship. Even the act of sexual intercourse was described as "knowing" (Matthew 1:25), which of course is physical interaction and intimacy, not mere fantasy and head knowledge. Furthermore, Jesus connected knowing the truth with action and doing. He said, "If you continue in My word, then you are truly disciples of Mine; and you will know the truth and the truth will make you free." (John 8:31,32). In these verses, Jesus connected the knowledge of truth with continuing to follow Him. Thus, this kind of knowledge cannot come from a mere scholastic study with a book, isolated from people and challenges. The truth, according to Jesus, comes while walking with Him consistently over time; obeying His commandments and following the assignment He has called a person to fulfill.

Ignatian spirituality, based on the life and example of Ignatius Loyola, the founder of the counter-revolutionary Jesuits of the Roman Catholic church was described like this, "The Ignatian approach to spirituality views God as one who is active in the world, inviting us to even closer collaboration. God can be sought and found in our own experience. The Ignatian God is busy, and is to be found not, or not only, in some static bliss, but rather in acting in the world."[241]

In keeping with the idea of Ignatius, research shows that there are various ways we attain knowledge. There is experiential knowledge, presentational knowledge, propositional knowledge, and practical knowledge. All such knowledge requires some sort of action on the part of the learner, for "In acting the body indeed is in action, but also the mind. Action is not blind....Action, then is a full concrete activity of the self in which all our capacities are employed."[242]

Knowledge involves experience, for "All knowing is based in the sensing, feeling, thinking, attending experiential presence of persons in their world. Any form of inquiry that fails to honor experiential presence-through premature abstraction, conceptualization and measurement, or through a political bias which values the experiences only of socially dominant or religiously likeminded groups, ignores the fundamental grounding of all knowing."[243] Some, like William Torbet argue that there are various levels of experience, or "The Four Territories of Experience. [244] However, one has to dedicate time to the task of arriving at answers, "Only ongoing, real time effort to attune to all four-through intentionally attending to single, double and triple loop feedback, in first-second, and third person research/practice, reveals incongruities and develops commitment to transforming toward a more awakening, more effective alignment."[245]

To conclude this chapter, we cannot separate action from knowledge, since action involves the heart, mind, soul, and body of an individual. Does this mean that Apostolic practitioners are off the hook and do not need to engage in serious ordered learning of Scripture, theology and the application of both in culture? Not at all. Apostolic leaders must make a concerted effort to do so. I will attempt to offer solutions or at least suggestions on how Apostolic leaders can become more effective.

In the next section of this chapter, I will lay out some practical ideas related to balancing scholarship and being a practitioner. This is based on over forty years of trying to juggle the two.

However, before we get to the next section there are some questions you need to ask yourself.

SOME QUESTIONS TO ASK YOURSELF

1. Is it possible to be both a practitioner and scholar?

2. Why is it easy for the tendency of a person to be either one or the other?

3. What are some of the challenges of a practitioner who doesn't take adequate time to reflect and study?

4. What are some of the consequences of a scholar who is not a practitioner?

5. What are some examples of apostolic scholars in scripture?

6. Who are some of the examples of pastor/scholars in church history?

7. What are some contemporary examples of pastor/scholars?

The Path to Creating a New synthesis Between Practitioner and Scholar: The Word and Spirit

In this discussion, I will lay out a framework that would help apostolic leaders as they seek to find a balance between being action-orientated as well as theologically sound, which will make them reflective practitioners.

There are many different approaches to arriving at a synthesis between action and study, (studying theology and applying theology), thinking and doing (being contemplative and being proactive).

For an example of the divergent approach, I asked some of my ecclesial centric friends who have extra local (Apostolic) influence how they combine work and study. Some questions I asked were:

1. Do you have a particular rhythm that you employ?
2. Do you take regular days off to study and write?
3. Do you carve out a certain number of days annually for intensive study and writing?
4. Do you weave a lifestyle of prayer, study and writing into your everyday life (my approach)
5. Or you just integrate all of the above as the need arises

Here are some of the replies to these questions:

Dr. Ron Cottle: "At this stage of my life I integrate it into the fabric of my daily life. In fact, it is a major part of my life on a daily and weekly basis, especially during the early hours. For years when I was younger and served as a pastor, I gave God the first half of my day in my study and gave His people, my staff, church members and community the second half. That was a winning formula that my ministry team, membership, and community, appreciated and honored. In fact, they were proud of that and literally protected me from unnecessary distractions. They partnered with me in the interest of a strong and genuine expository word from the Lord on Sundays and Wednesdays."

Dr. David Cannistracci: "I write two days per week in regular slots. With regards to sermons, we do much through preaching teams. We compose together for multi-site campuses. I also schedule regular days off, time with key staff, leadership development, and mentoring. If it is not scheduled as a priority, it remains optional!"

Alan Hirsch: "When I have a project, I dedicate significant time to writing when I am at home, I'm terrible on the road. Sometimes I'll clear a week or two to get slabs of work done. Also, I have given away my library and only use electronic books."

Dr. Mark Chironna: "I have to carve out days first as a priority since my days tend to be hectic when I am on the road. My assistant carves those days out with me ahead of time. When I do get free time on planes or on the road in hotels, I make the most of it, doing what I can."

Dr. Michael Brown: "Besides reading the Word daily, my study habits are driven by the subject matter I am working on: perhaps writing a commentary; perhaps working on a polemical paper; preparing for a debate, focusing on a controversial issue; perhaps researching for an academic book project. Through my Ph.D. years, my studies were driven by class content and the latest language I was learning. In the decades since, my studies have been more eclectic."

Joseph Mattera: As I have analyzed how I have approached this in my own life, I have rarely carved out days for study and prayer. My life is too busy, and I have too many responsibilities to take significant time off to study. In forty years, I can remember only going away a handful of times to study. What works better for me is to integrate a lifestyle of prayer and study into the everyday life I have as an apostolic leader, husband, and father to my biological children. Usually, I spend the first 2-3 hours every day praying, listening to Scripture, and seeking the face of God. I do not let anything get in the way of dedicating to God the first few hours of each day. I protect these hours; my spouse, children and staff aid in protecting this time for me.

In addition, I am constantly pouring over major news outlets at least three times per day (during breakfast, lunch, and dinner); I eat and read at the same time unless of course, I am eating with my family or friends. I am always looking for opportunities to read secular and Christian news sources throughout the day. Perhaps most importantly, I am always contemplative. No matter what I am doing, I am analyzing what is happening, thinking through the issues at hand, and discerning the will of God for the present and future for each of the organizations that I lead. As I walk with God in my everyday life I am also thinking and writing notes to myself on things I have to work on and things I have to write about. Also, in the midst of my busy schedule, I attempt to steal a few hours either on a Monday or Tuesday to write a weekly article/newsletter that gets sent out through MMI (Mattera Ministries International). When I am in transit on an airplane, I rarely if ever watch a movie (unless my brain is fried!). Instead, I have a collection of books or writings scheduled to read which I devote myself to so that I am not wasting any precious time.

Ways Apostolic Leaders Can Integrate Study and Work

To summarize and add to the thoughts mentioned above, I want to lay out some ideas for busy apostolic leaders in a way that does not compromise their time capacity for accomplishing tasks nor their potential for spiritual Christlike formation.

1. Set times should be prioritized for study, no matter how busy a leader is. Paul's mandate to Timothy is appropriate here, "Be diligent to present yourself approved to God as a workman that does not need to be ashamed accurately handling the word of Truth" (2 Tim.2:15) (NKJV)

2. Adequate study should be intensified, and days carved out if there is a project (like a book or paper) due.

3. All leaders should become a contemplative practitioner that seamlessly integrates prayer, and discernment of the will of God. Specific times should be set daily for study and prayer that are compatible with the habits and proclivities of the Apostolic leader.

4. All apostolic leaders should participate in some kind of hermeneutical community that can help sharpen their theological insight. Such a community should hold them accountable to what they teach and believe. This can be a regular zoom video meeting with other apostolic leaders, with elders or mature leaders within their local church or with a spiritual guide or theological mentor. Such persons should inquire about what they are reading and be able to tweak their application and interpretation.

5. All Apostolic leaders should be accountable to some kind of consistent small group dynamic that will feed their soul and keep them on the cutting edge prophetically.

The Apostle Paul. As we read the accounts of Paul's life in the various passages in the New Testament, we see that Paul seemed to walk in all of the points noted above. How he lived his life was also a sort of catechetical Didache for the body of Christ (1 Thes. 2:1-12; 2 Tim. 3:10,11).

1. He prayed without ceasing, which meant that he integrated his spirituality with his activities and life (1 Thes. 5:17).
2. He always had traveling companions or received from others in the local church. This ensured that he was always getting edified by others (Romans 1:12).
3. He submitted his understanding of the Gospel and Scripture to other leaders (Galatians 2).
4. He carved out long periods of time to be alone with the Lord and receive revelation from Him (Galatians 1:15-17).
5. He always attempted to study and did not waste time when the opportunity arose (2 Timothy 4:13).

The Apostolic Stewardship and Calling to Be Preachers and Teachers

I am of the opinion that all who have an assignment from God to communicate the Word and feed the flock of God should develop a system or pattern of study so they can accurately communicate the Word of God (2 Tim. 2:15). The Apostle Peter said, "whoever speaks, is to do so as one who is speaking the utterances (or words) of God" (1 Peter 4:11 paraphrased).

The Apostle James said, "My brethren, let not many of you become teachers, knowing that we shall receive a stricter judgment." (James 3:1 NIV). In light of the divine injunctions above, it should behoove all communicators of the Word to engage in some system of serious ordered learning. This is vital since we will be judged based on how much our teaching is derived from God. Our teaching should not be based on mere opinion or speculation, which can sometimes be based on ignorance, which reveals a lack of study. Truly, the preacher is called both to think and teach God's thoughts after Him. As the apostle Peter stated, we are called to speak His very words!

In my next chapter I will examine whether or not the global apostolic movement is the future hope of Christianity. According to the present and future trends -the answer seems to be yes which means it is all the more important to understand the way of Christ and His apostles so we can build according to the N.T. pattern.

SOME QUESTIONS TO ASK OURSELVES:

1. Do you have a particular rhythm that you employ to balance work and study?

2. Do you take regular days off to study and write?

3. Do you integrate a lifestyle of prayer and study in your life ?

4. What are some of the ways apostolic leaders can integrate study and work?

5. What are some of the ways the apostle Paul integrated study and work?

6. Should pastors and spiritual leaders prioritize studying the word of God ?

Chapter 10

Is the Global Pentecostal Apostolic Church the Future Hope of Christianity?

The vast majority of leaders initiating the expansion of global Christianity fit the rubric of the apostolic leader. Is this a trend that will continue or something short-lived? In this chapter, we will analyze whether or not global Pentecostal apostolicity is the future of Christianity.

According to Doug Geivett and Holly Pivec in their book, *A New Apostolic Reformation*, the New Apostolic movement is no shooting star and is here to stay:

The short life of the Latter Rain movement raises the question: Will the NAR also fizzle out or will it last? It appears that it will last, in spite of the continuing opposition from Pentecostal denominations. NAR already has outdistanced the Latter Rain Movement, and it shows no signs of decline. Whereas the Latter Rain revival lasted only a few years, NAR has been around for more than thirty years, since the 1980's, when the office of prophet began to be restored. NAR teachings have gained enough momentum for an entire generation of young people to be raised in churches that promote them. For these people, NAR teachings are at the heart of Christianity."[246]

Many thought that the so-called Apostolic movement would be rejected by the American Church. In 2004, in Kiev, Ukraine, while ministering with Apostle Sunday Adelja on the 10th anniversary of "The Embassy of the Blessed Kingdom of God for All Nations", the president of the National Association of Evangelicals, Ted Haggard, expressed such sentiments to me.

However, some of the latest research, as demonstrated in the book, *The Rise of Network Christianity: How Independent Leaders Are Changing the Religious Landscape*,[247] reveal that the Apostolic movement is not only alive and well in the USA, but that it is also the fastest-growing expression of Christianity in North America. To quote from a prominent Evangelical magazine, Christianity Today, interview[3], the authors state, there is "a quiet revolution is taking place in America religion."[248]

This Apostolic Revolution is impacting the Churches. "Largely behind the scenes, a group of mostly self-proclaimed 'apostles,' leading ministries from North Carolina to Southern California, have attracted millions of followers with promises of direct access to God through signs and wonders...Their movement, which Christerson and Flory called "Independent Network Charismatic" or "INC" Christianity, has become one of the fastest-growing faith groups in the United States. Apostles like Bill Johnson[249], Mike Bickle, Cindy Jacobs, Chuck Pierce, and Ché Ahn claim millions of followers. They're also aided by an army of fellow ministers who fall under their "spiritual covering."

Many of these apostles run megachurches, including Bethel Church in Redding California, Rock Church in Pasadena, and the International House of Prayer (IHOP) in Kansas City. But their real power lies in their innovative approach to selling faith. They've combined multi-level marketing, Pentecostal signs and wonders, and post-millennial optimism to connect directly with millions of spiritual customers. That allows them to reap millions in donations, conference fees, and book and DVD sales. And because these INC apostles claim to get direction straight from God, they operate with almost no oversight. Christerson states that this INC movement, "is unique in that they really think God has put these apostles on earth to basically transform the world. It's a sort of trickle-down Christianity, where these apostles are at the top of the mountain, exercising this power from the top down. That's how the kingdom of God comes in."[250]

I strongly disagree with the authors, Christerson and Flory, that the Apostolic movement in the USA is represented only by those leaders whose focus is primarily on "signs and wonders." In fact, USCAL, a rather large network of Apostolic leaders, does not eschew, nor does it give undue attention to "signs and wonders". The fact is that probably the fastest-growing segment of Evangelical Christianity, especially for young people, is an expression of the Church that would fall under the rubric of Apostolic Christianity.

The truth is that many charismatic churches that are considered part of the mainstream Evangelical movement in North America are also embracing the burgeoning Apostolic movement. One such example of this is Gateway church in Dallas Texas led by Pastor Robert Morris.[251] In 2018 they convened several meetings with approximately thirty well-known leaders of church networks.

Apostle John Kelly, as the International convener of ICAL, along with myself, were included in meetings. This meeting occurred after their initial meeting which also included a "who's who" of some of the most influential apostolic leaders in the charismatic church. The purpose of the meeting was to discern the will of the Lord in regard to the need for a coalition that can serve as a "Network of Networks." We discussed the need to create a unified nomenclature, along with definitions, and a conceptual framework we can all agree upon regarding apostolic and prophetic ministry function, networks and protocols.

The General Superintendent of the International Pentecostal Holiness Church (IPHC) Dr. A.D. Beacham, Jr. wrote a book called, Rediscovering the Role of Apostles and Prophets..[252] When I asked him to comment regarding the impact of the apostolic function in his denomination he said this:

"The International Pentecostal Holiness Church (IPHC) began in 1898 as a Wesleyan holiness movement. Following the Azusa Street revival in 1906, IPHC became a Pentecostal denomination. Throughout its history, there have been times when apostolic ministry was part of the conversation regarding how the denomination serves the cause of Christ. Much of this was described in Doug Beacham's 2003 book, *Rediscovering the Role of Apostles and Prophets*. "IPHC continues to critically reflect in the 21st century regarding how to faithfully understand and operate in the Biblical descriptions of apostolic ministry. Part of that reflection includes discerning the insights of leaders such as Joseph Mattera. I am personally grateful for his godly voice as the body of Christ continues to faithfully minister in these challenging times."

Within the Assemblies of God, there have also been discussions concerning the Apostolic Movement. I was told that the AOG is making changes to reflect the present Apostolic movement. One such change (according to my source) is their transition away from the name "district", which describes a cluster of churches, to the term "Network." This demonstrates the impact the Apostolic movement is having on mainstream Pentecostal denominations.

One of my close associates whom I will leave nameless has been participating in our apostolic networks for the past several years and was recently named the head presbyter of a district for the Assemblies of God. This was a remarkable move considering the fact that he is bold in his position regarding the need for Apostolic reform in the Body of Christ. He believes that the Church today must reflect the first century Church with its embrace of the function of five-fold ministry gifts of Ephesians 4:11.

The Pentecostal Church of God is also rethinking this issue. "The Pentecostal Church of God is in the process of addressing the issue afresh: however, their official doctrinal statement indicates that they do allow for the charismatic apostolate on the basis of their reference to 1 Corinthians 12:27-28 and Ephesians 4:11,12.[253]

In *Apostles Today*, Wagner states, "The International Pentecostal Holiness Church at their General Conference in 2005 made an assignment for appointed scholars and theologians to do a biblical/theological study of the Apostolic Movement. The result of this was the paper they produced in 2007. In summary, it affirmed the ongoing validity of apostles today, however, they made a clear distinction between what they term foundational and functional apostles."[254]

In addition, the "International Church of the Foursquare Gospel" has been impacted by the Apostolic Movement, "The International Church of the Foursquare Gospel does not have a specific statement in regard to the ministry of the apostle, but affirm the ongoing need and presence of apostles on the basis of Ephesians 4:11-13."[255]

There is a current re-evaluation regarding the Apostolic in the historic "Church of God" (Cleveland), "[T]he Apostolic Restoration Movement of the 1990's has caused many denominations to rethink their verbal positions. Within the Church of God, there are a growing number of individuals like myself who see the reality of the continuance of the ministry of Apostle."[256]

Again, Wagner states, "In summary, the American Historic Pentecostals are feeling a challenge from the New Apostolic Reformation to reevaluate their perspectives on Apostles, which they all accept as still being given to the church."[257]

In the UK, the AOG believes that the Apostolic ministry is still valid today. "According to David Petts, 'in practice, we have always believed in apostles today...there has been more talk in recent years of the need for apostolic ministry today and although opinions vary there is certainly general agreement as to the existence of these important gifts in our churches'...As a result, the Assemblies of God in Britain seem perfectly content to speak of their National Leader as having been a pastor and apostolic leader."[258] There are also numerous Apostolic leaders of networks in the UK (like the recently deceased Gerald Coates), who have been teaching and influencing the Body of Christ in their spheres of influence for many years. In summary, the apostolic movement in Britain is not as influential as in the USA, but the historic Pentecostal denominations are starting to think and speak more about this ministry.

Regarding the nature of the exponential growth of Christianity in Africa being a renewal of 1st Century Apostolic Christianity, Philip Jenkins states, "[S]econd century Christianity (and third-century, and even first-century) can still be witnessed and shared in, namely in contemporary Africa...The idea that Southern Churches are living in something like a renewed apostolic age inspires nothing short of awe, and it would be easy to write of all these developments in a thoroughly supernatural, even credulous way.... A religious believer might accept that God really is inaugurating a new era of signs and wonders, to give Christianity a kind of rebirth."[259]

The fact that the expansion of the Global Church is largely as a result of a renewed interest in the apostolic church of the first few centuries is incontrovertible. All one has to do is visit the largest churches and church movements in Latin America, Asia, and Africa. I have also witnessed this phenomenon as I have preached since the early 1990s in some of the most influential churches and church networks in Latin America, Africa, Asia, and Eastern Europe. I have witnessed firsthand the attempt to jettison the old, inhibiting structures of traditional denominations and embrace the way of Christ and His Apostles.

For example, in 1987 In Kiev, I met with one of the primary leaders of the underground House Church movement in the

Old Soviet Union, Bishop Ivan. He informed me about the vast network of millions of believers he gave direction to as a Bishop; his movement was apostolic in nature.

Another example was seen between the years 1991-1998 while ministering in the Dominican Republic. In 1992, I felt led by the Lord, in a pastor's gathering, to teach on Apostolic Unity and to help launch an Apostolic Network. This Santo Domingo network grew to about 250 pastors under the leadership of the late Apostle Jorge Reynosa. Also, around that time I ministered in an Apostolic Network in Puerto Rico of about 20 churches led by the late Apostle Mario Gonzalez.

From 2010-2015 I went to Kampala Uganda to train a loosely affiliated Apostolic network of over two thousand pastors. In addition, I went annually to a megachurch, Zion Temple, led by Apostle Paul Gitwaza in Rwanda, to teach 500 pastors from all over Africa. In addition, I was privileged to go several times to South Africa to teach thousands of leaders in Cape Town, Johannesburg and Durban. Those ministries were led by Apostolic Leaders Segie Govendar and Thamo Naidoo.

In 2003-2006 I taught in Riga Latvia to an Apostolic Network of 300 pastors, led by Aleksy Ledyaev. In November 2019 they celebrated the 30th Anniversary of "New Generation Network." In 2004 I spoke to an apostolic network of 50 pastors in the city of Amsterdam in the Netherlands. While that network no longer exists the apostolic is continuing to expand and develop through various streams that have emerged. In the same year, I spoke to an Apostolic Network of 900 pastors in Havana Cuba led by Bishop Samuel Ramos. That year I also spoke in Europe's largest church, The Embassy of the Blessed Kingdom of God for All Nations, for their 10th anniversary. This became a huge network of churches across the Old Soviet Union and Europe, led by Apostle Sunday Adelaja.

Through the years I conducted training for an apostolic network of 50 churches in France led by Jean Marc Ponti, in Brazil for Apostle Rene Terra Nova,[260] as well as many apostolic networks and conferences in Latin America and the Caribbean (In Honduras, Colombia, Argentina, Brazil, Panama, and beyond).

In 2005 I studied the massive, apostolic house church movement, which is the underground church in China, in the cities of Beijing, Sion and Shanghai. I studied with Urbanologist, historian, Dr. Ray Bakke.

The point I am trying to make here is that I have also had an eyewitness account of the burgeoning, massive Apostolic revolution that is taking place across the globe, which in my opinion, is obviously the future of Christianity.

In conclusion, my participation in being the founder and national convener of the United States Coalition of Apostolic Leaders (which has several hundred independent network leaders and apostolic types in both the church and workplace), as well as participating in the International Coalition of Apostolic Leaders (which has several thousand members as well as about 16 national coalitions affiliated with it), has given me a front seat as it pertains to the Apostolic Movement. I believe this is the greatest expression of the expansion of Global Christianity in the world today. I do not see it waning (like the Latter Rain Movement and others Pentecostal movements and renewals of the 20th Century), rather I perceive that it is in the beginning stages of its growth (especially in North America and Europe).

The Contemporary Church Today-Moving Forward

1. The contemporary Church needs to adopt the metanarrative of Scripture for biblical interpretation and preaching if it is to recapture the way of Christ and His apostles. Just a quick listen to many of the popular Evangelical preachers today demonstrates that their preaching (mostly topical)

is likely being informed through a systematic theological approach to biblical study. The result is preaching that pulls passages from various parts of the Bible without progressively making a case for their positions. This kind of preaching/teaching fails to teach church members how to interpret the Bible for themselves. This hurts the ability to mature members as disciples of Jesus.

2. The church needs to recapture the "Way of Christ and His Apostles" in local church movements. Again, since we already spent a lot of time on the need for complex apostolic networks, I will only mention it briefly again. Most regional church networks are only very loosely affiliated groups of pastors who meet regularly for fellowship, prayer and occasional events. If we are going to reflect the New Testament Apostolic pattern of Paul, effective networks need to have the following characteristics.

- They need to be missional: They need to have a cause related to church planting, disciple-making, and providing mutual support. (When I recently planted a church, I utilized three of the apostolic leaders from my network, Christ Covenant Coalition, to help me with the preaching and theological training. This was helpful because my itinerant ministry precluded my ability to properly launch a new church all by myself.

- They need to study scripture together to form a hermeneutical community: This keeps the spiritual leaders fed, motivated, educated, and held accountable as it relates to what they are preaching to their congregations. (Christ Covenant Coalition has weekly zoom meetings, an annual retreat and an annual leadership table in which our affiliated apostolic leaders of networks unpack scripture together and share ideas related to best practices and the application of scripture in culture.)

- They need to pray together and hear what the Spirit is saying to the churches, similar to the experience of the seven churches in Revelation chapters 2,3.
- They need to form apostolic teams in which they do seminars and missions together.

3. The Church needs to embrace a "Christological Ecclesiology"

What I mean by embracing a "Christological Ecclesiology" is the fact that the church needs to focus on the implications of being the "Body of Christ" more than merely embracing New Testament missional methodologies and strategies. The fact that believers are called Christians, (little anointed ones or little Christ) also illustrates this need. What do we mean by the term Christian? I believe it is clear by reading Scripture that Jesus is the fulfillment of the Story of Israel and the church -which is why our ecclesiology should be centered on His life and mission.

"[Karl] Barth calls the foundational concepts of his theology of the church 'christologico-ecclesiology', with the peculiar being, life, action, and history of Jesus Christ forming the determinative framework for the being of the community that He takes to Himself as His body. It is upon this foundation that all his ecclesiology is built. The theology of the church is second-order in that it derives from the primary work of Christology. Significant contrast may be made with the claims of Farrow at this point, who claims that ecclesiology is determinative of Christian theology. Barth's approach is clearly very different."[261]

In light of the Christ-centered approach in not only the Gospels but in the whole New Testament, it is important in my opinion that all theological constructs begin and end with Jesus the Messiah. Jesus is the head of the Church, without Jesus there is no brain, no direction, no order, no

communication, and no purpose. Christology is everything to the church, "Barth uses this phrase, to sum up his
description of the foundation of the being of the church in
the agency of Jesus Christ. Thus it means 'that the Christian community is the human fellowship in which Jesus as
the head is the primary subject.'"[262]

Consequently, the implications of this view are enormous.
This means that the Lord Jesus should always be the plumb
line and measuring stick to ensure the validity and integrity
of the ecclesia. Catholic theologian, Hans Balthasar, states,
"[T]his idea of Christ as 'standard of measure'...because the
Spirit is of course the Lord, He alone is able to point out
and to maintain the tension between the Christological
norm that remains valid in every era of the Church and
the ecclesiological variations of today's era. If the builders
do not build their bridge using this span, then they build
in vain. So first we must speak in Christological terms, for
that is decisive; it alone is the standard. Only then may
we speak of ecclesiological obedience, which will always
remain the rule that is ruled [*norma normata*], that is,
ecclesial obedience is always that which is measured by the
standard, as it takes into account all of the pressing questions of the day."[263]

Without a continual, robust reflection on the nature,
mission, and methodologies of Jesus, the Church will be
left trying to pivot itself in the air. Historically, mainline
Protestant churches have greatly diminished whenever they
veered away from Jesus as their primary focus (The liberal
Protestant churches whose sole focus became societal and
humanitarian causes experienced a rapid decline in the
20th century).

Balthasar also said, "Things already get murky if we start
out by ignoring the specifically New Testament element

in the constitution of the Church ("the People of God" is primarily an Old Testament concept and is thus unsuited, when taken alone for its own sake, to bring the decisively Christological element into view). The real danger would be to act as if the Church, even for a moment, could reflect on herself without holding herself up before the mirror that is Christ (2 Corinthians 3:18); only there can she find out what or who she is and how she is to act, both in general and more specifically today. Insofar as "the Lord is Spirit", his presence (assuming the Church chooses to perceive it) will suffice to provide her with direction for today and the appropriate way she can reflect back Christ without distortion in terms of contemporary needs. This is why I now use the term body of Christ a whole lot more.... it provides the Christological focus."[264]

In my opinion, the above quotes from these two notable theologians (one Roman Catholic and the other Protestant). highlight what ought to be the center of the apostolic church's concern, which is to embody Christ! After all, we are speaking in this section of recapturing the way of Christ and His apostles as opposed to just doing church.

How to Have a Christological Ecclesiology

We must have a Christological Ecclesiology if we are going to function as a true community of Jesus. First of all, we have to understand that the very nature and essence of the Gospel is the proclamation (kerygma) of the Good News. Such proclamation is about none other than Jesus. It cannot be overemphasized that Jesus is the gospel. The gospel is not just about the finished work He accomplished for humankind in His death, burial and resurrection. The Gospels are replete with sayings that have to do with repenting, believing and following Jesus as the promised Messiah who would eventually restore Israel and set up His Kingdom. Jeff Reed states, "Jesus became the *kerygma*. He proclaimed it and became it. The community was built around Him. They were to wait for the Spirit. And just as John the Baptist, and just as Jesus, they were to proclaim the good news, which Peter would soon begin doing! So the very essence of their existence was defined as being witnesses."[265]

Having a Christological Ecclesiology

Recently, as of the writing of this book, the Lord has been giving me insight related to the fact that the church is His Body, that is to say, believers are an extension of Jesus on the earth. That being said, we need to reinterpret the Church as the body of Christ by extending the life and teachings of Jesus in the present day through the faith and practice of his people. The communities that the Apostolic writers of the New Testament started, were really supposed to function as Jesus communities, not mere gathering places as we see today in the contemporary church scene. It is evident that Paul focused a lot of his attention on the finished work of the cross and the implications of it in the life of the believer. However, some scholars debate whether he spent much time with regards to the ethical practical implications of taking each of the Gospels and unpacking it ecclesiologically.

Unfortunately, when we think of the word gospel, most Protestants merely think of the last six hours on the cross and concomitant post-resurrection implications. However, it tells us in Mark chapter 1 that Jesus began preaching the gospel of the kingdom. That is to say, the gospel at that point could not be referring to his death burial and resurrection but had to be something that was presently good news to his hearers. Consequently, this can only mean that the gospel is the life of Jesus, not just regarding His death, burial and resurrection. Rather, the gospel is all-inclusive regarding the person, life and actions of Jesus; this is the essence of the gospel; this is what and who we proclaim, as His witnesses.

This has huge implications! This means that we could look at each chapter of the Gospels and understand the relevance that it has in terms of church practice, thought, belief and essence. Christological ecclesiology needs to be our ultimate focus. This stretches the basic kerygma to include other parts of the kerygma. This is necessary if we are to apply the context of Jesus' sayings with the community of disciples He walked with (a sort of pre-community ecclesial) before the full-blown Spirit infused church on the Day of Pentecost. This can also line up with what Paul said about himself when he, as a believer in the post-resurrection epoch, said that it was "not I who lives but Christ who lives in me and the life which I now live I live by faith in the Son of God who loved me and gave himself for me" (Galatians 2:19-21 paraphrased). Of course, this was said in his earliest letter that was focused primarily on grounding the new church in the kerygma. However, Paul also said he counted all things dung so that he may attain Christ, which means that his whole life was consumed, lost and hidden with God in Christ (Colossians 3:1-4). This was said in one of his middle epistles which consisted of applying the kerygma to church and family life which many refer to as "the Didache."

Paul also said that the ultimate goal that God the Father had in choosing the church was that they might be conformed to the image of his Son (Romans 8:29,30). The biblical commitment to Jesus and His community as seen in the gospels was so great, that it involved ties with Christ-followers that transcended the family and ethnic norms of the day (Mark 3:31-35; 10:28-30). Jeff Reed states, "The narrative of Mark to this point hints at a new social world in the making that began with Jesus calling disciples...The passage as a whole (Mark 10:25-35) may be read as reflecting or legitimating the social displacement and relativization of social norms that members of the audience have experienced as they moved from communities based on ties of kinship and traditional ethnic identities to voluntary associations of followers of Jesus."[266]

Consequently, any church, program, leadership training, practice, discipleship process that doesn't ultimately lead to Christlikeness is in of itself in vain (even if there are a lot of people and success attached to it and the result was a quality of life transformation in a community). The plumbline for all ministry and discipleship must be "Christ-likeness", not merely the advocating of a biblical worldview in politics, economics, community development for a societal transformation to advance our view of the Kingdom; it is not even the making of disciples who plant churches and start a movement. Any movement is only biblically valid to the extent that its disciples model and receive their life and strength from Jesus Himself. If we merely focus on mission or community transformation, then we merely have kingdom principles without a king. This explains why so many conservative leaders lead double lives and fall into a scandal! As Revelation 2:1-9 indicate, we can do everything right as a church and still abandon our first love.

In summary, part of what I see happening in the Apostolic movement in the coming decades is an alignment with the metanarrative of Scripture, which is that everything in heaven and earth is being summed up in Christ (Ephesians 1:9-11). This should move our eschatological focus towards a high Christology in our ecclesiology.

Paradigms the Global Church Must Restore to Function According to the New Testament Pattern

As I conclude this book, there are several paradigms the Church must restore to function according to the New Testament Apostolic Pattern. Since all of these points were already dealt

with in other parts of this book, this final section merely serves
to accentuate and summarize some of the salient issues related
to the theme of this book. The following are some of the main
paradigmatic changes that must occur for the contemporary church
to follow the exemplar of the way of Christ and His apostles.

1. **The restoration of theological education through the
   church.** A long time ago I concluded that I was primarily
   called to be a theologian "of the church for the church"
   instead of an academic theologian. Consequently, my focus
   has been to practically influence the church more than
   trying to have a voice in academia. While academic theologians are a blessing and are necessary for helping to uphold
   and explain biblical faith, they are often viewed as professionals who serve an entity (university) that is separate and
   distinct from the local church.

   Academia, in general, has been a syncretistic construct influenced more by the enlightenment (in terms of the verification of truth by the empirical scientific method), as well
   as the Greek Philosophical Academy of the second century
   onward (when Christian apologists attempted to show the
   superiority of Christianity to the Hellenistic culture by
   adopting Greek philosophical language and methods to
   preach and defend the gospel).

   The New Testament model of doing theology is found in
   the trenches of the local church. The apostle Paul made
   disciples and trained Christ-followers like Timothy in the
   context of the churches he was founding and overseeing.
   When we separate theology from the church, it is often
   not practical to the average church member and is only
   relevant for those called to be professional church ministers. I believe God is now changing this paradigm and
   bringing non-formal biblical education back to the local
   church. This does not eradicate seminaries but redefines

their role as an entity that exists solely to supply the local church with resources- instead of an entity in and of itself. This is a huge paradigm shift that many academic institutions will fight tooth and nail out of fear they will lose their jobs! However, the highest goal of educators in the church should be to aid local congregations, not replace congregations as the primary vehicle for biblical training.

2. **The role of the pastor.** As we examine the New Testament pattern of a shepherd, we find that the pastor/teacher is one of the cluster gifts mentioned in Ephesians 4:11. Their primary objective is not "to do the work of the ministry" but to place and equip the saints for the work of the ministry (4:12). This puts more of a burden on secondary leaders like elders, deacons and committed members since they should be the primary leaders edifying and ministering to the congregation. This is a huge paradigm shift that must take place in order for church leadership to maximize and fulfill their divine purpose

3. **Missionary agencies and the role of the church.** The mission of the church should never be exported to mission agencies and para church entities. When we read the Bible, the primary reason for the church was to be His witnesses to the ends of the earth (Acts1:8,9).

There was never a separate mission agency but a holistic understanding of the inextricable, organic integration between the local church that resulted in evangelization and multiplication.

This huge paradigm shift means that mission agencies should become arms of the local church and not vice versa. This shift away from missionary agencies will enable indigenous churches to understand their stewardship of the gospel and be responsible for equipping Christ-followers to go to all the world and preach the Good News. Paul understood that his ability to spread the gospel was dependent upon the church being established and strengthened (2Cor.10:10-14).

The notion of a separate entity fulfilling this role was foreign to the biblical narrative

4. **The Apostolic versus the contemporary church.** The typical local church is only focused on its own congregation and its own community. The apostolic church of the New Testament was constantly on the move, expanding and multiplying disciples and churches.

   Furthermore, the local churches were always connected to a global vision by partnering with their apostolic leader to reach the world. The apostle Paul had about 35 people mentioned in the book of Acts who traveled with him, all of whom came from the local churches he founded.

   Hence, the church (the modality) was focused locally but participated globally while the apostolic leader had a global focus (sodality) with local participation.

   Contrary to this New Testament pattern, the contemporary church is usually led by pastors who have only a local focus. They send church members off to a missionary enterprise if they sense a global call on them; they usually have no connection to an apostolic leader who functions as their Sodal expression for kingdom advancement. For the church to bless the world, it needs a huge paradigm shift towards the first-century apostolic church model.

5. **Leadership development.** The present-day protestant church usually sends aspiring church leaders to seminary or bible college to matriculate towards ordination. Hence, we farm people out of their native and church context to be trained as leaders through academic study and tests.

   As a result, leadership competency is separated from the grid of character development which is most effective in the cauldron of a local congregation. The original church that turned the world upside down, didn't utilize separate entities such as a bible school to train leaders.

They also didn't depend upon para-church organizations to make disciples and train leaders.

Emerging leaders were nurtured while serving in the context of the local church and managing their biological families (1 Tim.3:1-8). They were equipped by a leader functioning in one of the cluster gifts (mentioned in Ephesians 4:11). The Pauline method for leadership development is summarized in II Timothy 2:2 and modeled throughout the book of Acts and the Epistles of Paul.

Furthermore, the present-day church has demonstrated, the past several decades, that it will never reach the world with clever marketing schemes and large crowds. The Body of Christ needs a paradigm shift towards the New Testament pattern of church centric leadership development if it is to experience biblical results

6. **The church and the kingdom.** Jesus taught us to pray for His Kingdom to come, not for His church to come (Luke 11:2-4). The kingdom of God is the reign of God that emanates from the throne of God. The church is not the kingdom but the main agent of the kingdom to represent God as Salt and Light to this world. Unfortunately, most pastors and churches don't understand this and merely focus on the needs of their congregation. The church will never reach the world until it experiences a dramatic paradigm shift which includes embracing its call to manifest the reign of God in every aspect of culture.

7. **Embracing the five cluster gifts.** A few centuries after the birth of Christianity, the Church gradually went from being led by apostolic and prophetic leaders to being led by Pastors and teachers. God set first in the church apostles

(1 Cor 12:28-29) because they have a pioneering spirit and are always expanding Kingdom influence for God. The primary concern of Pastors is not expansion but protection and care. Consequently, when the pastoral gift became the predominant leader in local churches, the missionary expansion, and entrepreneurial spirit were slowed down. Local church pastors who pattern their church according to the missional focus of the Book of Acts should never solely focus on protection and care, but also on expansion and multiplication of disciples and churches. For this to happen, lead pastors need to be apostolic in their function and focus. If they are not apostolic, then perhaps they need to serve in an associate role and allow an apostolic-type pastor to take the lead.

My prayer is that these seven paradigms will soon be restored to the church so that we can manifest the reign of God on earth as it is in heaven

In the next chapter I am going to honestly assess some of the challenges the apostolic church has in regard to reaching the next generation. This may be the most crucial part of the book since every movement is only one generation away from extinction if it does not nurture young leaders who will continue the movement on after their founders have passed on.

QUESTIONS TO ASK YOURSELVES:

1. Is the global Pentecostal apostolic movement the future of Christianity?

2. Why are many historic Pentecostal denominations rethinking the role of the apostolic?

3. Is the global expansion of the church connected to renewed interest in the apostolic church of the first few centuries?

4. Why does the apostolic church have to adopt utilizing the met-anarrative of Scripture for preaching and biblical interpretation to align with the way of Christ and His apostles?

5. What does it mean to have a christological ecclesiology?

6. What are some of the macro paradigms the church must restore to walk in the way of Christ and His apostles?

Chapter 11

The Millennial Challenges to Global Apostolic Pentecostalism

In this chapter, we will analyze how the present-day Millennial generation of young people oppose many of the values of the contemporary Apostolic Church model. This is a major hurdle that can slow down the growth of the contemporary apostolic church, especially among the educated in First and Second world nations.

Next Generation Challenges

The so-called "millennium generation" has seemed to have developed certain presuppositions that are presently a huge challenge to the Body of Christ. If it is not addressed wisely, it will hinder the continuation of the present Apostolic movement in North America and beyond.

I have also observed some of the ways many Apostolic leaders function that is a challenge to the present mindset of millennial leaders in the Body of Christ. Whether we agree with these young people or not, the fact is that apostolic leaders must overcome these challenges if they are going to successfully perpetuate apostolic vision into the next generation. This is especially needed in developed nations, and among the educated in developing nations. (Irrespective of what nation a young person lives in, the more educated they are, the more they tend to think along the lines illustrated below). To help overcome this challenge, we have formed "The Futures Alliance". This Alliance exists to connect and converge with the top leaders, under 40, in our nation. This group has been beneficial to me and others, as we are constantly receiving input from them so that we can understand how they think and devise ways we can effectively work together for the kingdom.

The following issues I have identified are meant to be very general hence, there are exceptions to every one of my points. I have also met many young people who do not espouse every one of these following views. (It is important to note that many of the African American millennial leaders in our network do not believe millennials in their churches share these same concerns).

Symbols of power

Millennials (including my two biological sons), often tell me how they are turned off by symbols of authority in the church services. Things such as elders sitting on a platform, pastors preaching from an elevated stage, the ministers wearing clergy attire and the like, are often complete turnoffs (The use of clergy attire is more in use amongst apostolic leaders in the more Episcopal traditions).

- **The dress code of churches.** While many apostolic leaders dress formally, young people (especially Caucasians), are extremely casual in their attire. Often, they are turned off by pastors and attendees in church services who dress formally (of course, my first point related to clergy attire can also fit here, but I used it in the previous point because it comports with vestiges of ecclesial authority, not mere formality in dress).
- **The use of religious language.** Many apostolic leaders continue to use the same expressions they used in church 20-30 years ago. Young people are turned off by excessive religious language in church services like the continual use of the words "amen", "hallelujah", "praise the Lord", etc. Along with those exclamations during the service, they register disproval to the intense shaking, shouting and physical gyrations seen in some services. They are viewed as unnatural and weird (I am speaking more about religious behavior and tradition, than a spontaneous response

to the undeniable presence and move of God in a church service).

- **The need for authentic relationships.** Apostolic leaders and visionaries are often focused more on accomplishing the mission than on building relationships with the people. Young people long for a church culture where relationships are deepened, in addition to having a strong sense of purpose and mission.

- **The challenge of top-down leadership.** Often, especially in developing nations and among certain contexts in North America, apostolic leaders function autocratically and lead from the top down. Young people are egalitarian and want to be respected and treated more like peers, not like mindless followers. I have also found that the more educated and empowered a congregation is (irrespective of age), the more they have learned critical thinking skills. As a result, they tend to shy away from leadership styles that are demanding, dogmatic and dictatorial.

- **The challenge of the culture wars.** While many apostolic leaders have been front and center in the culture wars, young people are wary of the right versus left culture war tussle. Unfortunately, many young leaders have gone too far and moved away from taking a position in their churches when it comes to serious moral issues, such as abortion, marriage and sexual ethics. While I agree with their concern about the Christian Right and Left going too far, interweaving the gospel with politics, I also believe the gospel is irrevocably connected to morality and societal ethics. This should result in maintaining certain biblical standards. Those who refuse to take a stand will eventually find their churches overrun with confusion related to sexual identity, immorality, and a progressive humanism that runs counter to the ethics of Scripture.

- **The desire for social justice.** While many apostolic leaders have been very vocal regarding socially moral issues, young people have been invigorated to fight against the sex slave industry, racism, economic injustice and the like. They are sick and tired of focusing on what the church is "against" and want to focus on what the church "is for". Any church that has the vision to love and empower humanity irrespective of race, gender, and economic status, will have an easier time garnering the attention of young people. While I realize that the term "social justice" is an old mantra for socialism, its meaning has also been expanded to include things that can coincide with the tenets of the biblical worldview.

- **The desire to serve the community.** Whereas many in the Apostolic Movement want to transform nations politically, many young people are not as interested in "reforming society" but feel more compelled to meet the practical needs of their community. Reaching others through art, music, mentoring and befriending the lost and lonely are things they have a passion for. Hence, while many Apostolic leaders are "macro", young people are "micro" in their approach as it pertains to seeing the renewal of all things on earth.

- **The desire for parish ministry.** Many Apostolic leaders and centers have a vision for reaching their region and beyond, while many young people focus more on reaching their immediate community. The difference in methodology is the apostolic regional church versus the parish church model. Young leaders tend to focus more on developing church campuses with each campus adopting a parish model with regards to concentrating on their own local community.

- **The challenge of the technological era for communication.** Older, apostolic leaders are utilizing social media and texting more and more, but young people have been born into this technological age and are as accustomed to connecting through social media as a fish is used to living underwater. Apostolic leaders need to continue to grow in their use of social media if they are going to connect with the next generation and young people and have to develop more in their face-to-face skills, if they want to be more balanced.

- **The mobility of next-generation leaders.** While most apostolic leaders have been located in the same region for decades, many young people are "cultural creatives" who are constantly in geographic transition depending on where they have the best opportunity. Even young pastors have more of a tendency to move geographically more often than the past generation, who often made a commitment to one community for decades.

- **The challenge of hierarchical structures.** While many apostolic leaders use ecclesiastical titles like "Apostle" and "Bishop", young people are uncomfortable with titles and anything hierarchical. They would much rather relate to other people on a first-name basis.

- **The challenge of the prosperity gospel.** While many apostolic leaders are visionaries with amazing fundraising skills, many young people connote a strong appeal for finances with the so-called prosperity gospel. Many even shy away from utilizing the scriptures that speak about God rewarding faithful tithers. Instead, they focus on giving to God purely out of love and generosity. Of course, the legitimate apostolic leaders I partner with are also uncomfortable with the notion of turning the church into a fundraising machine or the use of God for personal gain and prosperity. The truth is, God does reward financial faithfulness and generously gives back more than we can ever sow into His Kingdom. However, our motives have to be pure before God as we are called to seek first His Kingdom.

- **Young leaders tend to be entrepreneurial.** One primary thing both apostolic leaders and millennial leaders have in common is, by nature, they both tend to be entrepreneurial. Apostolic leaders who understand this should focus on empowering creativity in young people. They need to realize that this is a generation with more knowledge, technology and the opportunity to be self-employed than any recent generation. Apostolic leaders who treat Millenials like stationary employees (like the factory workers and unionized workers of their own era), will miss a great opportunity to connect the next generation with the present apostolic movement.

There are more points that can be made but the few issues related above are a snapshot of some of the hurdles older leaders like myself face when attempting to pass the values, vision, and patterns of the New Testament Apostolic church down to the next generation of leaders.

In the next chapter I will explore whether the apostolic church can contribute to the unity of the faith in accordance with Ephesians 4:13. The importance of this subject cannot be overstated since Jesus said that the world will not believe until the church walks in oneness. (John 17:20-24)

SOME QUESTIONS TO ASK YOURSELF

1. What are some of the ways an apostolic leader can be a stumbling block to young leaders?

2. Which of the criticisms of the millennial generation do you think are valid?

3. What are ways we can reach the next generation without compromising the gospel?

4. What are ways we can cultivate young entrepreneurial leaders?

5. Are there certain teachings or methods we should modify in light of Scripture?

Chapter 12

Cacophony or Symphony: Will Apostolic Pentecostalism, Denominationalism, and Independent Evangelicalism Converge?

In this chapter, I will analyze the recent collaborative attempts made amongst Denominational, Evangelical, and Pentecostal Apostolic expressions of Christianity. I will also attempt to answer the question of whether this greater unity will eventually lead to a greater theological synthesis in the global Body of Christ.

I am of the opinion that Jesus has been building His church for the past 2000 plus years! (Matthew 16:16-19). That being said, I believe that Jesus will finish the work He started when He initiated His global movement on the Day of Pentecost (Acts 1:8-10, 2:1-40). According to Ephesians 4:1-16, one of the primary ways He builds His church is shown in Ephesians 4:7-11. This is His Ministry DNA, which is embedded in the non-believer through creation grace, as well as the Believer whom it was bestowed on after His ascension (Ephesians 4:9,10).

Consequently, He will continue to bestow these gifts until the five-fold ministry gifts are fulfilled; this relates to the Church coming to the unity of the faith, to the perfect knowledge of the Son of God and to the fullness of the stature of the measure of Christ.

With all of the movements towards the restoration of the Apostolic among historic Pentecostal denominations and Independent Evangelical networks, I see this trend continuing to garner influence until the (global) gospel confessing Body of Christ (whether denominational or nondenominational) morphs into the New Testament pattern of the way of Christ and His apostles. This will take place in various forms and levels of maturity depending upon the leadership and denominational expression of the organization.

Basically, I see God gradually restoring biblical truth, as He did in the Protestant Reformation in the 16th century, and in which "the Reformed church will continually reform itself". Hence, this restoration is not limited to merely the fivefold ministry gifts (Ephesians 4:11) but includes the restoration of all biblical truth, in both Testaments. This restoration will continue until the Church grows to be the mature sons of God (Romans 8:19-22). This will eventuate in the second bodily advent of the Lord, which will culminate in all things in both heaven and earth being united in Christ (Ephesians 1:9-11).

In my journey as a Christian since 1978, I have witnessed the huge divide between Charismatics and Cessationist Evangelicals gradually narrow. Most Evangelicals are now open to all the gifts and manifestations of the Holy Spirit, having become less dogmatic Fundamentalist Cessationists. More and more respected Evangelical theologians and scholars have embraced the Pentecostal experience (such as Wayne Grudem, J.I. Packer, Jeffrey Niehaus, S.M.Burgess, Charles H. Craft, David Lewis, John White). Several of these theologians even collaborated several decades ago to write, *The Kingdom and the Power*.[267] This book was written to demonstrate the healing and spiritual gifts used by Jesus and the early Church were still meant for the church today. One of the primary reasons for the move towards the acceptance of the gifts is the incontrovertible evidence that the primary growth and expansion of global Christianity is happening through the Pentecostal church. Evangelical leaders who hold to a view of Cessationism regarding the manifestations of the Holy Spirit (1 Corinthians 12:4-8) and of the cessation of "apostles and prophets", will either have to say that the devil is growing

Christianity through the Pentecostal Apostolic movement and or they will have to admit that God is actually behind what is happening. Jesus said, "a house divided cannot stand and if Satan is divided against himself his kingdom cannot stand" (Matthew 12).

My dear friend and theological mentor, Jeff Reed,[268] is an example of a Cessationist Evangelical scholar who became convinced of the legitimacy of the global Pentecostal Apostolic Movement (including the Charismatic gifts mentioned in 1 Cor. 12), through his vast experience working with Pentecostal groups worldwide and observing the global Church trends. I was shocked, when at a recent USCAL conference, the late notable Sessationist, Reformed Economist/Theologian Gary North, attended our Bridge Summit 2018 in Atlanta. Much of the preaching seems to have resonated with him. He indicated to me privately that he cannot deny what God is doing through Charismatic Churches in the world today.

In my teachings of the Apostolic movement, as it relates to the Kingdom of God, I have had many Reformed theologians tell me how they greatly enjoy what I taught, even purchasing my books. Furthermore, I have spoken in leadership conferences in Latin America, North America and Africa with thousands of participants, which included many developing world Bishops, theologians, and denominational leaders. My messages have also resonated with them, and they respond to the call of bringing the Body of Christ back to the "Way of Christ and His Apostles."

In the year 2005, I participated in the "Centurions program" under the auspices of the late Chuck Colson, a notable political insider, public intellect, scholar and the founder of "Prison Reform." As a result of this, I had much interaction with Colson and other notable non-Charismatic Evangelical theologians, academics and scholars who were part of the faculty. They all were intrigued and very supportive of my work in the Charismatic Apostolic movement. They even went so far as to post my weekly articles on their websites and promoted my teachings and books among their Alumni.

In the spring of 2018, I had a one-hour video meeting with some of the leaders of the International Lausanne Movement who invited me to share my thoughts on what is the apostolic ministry, its function, and networking. They then invited me to become a delegate, representing the Apostolic movement in the USA, to the International Lausanne Gathering in Manilla, the Philippines in June of 2019. I attended their global workplace gathering in Manila, met with the global leader of Lausanne (Michael Oh) and have been in talks with them in regard to how to relationally connect ICAL with the Lausanne movement. I consider this to be a major breakthrough for the Apostolic Movement since only traditional Evangelical Denominational leaders and representatives of the Pentecostal and Evangelical church are invited as delegates to the Lausanne convention. Also, as of the writing of this section we are in dialogue with the General Secretary of the WEA, Thomas Shirrmacher regarding the possibility of ICAL becoming a global partner with the WEA. This is another significant example of the apostolic being embraced by the Evangelical community at large.

My friend, Alan Hirsch, is perhaps the greatest proponent of the need for the Apostolic to be restored in the church so that we can have a "Permanent Revolution" and not routinize and institutionalize like many apostolic movements have done so in Church history.[269] His scholarly and brilliant writings have impacted the Missional Church Movement, Evangelical Church planting movements (ex. "Exponential" led by Dave Ferguson) and leadership networks. Hirsch's books are featured on the website of the "Leadership Network" founded by Bob Buford and have been endorsed by significant Evangelical leaders. As of the writing of this book, Alan has moved to New York City to be a consultant to "City to City", a church planting network that was founded by Tim Keller of Redeemer Church.

Another one of my friends, Dr. Michael Brown, is an Apostolic leader who has written many scholarly books as well as host of a Radio show called "Line of Fire." He is a member of USCAL. He has friendships with many mainstream Evangelical leaders and theologians.

Another colleague and USCAL member, Dr. Mark Chironna, is in a Ph.D. program with the University of Birmingham. Chironna has launched a movement of Charismatic practitioners and scholars called "The Issachar Initiative." His goal is to unite Charismatic movements like USCAL to Charismatically inclined Evangelical scholarship. Doug Geivet and Holly Pivac also have made note of the fact[270] that the NAR is mainstreaming (to the dismay and or concern of some Evangelicals) in the societal spheres of Christian Media, the Internet, Academia, as well as through massive youth movements such as "The Call" (founded by Lou Engle).

In my estimation, through these and other efforts amongst those related in some respect to the burgeoning Apostolic movement, this will eventuate in said Apostolic movement becoming part of the theological and methodological mainstream of Evangelicalism within the next two decades or less.

The Unity of the Global Church

Also, since the council of Chalcedon in 451, the global church started to fragment. The culmination of this fragmentation was when Islam conquered the Christian nations of North Africa. Regarding the start of this divide. I will summarize historian Andrew Wall's observation that the council of Chalcedon of 451 defined safe areas for Christology but resulted in dividing those who did their thinking in Greek and Latin from those whose theological vocabulary was in Coptic or Syriac, who felt left outside. Terms such as Nestorian, Monophysite, Melkite were concepts used to cast aspersions towards other Christians.

This resulted a century later in the church splitting three ways along cultural and linguistic lines: Greco/Latin; Syriac and Coptic.[271]

This weakened the unity of the church and made the Christians residing in North Africa more vulnerable to the attacks from the Muslims a few centuries later. Consequently, I believe that one of the greatest developments we have seen starting in the 20th century is the possibility that the global church will unite once again for the first time in approximately 1500 years!

Presently movements like ICAL led by John Kelly and BILD. org<http://BILD.org> led by Jeff Reed are forging unified efforts between apostolic leaders from the continents of Africa, Asia, and Latin America. General Secretary of the World Evangelical Alliance and friend, Thomas Schirrmacher is also an amazing apostolic leader/scholar who is doing much to unite the body of Christ as is my friend Brad Smith, the president of Bakke university who sits on the board of the WEA and is also very influential with the Global Lausanne movement.

In the next chapter we will compare contemporary expressions of the church with the first century pattern of church based on the Way of Christ and His apostles.

QUESTIONS TO ASK YOURSELF

1. Do you see signs of hope now that Jesus is uniting His church?

2. Do you believe the apostolic has a role in bringing unity to the global church?

3. What are some of the huge theological divides that have been healed in the evangelical church the past fifty years?

4. What are some evangelical movements that are presently open to the apostolic movement?

5. Who are some of the contemporary scholars that God is using presently to bring unity in His church?

Chapter 13

Comparing The Way of Jesus And The Apostles With The Present Day Global Apostolic, Denominational, and Fragmented Evangelical Models

In this chapter, we will analyze the first century Church model with the present-day Denominational, Evangelical, and Pentecostal Apostolic Church models.

Recapturing the Way of Christ and His Apostles

In order to recapture the New Testament model of apostolicity, there are several areas where the Church must mature. I believe the Spirit is shedding light on these areas so that His Bride can be perfected. Here are the following areas:

1. **I believe we need to embrace an egalitarian spirit of team ministry and co-collegiality in our local churches and networks.**[272] This includes having a Christological Ecclesiology that incorporates a culture of service. Implicit in this is the practice of lateral leadership as opposed to only vertical leadership.

2. **We need to have an understanding of the "Cultural Mandate" (Genesis 1:28) that precludes top-down Dominionism.** This Mandate must be interpreted through the lens of the New Testament. An example of Jesus' style of leadership is seen when He washed the feet of His disciples, telling them to imitate Him. We also have to understand that the "Cultural Mandate" is only part of the metanarrative of Scripture. The Church also needs to understand and proclaim the "Big Story" of God as it relates to Christology and redemption. This is necessary

if it is to make disciples who will properly interpret the Word and function as "salt and light" to the world. While applying the biblical worldview to the culture we also need to be aware of and respect cultural diversity and pluralism, without compromising the essence of Jesus' message and movement.

3. **The Apostolic Church must apply theology in culture by practicing incarnational mission in their community.** One of the most important elements needed to recapture the way of Christ and His apostles is to embrace an incarnational (or missional) approach as it relates to having a local church presence in the community (John 1:14, Jeremiah 29:4-7). This involves going from being Church centric to community-centric as it pertains to missions.[273] For the church to be community-centric as opposed to being merely self-focused, the body of Christ must move away from dispensational escapist theology.

4. **An incarnational ministry must release the congregation to serve God by serving their community.** They must harness all the gifts of the Body so that the Church can serve as a benefactor community to the surrounding community. This will result in churches and believers having favor with God and men. Because so many of the churches in local communities are inbred, (only focused on their own members, buildings and programs), they have opened a door to the accusation from unbelievers. This is the main reason why community boards and elected officials often use zoning laws to stop churches from having more land. They view the church as an irrelevant, tax revenue-sucking leech, that contributes nothing to the life of the community. (The church was originally granted tax-exempt status because it was seen as beneficial to the life of communities. The redeeming nature of its work with

individuals and neighborhoods aided society.) I will use my church as an example of a local church having favor with both God and men due to our commitment to serving our community.

The mother church we founded in 1984 (Resurrection Church of New York), dealt with some contextual zoning limitations regarding our plans to construct a new edifice for our congregation. Contrary to the numerous war stories we hear around the country of Churches not being able to attain zoning permits, we were successful. The elected officials and community leaders in charge of zoning in my community banded together to help us avoid zoning limitations. This resulted in our church being "upzoned", which increased the property value of the church. This was because our church has had a history of serving our community. It was no secret to some city officials that our church's work contributed to a quality-of-life transformation in its Sunset Park, Brooklyn neighborhood. Much of the improvements started in the 1980s to the 1990s, occurring without gentrification!

Consequently, when the Church has an incarnational/missional purpose, the Church's main cause becomes the community. If we don't do this, it would be impossible to make true disciples of Christ because we have to give believers a sense of purpose as it relates to their call to make an impact outside the Church walls. Also, if we don't focus first on reaching our surrounding community, why should we attempt to do missions in other nations? Jesus told the Church to first affect Jerusalem before going to Judea and Samaria (Acts 1:8) Unfortunately, much of the Body of Christ spends millions of dollars every year with mission trips while neglecting their own local community. Many of them do this to cover their lack of community impact.

It's unfortunate that many congregations will send a person to Africa to minister but ignore the African-American families in their proximity.

As apostolic leaders survey the gifts and abilities of their congregations, the Body of Christ can utilize their members to serve according to their natural and spiritual gifts. This then allows them to contribute their expertise to their communities in such areas as economics, the environment, law, etc. When our burden is for the community, we train our church in a practical manner and not just a mystical manner. These church members who are called to the marketplace should be honored in the church as ministers in the same way we may honor the diaconate in the church. God calls the civil authorities in Romans 12:4 His servants ("deacon" in Greek means servant). This paradigm will give the church membership motivation to be trained as leaders because it will take the utilization of every gift possible to meet all the vast needs of a community. This paradigm has a double-edged sword since it enables the church to simultaneously affect both the local congregation and the community in its discipleship process.

Part of the process of the church embracing an incarnational approach is when "common grace"[274] issues become a common ground for the church to connect with key community leaders and initiatives. From my own experience, most pastors and apostolic leaders have no clue as it pertains to the concept and outworking of "creation grace". The incarnational missional apostolic church has a discipleship making movement that mobilizes and releases the "church gathered" on Sunday to be the problem solvers and leaders as the "church scattered" on Monday.

In my opinion, this is one of the most important theological awakenings pastors can have since they realize that they can work with leaders in various levels of authority in society (including the unsaved), without compromising their faith because of the fact that God extends His common grace to all involved in the stewardship of a community. Truly, the light of Jesus extends to all men, not just saved men (John 1:4). Jesus is the Truth (John 14:6), not only biblical truth but the truth for all issues related to the created order. The radical result of this creation grace illumination is that it would motivate pastors of congregations to begin serving in a dual role as both a Chaplain/Statesman to their Community as well as their flock.

I came into a revelation of this common grace concept in the mid-1990s. As a result, I began serving as one of the primary spiritual leaders of our community of about 165,000 people. I served on the regional management team with the NYPD. There, I personally ministered to all of the commanding officers of our local police station. In addition, I worked with all the major elected officials, served for three years on the local community board. I was the one they called to open in prayer for the major community feasts, and to help mediate problems between community leaders (we used our church to hold said meetings). I was called upon for advice and had a say regarding pending legislation when called upon by some significant political gatekeepers of our community, city, and state. Understanding the distinction between common Grace and saving Grace gave me theological permission to serve with unchurched leaders, for the sake of the quality of life of our city.

When The Church Becomes a "City on a Hill" and the "Light of the World"

The implications of the Apostolic Missional Church which possesses an incarnational methodology is significant! This kind of church employs a holistic approach to ministry. This kind of church takes advantage of the social structures and outreaches already present in a community and releases servant leaders into those structures to bless and transform from within. The apostolic incarnational church recognizes the fact that even as individuals-congregations have specific redemptive gifts for humanity, and communities and cities (and nations) are also endowed by God's common grace with a redemptive gift to be a blessing to all its inhabitants. Consequently, instead of the isolationism of the twentieth century, the twenty-first century Church is going to learn how to both appreciate and capitalize on all the resources presently available in their cities. They will do things because they understand the purpose of serving, leading, and transforming all systems with the goal of reflecting God's purposes.

The churches that follow the way of Jesus and His Apostles don't only try to build and fill their own megastructures but seeks to fill everyone else's buildings with disciples of Jesus! Their credibility comes not from erecting huge church edifices and building their own kingdom but come when they love and exhibit a spirit of excellence in the workplace. Instead of employing only one strategy, (e.g. preaching on the street), this kind of church reflects what Daniel did when he gained favor and built a platform to evangelize a nation by serving a pagan king in a pagan system. He served with wisdom, faithfulness, and prophetic insight. The twenty-first century Church will love the city (community) even as God commanded Israel to love a pagan city some 2,700 years ago (Jeremiah 29:7).

Consequently, the typical "Christian Right" methodology of merely emphasizing politics and moral issues will never work in most urban areas of the Northeast United States. The Daniel model of disciples of Jesus serving with excellence in the context of a pagan culture is the only one that works in a post-Christian or humanistic environment.

The Apostolic Church Penetrates and Transforms Culture Before It Emphasizes Politics

The first century Apostolic Church never attempted to circumvent the Roman Empire politically but conquered Rome by refusing to worship any god other than Jesus. They did this by refusing to burn incense to an image of the Roman emperor and by serving their neighbors with acts of kindness and by proclaiming the Gospel of Christ with boldness. Even so, the present-day Church must walk in the way of Jesus and His apostles so that they can transform their cities and nations.[275]

Some Cautions Regarding the "Church in Community" Model

If the contemporary Apostolic Church is going to continue to walk in the way of Christ and His Apostles, there have to be boundaries to ensure its integrity to Jesus's mission. In my decades of experience, I have seen pastors become inebriated because of their proximity to power, resulting in them compromising their call to proclaim the fullness of the Scriptures. The result is that they no longer speak out on certain culturally controversial biblical issues because of the fear they will relinquish their access to political gatekeepers and potential donors. Unfortunately, I have witnessed firsthand pastors who initially were prophetic, turn into puppets of the political establishment. Sadly, this resulted in these pastors and their churches becoming part of the systemic problem!

To avoid this from happening, the following are some important cautions to consider before launching out into the missional world of serving and impacting the culture:

1. **The Pastor and Sent-Out Community Leaders Must Be Theologically Grounded**

The reason for this is when Christians begin to get involved in a community, they will be exposed to all sorts of belief systems, power, money, and political corruption. If a person is not rooted and grounded in the Word then they may either get confused or compromise in order to accommodate.

2. **The Church Must Be Grounded in the Cultural Mandate of Genesis 1:28**

   The reason for this is that if the Church doesn't emphasize the lordship of Christ over all, then all service in the community collapses down to humanism and the church will be no different in function and essence then secular community service organizations.

3. **The Church Must Never Stop Emphasizing Saving Grace Methodologies of Discipleship and gospel proclamation.**

   In spite of the vast needs and opportunities of ministering to a community, the Church should never stop preaching the Gospel, saving the lost, healing the sick, and producing full-time ecclesial ministers.

4. **The Church Must Understand Saving Grace/Common Grace Distinctions and protect itself from secular humanitarianism.**

   The Church in the early 1900s fell into a social gospel in which the preaching of the cross was gradually supplanted by just doing good works. The fundamentalist approach reacted to the social gospel and eschewed common grace methodologies because their hyper-dispensational end-time eschatology taught that it was a waste to "arrange the chairs on the Titanic." In light of these two extremes, the Apostolic Church endeavors to maintain a balance between keeping their essence as a church and the doing of good works in and for the community (Galatians 6:10, Ephesians 2:10).

As the Church begins to integrate itself and its programs into the community with various partnerships, the temptation will be to allow those with money, power, influence, or smarts to control their governing boards and leadership committees. This is why many or most of the Christian organizations that started off preaching the Gospel stop doing so in the second or third generation of their existence. In the first generation, the pastors usually lead these social service entities through their local church, with spiritually mature leaders on the governing board, making it a 501C3 organization. As the program gained more notoriety, the pastors typically allowed the businesspeople on the board to separate it from the local church. For the sake of being "pragmatically" focused more than a biblical focus, the organization was gradually steered away from its Christian foundations (This has been the story of many Ivy League schools, hospitals, and charitable organizations, like the YMCA, and the Red Cross).

It is imperative that both the Apostolic leader and church members keep the balance between community and congregational ministry, between the true Apostolic mission and the Apostolic family of families. Unfortunately, the tendency of many spiritual leaders when they learn a new truth is to go to extremes. In this regard, pastors must make sure they don't only emphasize the community to the neglect of their local church's internal needs.

QUESTIONS TO ASK YOURSELF

1. What are some of the areas the church must embrace for it to follow the way of Christ and His apostles?

2. What is the cultural mandate and why is it so important?

3. Why must the apostolic church practice theology in culture by practicing incarnational mission?

4. What is common grace?

5. Why is understanding the concept of common grace essential for finding common ground with secular leaders?

6. How does the church function as the light of the world?

7. Why must the church transform culture before it focuses on politics?

8. What are some of the cautions regarding the church and community model?

A Final Word

My prayer is that this book will give a contemporary, practical, robust understanding of the true nature of apostolic ministry that will challenge static religious church models, shift mindsets, and motivate the building of churches and movements according to the way of Jesus and His apostles.

I contend that God is calling the church back to her missional apostolic roots that will result in a local church-based disciple making movement empowered by the Holy Spirit that is rooted and grounded in both the *kerygma* and the *dedache*.

I pray this book can also serve as an easy to replicate blueprint that will help shape theological and church planting discussions that will advance the Kingdom of God in every nation and context until He comes, Amen.

Bibliography

"About BILD International." Bild. Accessed April 21, 2020. https://bild.org/.

"Abraham Kuyper." Abraham Kuyper. Accessed April 22, 2020. https://abrahamkuyper.com/.

Anderson, Allan. "An Introduction to Pentecostalism: Global Charismatic Christianity" Cambridge: Cambridge University Press, 2016.

"Antioch School of Church Planting and Leadership Development Grants Degrees for Church-Based Theological Education." Antioch School of Church Planting and Leadership Development grants degrees for church-based theological education. Accessed April 21, 2020. http://www.antiochschool.edu/.

Augustine, and Marcus Dods. "The City of God." Lexington, KY: Amazon CreateSpace, 2018.
b777. "Christian Apologetics & Research Ministry." CARM. org<http://CARM.org>, March 29, 2017. https://carm.org/pelagianism.

Baker, Wayne E. Networking Smart: "How to Build Relationships for Personal and Organizational Success." New York: iUniverse. com<http://iUniverse.com>, 2003.

Bakke, Ray. "A Theology as Big as the City" Downers Grove, IL: InterVarsity Press, 1997.

Bakke, Raymond J. "A Biblical Word for an Urban World: Messages from the 1999 World Mission Conference." Board of International Ministries, American Baptist Churches in the U.S.A (2000), 2000.

Balthasar, Hans Urs von. "Explorations in Theology" San Francisco: Ignatius Press, 1993.

Barabási Albert-László. "Linked: How Everything Is Connected to Everything Else and What It Means for Business, Science, and Everyday Life" New York: Basic Books, 2014.

Beacham, Doug. "Rediscovering the Role of Apostles and Prophets." Franklin Springs, GA: LifeSprings Resources, 2004.

BioLogos. "God's Word. God's World." BioLogos. BioLogos, August 28, 2018. https://biologos.org/?modal=about.

Bosch, David Jacobus. "Transforming Mission: Paradigm Shifts in Theology of Mission." Maryknoll, NY: Orbis Books, 2011. Burgess, Andrew R. "The Ascension in Karl Barth. Abingdon, England: Routledge, 2017"

Burgess, Stanley M. "Dictionary of Pentecostal and Charismatic Movements" Grand Rapids, MI: Zondervan, 1998.

Cahill, Thomas. "How the Irish Saved Civilization: the Untold Story of Irelands Heroic Role from the Fall of Rome to the Rise of Medieval Europe" New York.: Nan A. Talese/ Doubleday, 1995.

Cannistraci, David. "The Gift of Apostle" Ventura, CA: Regal Books, 1996.

Cartledge, David. "The Apostolic Revolution: the Restoration of Apostles and Prophets in the Assemblies of God in Australia" Chester Hill, NSW, Australia: Paraclete Institute, 2000.

Christerson, Brad, and Richard W. Flory. "The Rise of Network Christianity: How Independent Leaders Are Changing the Religious Landscape" New York, NY: Oxford University Press, 2017.

Clifford, Alan C. "John Wesley (1703–91)" Oxford Scholarship Online. Oxford University Press. Accessed April 22, 2020. https://www.oxfordscholarship.com/view/10.1093/acprof:oso/9780198261957.001.0001/acprof-9780198261957-chapter-4.

Coghlan, David. "Ignatian Spirituality as Transformational Social Science - David Coghlan, 2005." SAGE Journals. Accessed April 22, 2020. https://journals.sagepub.com/doi/10.1177/1476750305049967.

Conner, Kevin J. "The Church in the New Testament" Portland, OR: City Bible Publishing, 1982.

Conner, Kevin John. "This Is My Story: With Lessons Along the Way" (version Amazon.com<http://Amazon.com> Services LLC), n.d. Accessed June 12, 2017.

Cook, Bruce. "Aligning With The Apostolic: An Anthology of Apostleship" Kingdom House, 2013.

David, Jonathan. "Apostolic Strategies Affecting Nations" Muar, Johor, Malaysia: The author, 2007.

Dearteaga, William. "Quenching the Spirit Examining Centuries of Opposition to the Moving of the Holy Spirit" Lake Mary, FL: Creation House, 1992.

Delph, Ed. "Church@Community" Lake Mary, FL: Creation House, 2005.

DeMar, Gary. "Americas Christian History" Powder Springs, GA: American Vision, 2005.

"DiSC Profile - What Is DiSC°? The DiSC Personality Test and Profile Explained." DiSCProfile.com<http://DiSCProfile.com>. Accessed April 22, 2020. https://www.discprofile.com/what-is-disc/overview/.

"Dr. Mark Chrionna." Mark Chironna. Accessed April 22, 2020. https://www.markchironna.com/.

Fletcher, R. A. "The Barbarian Conversion: from Paganism to Christianity" Berkeley, CA: University of California Press, 1999.

Ford, Lance. "Unleader: Reimagining Leadership-- and Why We Must" Kansas City: Beacon Hill Press, 2012.

Ford, Lance. "Unleader: Reimagining Leadership--and Why We Must" Kansas City: Beacon Hill Press, 2012.

G., McNair Scott Benjamin. "Apostles Today: Making Sense of Contemporary Charismatic Apostolates: a Historical and Theological Appraisal" Cambridge: The Lutterworth Press, 2014.

Gadamer, Hans-Georg, Carsten Dutt, and Richard E. Palmer. "Gadamer in Conversation: Reflections and Commentary" New Haven: Yale University Press, 2001.

Geivett, R. Douglas., and Holly Douglas. Pivec. "A New Apostolic Reformation?: a Biblical Response to a Worldwide Movement" WOOSTER, OHIO: WEAVER Book Company, 2014.

Hamon, Bill. "The Eternal Church: a Prophetic Look at the Church--Her History, Restoration, and Destiny" Shippensburg, PA: Destiny Image, 2003.

Hiestand, Gerald. "The Pastor Theologian: Resurrecting an Ancient Vision" Grand Rapids, MI: Zondervan, 2015.

Hill, Jonathan. "What Has Christianity Ever Done for Us?: How It Shaped the Modern World" Downers Grove, Illinois (USA): InterVarsity Press, 2005.

Hirsch, Alan. "The Forgotten Ways: Reactivating the Missional Church" Grand Rapids, MI: Brazos Press, 2008.

Hirsch, Alan. "The Permanent Revolution: Apostolic Imagination and Practice for the 21st Century Church" C. John Wiley & Sons, 2012.

http://www.christcovenantcoalition.com/leadership, n.d.

http://www.uscal.us/, n.d.

https://resurrectionchurchofny.com/about/, n.d.

https://www.biblicalstudies.org.uk/pdf/ref-rev/07-4/7-4_
mcgoldrick.pdf, n.d.

https://www.sparknotes.com/us-government-and-politics/
political-science/nations-and-states/section2/. SparkNotes.
Accessed April 21, 2020. https://www.sparknotes.com/us-
government-and-politics/political-science/nations-and-states/
section2/.

Hunter, George G. The Apostolic Congregation: Church Growth
Reconceived for a New Generation. Nashville, TN: Abingdon
Press, 2009.

Hunter, James Davison. To Change the World: the Irony,
Tragedy, and Possibility of Christianity Today. New York: Oxford
University Press, 2010.

Jenkins, Philip. The next Christendom: the Coming of Global
Christianity. Oxford.: Oxford University Press, 2011.

Keller, Timothy. Center Church - Doing Balanced, Gospel-
Centered Ministry in Your City. Zondervan, 2012.

Kuiper, B. K. The Church in History. Grand Rapids: Eerdmans,
1995.

Küng Hans, and David Tracy. Paradigm Change in Theology: a
Symposium for the Future. Edinburgh: T. & T. Clark, 1989.

Küng Hans. Theology for the Third Millennium: an Ecumenical
View. New York: Doubleday, 1990.

Küng Hans. Theology for the Third Millennium: an Ecumenical View. New York: Doubleday, 1990.
Küng Hans. Christianity: Essence, History, and Future. New York: Continuum, 2003.

Küng Hans. Great Christian Thinkers. NY, NY: Continuum, 2006.

"Love Wins: A Book About Heaven, Hell, and the Fate of Every Person Who Ever Lived: Bell, Rob: Amazon.com.au<http://Amazon.com.au>: Books." Love Wins: A Book About Heaven, Hell, and the Fate of Every Person Who Ever Lived: Bell, Rob: Amazon.com.au<http://Amazon.com.au>: Books. Accessed April 21, 2020. https://www.amazon.com.au/Love-Wins-About-Heaven-Person/dp/006204964X.

Macmurray, John, and John Macmurray. The Self as Agent. Amherst, NY: Humanity Books, 1999.

MacPherson, Dave. The Rapture Plot. Simpsonville, SC: Millennium III Publishers, 2000.

Mattera, Joseph. "Understanding the Wineskin of the Kingdom." Place of publication not identified: EGEN CO LLC, 2016.

Mattera, Joseph. "Ruling in the Gates" Lake Mary, FL: Creation House Press, 2003.

Mattera, Joseph. "Kingdom Awakening: A Blueprint for Personal and Cultural Transformation" Shippensburg, PA: Destiny Image Publishers, 2010.

Mattera, Joseph. "Kingdom Revolution: Bringing Change to Your Life and Beyond" Shippensburg, PA: Destiny Image, Inc., 2011.

Mattera, Joseph. "Walk in Generational Blessings: Leaving a Legacy of Transformation through Your Family" Shippensburg, PA: Destiny Image Pub., 2012.

Mattera, Joseph. "An Anthology of Essays on Apostolic Leadership" CreateSpace Independent Publishing Platform, 2015.

Mattera, Joseph. "25 Truths You Never Heard in Church: Becoming a Kingdom Focused Believer" Micro65, 2017.

Mattera, Joseph. "The Divided Gospel: The Consequences of Separating the Gospel from the Kingdom" Micro65, 2018.

Maxwell, John C. "The 21 Irrefutable Laws of Leadership: Follow Them and People Will Follow You" Nashville, TN: Thomas Nelson, n.d.
Newbigin, James Edward Lesslie. "The Gospel in a Pluralist Society" Grand Rapids: Eerdmans, 1989.

Newbigin, Lesslie. "The Gospel in a Pluralist Society" London: SPCK, 2014.

O'Donnell, James. "St. Augustine" Encyclopædia Britannica. Encyclopædia Britannica, inc., February 19, 2020. https://www.britannica.com/biography/Saint-Augustine.

"Our Team." Bild. Accessed April 22, 2020. https://bild.org/about-us/team.

Palmer, Parker. "To Know As We Are Known-Education As Spiritual Formation" n.d.

Payne, Jervis David. "Roland Allen: Pioneer of Spontaneous Expansion" United States: J.D. Payne, 2012.

Podder, Api. "This Award-Winning Activist Has Been Serving NYC Youth For Almost 4 Decades." Your Mark On The World, May 23, 2018. https://yourmarkontheworld.com/this-award-winning-activist-has-been-serving-nyc-youth-for-almost-4-decades/.

Raschke, Carl A. "The next Reformation: Why Evangelicals Must Embrace Postmodernity" Grand Rapids, MI: Baker Academic, 2004.

Reason, Peter, and William R. Torbet. "The Action Turn: Towards A Transformational Social Science. Concepts and Transformation" n.d., 1–37.

Reed, Jeff. "Uneducated Apostles: Orality, Literacy, and Leadership in the Early Church." A BILD Encyclical, n.d.

Reed, Jeff. "Kerygmatic Communities: Evangelism and the Early Churches" A BILD ENCYCLICAL, November 3, 2011.

Reed, Jeff. "Global Pentecostalism and the Spirit: The Progress of the Gospel in the 21st Century," A BILD Encyclical, November 7, 2019.

"Restoration Ministries." Restoration Ministries, October 9, 2018. https://restorationministriesbrazil.com/.

"Resurrection Church" Resurrection Church. Accessed April 21, 2020. https://resurrectionchurchofny.com/.

Ringenberg, William C., and Mark A. Noll. "The Christian College: a History of Protestant Higher Education in America" Grand Rapids, MI: Baker Academic, 2006.

"Robert Morris." People. Accessed April 22, 2020. https://gatewaypeople.com/staff/robert-morris.

Schmidt, Alvin J. "How Christianity Changed the World" Grand Rapids: Zondervan, 2004.

Schnabel, Eckhard J. "Paul the Missionary: Realities, Strategies and Methods." Amazon. IVP Academic, 2008. https://www.amazon.com/Missionary-Methods-Pauls-Church-Provinces/dp/152149665X.

Silvoso, Ed. "Anointed for Business" Bloomington, MN: Chosen Books, 2014.

Smietana, Bob. "The 'Prophets' and 'Apostles' Leading the Quiet Revolution in American Religion." ChristianityToday.com<http://ChristianityToday.com>. Christianity Today, August 7, 2017. https://www.christianitytoday.com/ct/2017/august-web-only/bethel-church-international-house-prayer-prophets-apostles.html.

Smietana, Bob. "The 'Prophets' and 'Apostles' Leading the Quiet Revolution in American Religion" ChristianityToday.com<http://ChristianityToday.com>. Christianity Today, August 7, 2017. https://www.christianitytoday.com/ct/2017/august-web-only/bethel-church-international-house-prayer-prophets-apostles.html.

"The Churches of the First Century: From Simple Churches to Complex Networks." A BILD Encyclical , November 5, 2009.

The Editors of Encyclopaedia Britannica. "Doctor of the Church." Encyclopædia Britannica. Encyclopædia Britannica, inc., December 31, 2018. https://www.britannica.com/topic/Doctor-of-the-Church.

"The Gospel in a Pluralist Society," n.d.

Vanhoozer, Kevin J. "Pastor as Public Theologian: Reclaiming a Lost Vision" Place of publication not identified: Brazos Baker, 2014.

Vanhoozer, Kevin J., and Owen Strachan. "The Pastor as Public Theologian: Reclaiming a Lost Vision" Grand Rapids, MI: Baker Academic, 2015.

Vines, Matthew. "God and the Gay Christian: The Biblical Case in Support of Same-Sex Relationships." Amazon. Convergent Books, 2015. https://www.amazon.com/God-Gay-Christian-Biblical-Relationships/dp/160142518X.

Wagner, C. Peter. "Apostles Today" Bloomington, MN: Chosen Books, 2014.

Willibald, Of Mainz. "Life of Saint Boniface" Place of publication not identified: Hardpress Publishing, 2012.

Wilson, Andrew. "Why Being a Pastor-Scholar Is Nearly Impossible." ChristianityToday.com<http://ChristianityToday. com>. Christianity Today, November 1, 2017. https://www. christianitytoday.com/ct/2015/september-web-only/why-being-pastor-scholar-is-nearly-impossible.html.

Wright, N. T., and Michael F. Bird. "The New Testament in Its World: an Introduction to the History, Literature, and Theology of the First Christians". Grand Rapids, MI: Zondervan Academic, 2019.

Endnotes

1   Regarding the size and scope of the movement, even opponents of one expression of the movement (called the NAR, an acronym for the "New Apostolic Reformation") state, "Unlike the Latter Rain Movement that was concentrated in revival hot spots and so had only a limited number of participants, NAR is worldwide in scope, with millions of participants. A movement of such size is not going away soon. NAR accounts for much of the phenomenal growth of Christianity taking place in the Global South-Africa, Asia, and Latin America. It is part of the fastest-growing segment of non-Catholic Christianity worldwide, a segment researchers call the Independent or Post Denominational segment, with more than 369 million participants. Only the Protestant segment is slightly larger. At its current rate of growth, researchers expect that NAR/Independent churches will soon overtake even the Protestants."

R. Douglas. Geivett and Holly Douglas. Pivec, A New Apostolic Reformation?: a Biblical Response to a Worldwide Movement (Wooster, Ohio: Weaver Book Company, 2014), 23.

Historian Philip Jenkins essentially said the same thing regarding current trends in Global Christianity when he described the New Christendom looking like the Apostolic church of the first century, "The idea that Southern churches are living in something like a renewed apostolic age inspires nothing short of awe." Philip Jenkins, The Next Christendom: the Coming of Global Christianity (Oxford.: Oxford University Press, 2011), 135.

2   Of course, the concept of the apostolate is nothing new in the church, even after the original 12 Apostles passed from the scene, "The Roman Catholic, Orthodox and Anglican churches hold that the bishop is the historic successor of the apostles, being the sole ministry able to ordain others, and possessing an apostolic sacramental ministry which they share with their co-workers the priests. Lutherans and Methodists hold to a form of apostolic succession but believe it can be validly passed on via the presbyterate. These churches clearly differentiate between those first apostles who were eyewitnesses of the resurrected Lord, instructed directly by Jesus, receiving revelation that was to be a part of the deposit of faith entrusted to all the saints and their successors." McNair Scott Benjamin G., "Apostles Today: Making Sense of Contemporary Charismatic Apostolates: a Historical and Theological Appraisal" (Cambridge: The Lutterworth Press, 2014)), 255, Kindle.

3   Also, it has been the practice of many Christian traditions to posthumously refer to a great saint or missionary as an apostle. Dionysius of Corinth was called the Apostle of France, Xavier was called the Apostle of the Indies, Hudson Taylor was called the apostle to China, John Eliot was called the Apostle to the Indians. I have also heard of people referring to leaders such as John Wesley, D.L.Moody, William Booth, Billy Graham and others as apostles posthumously.

Also, most Pentecostal denominations believe in Apostolic ministry, like the Assemblies Of God and Foursquare. However, they often make a distinction between "foundational and functional" apostles. Foundational refers to the original 12 Apostles plus Paul, and functional refers to those who do apostolic work, such as, church planting and missionary work.

4 My experience is that most Apostolic practitioners, use apostolic language. They may use "apostolic lingo" and have a Charismatic church with great worship, preaching, believe in the ministry of apostles and prophets, have independent networks, etc., but in many ways fail to teach and pattern their structures related to church planting, fail in the multiplication of disciples and fail in securing a strong church government. In other words, they fail to build according to the way of Christ and the Apostles.

   Also, it must be said at the onset of this book that I am not a proponent of some of the teachings that have emerged out of the NAR because of my understanding of Scripture and the Way of Christ and His Apostles.

5 My wife, Joyce and I established Resurrection Church in 1984 https://resurrectionchurchofny.com/about/, n.d).

6 Christ Covenant Coalition was established in 1999. http://www.christcovenantcoalition.com/leadership, n.d).

7 Birthed in 2015, USCAL is one of the largest apostolic networks in the United States. http://www.uscal.us/, n.d).

8 David Cannistraci, *The Gift of Apostle* (Ventura, CA: Regal Books, 1996), 82-85.

9 Such as top-down leadership, hyper dominion rhetoric, the use of apostle as a title rather than a description, and the practice of laying hands on leaders proclaiming them to be apostles over regions and nations.

10 Cannistraci, *The Gift of Apostle*, 11.

11 Read Ephesians 4:11-16 for the entire context.

12 Wagner, *Apostles Today*, 10.

13 Bill Hamon, *The Eternal Church: a Prophetic Look at the Church--Her History, Restoration, and Destiny* (Shippensburg, PA: Destiny Image, 2003), .234.

14 Wagner, *Apostles Today*, 10.

15 The Pietist movement started by Philipp Jacob Spener (1683-1719) and August Franke (1663-1727) both out of the University of Halle were German theologians of the Lutheran Church.

16 It is interesting that the word "mission"(Latin:missio) is a translation of the Greek Apostle, a sending, hence, an apostle (Apostolos) is one commissioned and sent to fulfill a special purpose.

17 Jonathan Edwards started "Concerts of Prayer" in New England and co-labored with Whitfield to enhance the First Great Awakening.

18 William Dearteaga, *Quenching the Spirit Examining Centuries of Opposition to the Moving of the Holy Spirit* (Lake Mary, FL: Creation House, 1992), 29.

19 Allan Anderson, *An Introduction to Pentecostalism: Global Charismatic Christianity* (Cambridge: Cambridge University Press, 2016), 1.

20 Allan Anderson, *An Introduction to Pentecostalism: Global Charismatic Christianity* (Cambridge: Cambridge University Press, 2016), 1.

21 Stanley M. Burgess, *Dictionary of Pentecostal and Charismatic Movements* (Grand Rapids, MI: Zondervan, 1998), 3.

22 Ibid.

23 Ibid.

24 Wagner, *Apostles Today,* 10.

25 Ibid.

26 Ibid.

27 Ibid. p. 12-16.

28 Ibid.

29 Ibid.

30 For more detail on the history of the Latter Rain movement, read pages 532-534 in, Burgess, *Dictionary of Pentecostal and Charismatic Movements.*

31 Bill Hamon, *The Eternal Church: a Prophetic Look at the Church--Her History, Restoration, and Destiny* (Shippensburg, PA: Destiny Image, 2003), .239.

32 Ibid. 234.

33 Ibid., Wagner, *Apostles Today*, 18.

34 Ibid.

35 Read chapters 14,15 in Kevin John Conner, T*his Is My Story: With Lessons Along the Way*, version Amazon.com Services LLC, n.d., accessed June 12, 2017.

36 Ibid., Geivett & Pivec, *A New Apostolic Reformation*, 39.

37 Ibid, p. 132.

38 Ibid.

39 Ibid, p.143.

40 Ibid., 143.

41 Ibid., 143.

42 Ibid. 139.

43 Ibid.

44 Ibid.

45 James Davison Hunter, T*o Change the World: The Irony, Tragedy, and Possibility of Christianity Today* (New York: Oxford University Press, 2010.

46 https://www.sparknotes.com/us-government-and-politics/ political-science/nations-and-states/section2/ (SparkNotes), accessed April 21, 2020.

47 https://www.sparknotes.com/us-government-and-politics/ political-science/nations-and-states/section2/ (SparkNotes), accessed April 21, 2020.

48 Ibid., p.94.

49 The word "apostle" is the Greek translation of the Latin word "missio", hence the missional essence of the word "apostle".

50 Ibid., Hirsch, 269-270.

51 Ibid.

52 The term "Super Apostles" is used to describe those who attempt to usurp authority over pastors because they operate under the belief that "Apostle" is an office, not a mere function. Although I am not in a relationship with any or know of any so called "Super Apostles", there may indeed be some in the Body of Christ.

53 See the application of broad ecclesial participation and partnerships in the New Testament Didache as seen in Ephesians 4:3; 1 Corinthians 1:10; 3:1-5.

54 I usually use the term as an adjective rather than an office.

55 Küng Hans, *Christianity: Essence, History, and Future* (New York: Continuum, 2003), 25.

56 Ibid., Wagner, 10.

57 Ibid.

58 Ray Bakke, *A Theology as Big as the City* (Downers Grove, IL: InterVarsity Press, 1997), 12.

59 Alvin J. Schmidt, *How Christianity Changed the World* (Grand Rapids: Zondervan, 2004), 272.

60 Ibid., p. 274. Additionally, after Emperor Constantine issued the Edict of Milan in A.D. 313, the influence of Christianity began to spread rapidly in Western Europe because it placed Christianity on equal footing before the law with all the other religions in the empire. Because of this vast influence, Christians gained political, military and social promotion. After A.D. 313 the Roman army even changed their emblem from the Eagle to the Cross. Although there are many who say this began the decline of the church, some historians believe this to be beneficial because before this edict many estimate that less than ten percent of the empire had converted to Christianity, and after between thirty-five and fifty percent converted.

61 Augustine and Marcus Dods, *The City of God* (Lexington, KY: Amazon CreateSpace, 2018.

62 Ibid., Schmidt, 274.

63 B. K. Kuiper, *The Church in History* (Grand Rapids: Eerdmans, 1995), 49.

64 R. A. Fletcher, *The Barbarian Conversion: from Paganism to Christianity* (Berkeley, CA: University of California Press, 1999), .68.

65 Ibid., Kuiper, 51.

66 Ibid., Jenkins, The Next Christendom, 17.

67 Ibid., Bakke, 12.

68 Historian, Glen Sunshine, in a *Centurions Residence Lecture*, January 21, 2006.

69 "After they were converted, they needed to know all there was to know about Christianity. They learned it in a language they never learned (Latin) and in a culture, they weren't familiar with. Romans had no spaces or punctuation marks in their writing, which was an unbroken string of capital letters. [After their conversion] the Irish began to separate the words and put little marks to show whether it was a question or a statement. The Irish are the ones who came up with the way we are writing today." Ibid.

70 Thomas Cahill, *How the Irish Saved Civilization: the Untold Story of Irelands Heroic Role from the Fall of Rome to the Rise of Medieval Europe* (New York.: Nan A. Talese/ Doubleday, 1995), 150-151.

71 Ibid., 196.

72 Of Mainz. Willibald, *Life of Saint Boniface* (Place of publication not identified: Hardpress Publishing, 2012.

73 Ibid.

74 Jonathan Hill, *What Has Christianity Ever Done for Us?: How It Shaped the Modern World* (Downers Grove, Illinois (USA): InterVarsity Press, 2005.

75 Ibid., Sunshine. Centurion Residency Lecture, January 21, 2006.

76   Gary DeMar, *Americas Christian History* (Powder Springs, GA: American Vision, 2005), 101.

77   William C. Ringenberg and Mark A. Noll, *The Christian College: A History of Protestant Higher Education in America* (Grand Rapids, MI: Baker Academic, 2006), 38.

78   Ibid., Kung, *Paradigm Changes In History,* 18.

79   Ibid., Kung, *Great Christian Thinkers*, 62.

80   Ibid, p. 63, "To overcome the platonic dualism of Hellenistic Philosophy, the center of Christianity went from the cross and resurrection of Christ to the incarnation and eternal pre-existence of the divine Logos (John 1:1) who alone could bridge the gap between things spiritual and natural, between heaven and the earth."

81   Ibid.

82   Ibid. 58-60.

83   Ibid, 65. "All these paradigm shifts to Hellenism explains why the messianic faith of Christians and Jews have drifted so far apart; why belief in Christ and His nature lead to so many splits in the church; why in the first millennium a deep gulf was opened up between the churches of the east and the west."

84   Ibid., Hirsch, *Permanent Revolution*.

85   Ibid., Bosch, "*Transforming Mission*", 190 -213.

86   This was a summary of the radical changes that took place as a result of the Church going from a Hebraic mindset to a Greek cultural mindset, as noted by David Bosch, Transforming Mission. 190-213.

87   Ibid., Kung, "*Christianity,*" 24.

88   Ibid, Bosch, The following is a summary of pages 243-259 in "Transforming Mission."

89   Küng Hans, *Theology for the Third Millennium: an Ecumenical View* (New York: Doubleday, 1990), 171-180.

90   Ibid., Cannistraci, T*he Gift of Apostle*, 188.

91 Ibid., 189.

92 Ibid., 190.

93 Acts 9:2.

94 Ibid., Keller, *Center Church*, 341.

95 "The productive use of networking principles is nothing short of revolutionary.

Networking organizations are replacing organizations built around traditional hierarchies." Wayne E. Baker, *Networking Smart: How to Build Relationships for Personal and Organizational Success* (New York: iUniverse.com, 2003), p.xvi.

96 Ibid., Keller, 154.

97 Ibid., Wagner, *Apostles Today*, 311.

98 Ibid., 313-315.

99 Ibid., Keller, 339.

100 Jervis David Payne, *Roland Allen: Pioneer of Spontaneous Expansion* (United States: J.D. Payne, 2012), 93-94 Kindle.

101 "Resurrection Church," Resurrection Church, accessed April 21, 2020, https://resurrectionchurchofny.com/

102 Api Podder, "This Award-Winning Activist Has Been Serving NYC Youth For Almost 4 Decades," Your Mark On The World, May 23, 2018, https://yourmarkontheworld.com/this-award-winning-activist-has-been-serving-nyc-youth-for-almost-4-decades/)

103 Ibid., Cannistraci, *The Gift of Apostle*, 188, 190, 194.

104 Ibid., Keller, *Center Church*, 24.

105 Eckhard J. Schnabel, "Paul the Missionary: Realities, Strategies and Methods," Amazon (IVP Academic, 2008), https://www.amazon.com/Missionary-Methods-Pauls-Church-Provinces/dp/152149665X

106 "The Churches of the First Century: From Simple Churches to Complex Networks," A BILD Encyclical, November 5, 2009, .8.

107 Barabási Albert-László, Linked: *How Everything Is Connected to Everything Else and What It Means for Business, Science, and Everyday Life* (New York: Basic Books, 2014.

108 Ibid., Reed, *The churches of the first century*; 34,35,43,45-47.

109 Such paradigms are especially seen in the Pentecostal circle.

110 Kevin J. Conner, *The Church in the New Testament* (Portland, OR: City Bible Publishing, 1982.

111 Ibid., 133-194.

112 Ibid., 94-96.

113 Ibid., 92-103.

114 Ibid., 124-132.

115 Ibid., 102.

116 Presented in Dallas Texas November 10th, 2011.

117 For ICAL, February 28-March 1st.

118 This was another paper presented at the annual ICAL gathering by Dr. Ron Cottle.

119 David Cartledge Published by Paraclete Institute; the year 2000.

120 Ibid.

121 Ibid.

122 David Cartledge, *The Apostolic Revolution: the Restoration of Apostles and Prophets in the Assemblies of God in Australia* (Chester Hill, NSW, Australia: Paraclete Institute, 2000, 39.

123 Ibid.

124 Ibid., 93.

125 Ibid., 69.

126 Ibid. 172.

127 Ibid.

128 Ibid., 173.

129 Ibid. 175.

130 Ibid. 175-176.

131 Ibid., 175-176.

132 Ibid., 185-190.

133 Ibid., 201-208.
134 Ibid., 222.
135 Ibid.
136 Ibid., 236-237.
137 Ibid. 393-394.
138 Ibid., 393-394.
139 Ibid, Hirsch, *The Permanent Revolution*.
140 Ibid.
141 Ibid., 8.
142 Ibid., 9.
143 Ibid., 16.
144 Ibid., 92-93.
145 Ibid., 102-104.
146 Ibid., 102-104.
147 Ibid., 111-112.
148 Ibid., 176.
149 Ibid., 218.
150 Ibid., Wagner, 32-33.
151 Ibid., 34.
152 Ibid., 103.
153 Ibid., 107.
154 Ibid., 108.
155 May 3, 2006.
156 Jonathan David, *Apostolic Strategies Affecting Nations* (Muar, Johor, Malaysia: The author, 2007.
157 Ibid.
158 Ibid., 363.
159 Ibid., 371.
160 Ibid., 373.
161 Ibid., 391.
162 Ibid., 422-428.
163 Ibid., 457-459.
164 Ibid., 475-477.

165 Ibid., 475-477.

166 Ibid., 489-491.

167 Joseph Mattera, *Ruling in the Gates* (Lake Mary, FL: Creation House Press, 2003).

168 Bruce Cook, *Aligning With The Apostolic: An Anthology of Apostleship* (Kingdom House, 2013).

169 I believe Cook reached out to approximately 300 known apostolic leaders in the church place and workplace and was able to successfully garner 70 out of that group.

170 Some may argue that a few of the writers do not have a clear ecclesiology.

171 Ibid., p. xliii, xliv.

172 John C. Maxwell, *The 21 Irrefutable Laws of Leadership: Follow Them and People Will Follow You* (Nashville, TN: Thomas Nelson, n.d.

173 Ibid.

174 See the New Testament Catechetical element for leadership based on servanthood found in Mark 10:41-45 and Phil. 2:4-12.

175 Ibid., Jenkins, "The Next Christendom", 19, 47-53. This is just a small sample of what I am referring to regarding the syncretistic mixture between Christianity and other religious and cultural practices and beliefs.

176 Jeff Reed, "Global Pentecostalism and the Spirit: The Progress of the Gospel in the 21st Century," *A BILD Encyclical*, November 7, 2019, 6.

177 Ibid.

178 The pre, mid and post-tribulation rapture theory was unknown in church history prior to 1823 when it was introduced by Edward Erving. He was a teacher with a dubious reputation and known for his extreme views based on visions and revelations. He received his view on the pre-trib rapture through a vision and revelation by a lady,

Margaret McDonald, who was attending his meetings. Dave MacPherson, *The Rapture Plot* (Simpsonville, SC: Millennium III Publishers, 2000.

179 Ibid., NewBegin, 185.

180 Ibid., Reed, *The Churches of the First Century.*

181 Carl A. Raschke, *The Next Reformation: Why Evangelicals Must Embrace Postmodernity* (Grand Rapids, MI: Baker Academic, 2004), 19).

182 For more on this subject read, Raschke, *The New Reformation.* It is partially a rebuttal of a book against postmodernism by Douglas Groothuis entitled, "Truth Decay: Defending Christianity Against the Challenges of Postmodernism." Also, read "The Gospel in a Pluralist Society" by Newbigin.

183 Ibid., Jenkins.

184 "Antioch School of Church Planting and Leadership Development Grants Degrees for Church-Based Theological Education.," Antioch School of Church Planting and Leadership Development grants degrees for church-based theological education., accessed April 21, 2020, http://www.antiochschool.edu/).

185 Matthew Vines, "God and the Gay Christian: The Biblical Case in Support of Same-Sex Relationships," Amazon (Convergent Books, 2015), https://www.amazon.com/God-Gay-Christian-Biblical-Relationships/dp/160142518X).

186 Read "The Stone Lectures" that Abraham Kuyper gave at Princeton University in 1898; Francis Schaeffer's, *A Christian Manifesto*; Charles Colson's, *How Now Shall We Live?*, and Nancy Pearcey's, *Total Truth*, are excellent books on having a biblical worldview.

187 For more information on this subject read: *The Emotionally Healthy Church*, by Peter Scazzero; *Invitation to Solitude and Silence and Sacred Rhythms*, by Ruth Haley Barton; *Invitation to a Journey*, by M. Robert Mulholland; all of the writings of Thomas Merton.

188 For more on this trend read *Return to Rome*, by Francis Beckwith; *The Rebirth of Orthodoxy* by Thomas Oden; *Evangelicals on the Canterbury Trail* by Robert Webber; *The Ancient Christian Commentary on Scripture*, general editor Thomas Oden; *Worship Old & New* by Robert E. Webber; *Listening to the Past: The Place of Tradition in Theology* by Stephen R. Holmes; *Evangelical Is Not Enough: Worship of God in Liturgy and Sacrament* by Thomas Howard; and *Retrieving the Tradition & Renewing Evangelicalism: A Primer for Suspicious Protestants* by D.H. Williams.

189 Hal Lindsey's dispensational, best-selling books like "The Late, Great Planet Earth".

190 For more on this view the lecture of N.T. Wright at the center for philosophy of religion entitled, *The meanings of history; event and interpretation in the Bible and theology.* https://www.youtube.com/watch?v=KII2rltbG58&feature=youtu.be

191 For more on this view the lecture of N.T. Wright at the center for philosophy of religion entitled, *The meanings of history; event and interpretation in the Bible and theology.* https://www.youtube.com/watch?v=KII2rltbG58&feature=youtu.be

192 For more on this read the book, "The Celtic way of evangelism" by George G Hunter III).

193 For more on this read the book, "The Celtic way of evangelism" by George G Hunter III).

194 Refer to the front page of the June 2011 edition of Christianity Today magazine, online at http://www.christianitytoday.com/ct/2011/june/historicaladam.html

195 BioLogos, "God's Word. God's World.," BioLogos (BioLogos, August 28, 2018), https://biologos.org/?modal=about).

196 See Scientist Stephen Meyer refute the concept of Theistic Evolution in a lecture at Biola University. https://www.youtube.com/watch?v=mN41M732I_I&feature=youtu.be

197 This is not to say that the word *ekklesia* was only used in Scripture to signify a political mandate or gathering (that would be a stretch), but it implied far more than just coming together on a Sunday to sing songs and hear preaching.

198 Jeff Reed (BILD.ORG) has also written extensively on this topic in His encyclicals. I don't have a lot of hope for this happening as much in American parachurch ministries but more so in the developing world where the gospel is exploding through the work of local church apostolic networks and movements.

199 Read Harvey Cox, "The Future of Faith".

200 b777, "Christian Apologetics & Research Ministry," CARM. org, March 29, 2017, https://carm.org/pelagianism).

201 For more on this, read the historical writings of St. Augustine refuting Pelagius's writings.

202 Compare the social pathologies in the public school system before the time they removed prayer and the teaching of the biblical account of creation (in the early 1960's) to the pathologies today. Any honest social scientist will have to admit that the increase in dehumanizing behavior amongst grade and high school students corresponds to our nation going from the sacred to the secular worldview.

203 Which is one reason why progressive liberals, programmed with a secular humanistic mindset, are attempting to discard America's founding documents in order to deconstruct the USA to reconstruct it as a nation without borders, boundaries and morals!

204 A great book on this subject is, "The End of Apologetics" by Myron Bradley Penner.

205 Richard Florida's book, "The Rise of the Creative Class".

206 Ibid., Hunter, "To Change the World".

207 Ibid., Mattera, "Ruling in the Gates".

208 Ibid., Wagner, "Apostles Today" 228-230.

209 Alan Hirsch, "The Forgotten Ways: Reactivating the Missional Church" (Grand Rapids, MI: Brazos Press, 2008.

210 Ed Silvoso, "Anointed for Business" (Bloomington, MN: Chosen Books, 2014.

211 Ibid.

212 Ibid., Mattera, "Ruling in the Gates".

213 Published by Mattera Media, "Kingdom Revolution: Bringing Change to Your Life and Beyond" (Shippensburg, PA: Destiny Image, Inc., 2011.

214 Published by Mattera Media, "Kingdom Awakening: a Blueprint for Personal and Cultural Transformation" (Shippensburg, PA: Destiny Image Publishers, 2010.

215 Published by Mattera Media, "Walk in Generational Blessings: Leaving a Legacy of Transformation through Your Family" (Shippensburg, PA: Destiny Image Pub., 2012.

216 Published by Mattera Media, "Understanding the Wineskin of the Kingdom" (Place of publication not identified: EGEN CO LLC, 2016.

217 Published by Mattera Media, "25 Truths You Never Heard in Church: Becoming a Kingdom Focused Believer" (Micro65, 2017.

218 Published by Mattera Medias, "The Divided Gospel: The Consequences of Separating the Gospel from the Kingdom" (Micro65, 2018.

219 Ibid., Wagner, "Apostles Today" 259-260.

220 Gerald Hiestand, "The Pastor Theologian: Resurrecting an Ancient Vision" (Grand Rapids, MI: Zondervan, 2015), 10.

221 Kevin J. Vanhoozer and Owen Strachan, "The Pastor as Public Theologian: Reclaiming a Lost Vision" (Grand Rapids, MI: Baker Academic, 2015), 161. Kindle.

222 "DiSC Profile - What Is DiSC®? The DiSC Personality Test

and Profile Explained," DiSCProfile.com, accessed April 22, 2020, https://www.discprofile.com/what-is-disc/overview/

223 Ibid.

224 Ibid.

225 The order of the books of the Hebrew Scriptures as Christ would have known them was according to the tripartite division: the Law, the Prophets, the Writings. The Law (*Torah*) includes the five books of the Pentateuch (Genesis, Exodus, Leviticus, Numbers, Deuteronomy). The Prophets (*Nevi'im*) comprises the Former Prophets (Joshua, Judges, 1 and 2 Samuel [counted as one book], 1 and 2 Kings [counted as one book]) and the Latter Prophets (Isaiah, Jeremiah, Ezekiel, the Twelve Minor Prophets [counted as one book]). The Writings (*Kethuvim*) consists of Psalms, Proverbs, Job, the Song of Songs, Ruth, Lamentations, Ecclesiastes, Esther, Daniel, Ezra-Nehemiah (counted as one book), 1 and 2 Chronicles (counted as one book).

226 The order of the books of the Hebrew Scriptures as Christ would have known them was according to the tripartite division: the Law, the Prophets, the Writings. The Law (*Torah*) includes the five books of the Pentateuch (Genesis, Exodus, Leviticus, Numbers, Deuteronomy).The Prophets (*Nevi'im*) comprises the Former Prophets (Joshua, Judges, 1 and 2 Samuel [counted as one book], 1 and 2 Kings [counted as one book]) and the Latter Prophets (Isaiah, Jeremiah, Ezekiel, the Twelve Minor Prophets [counted as one book]). The Writings (*Kethuvim*) consists of Psalms, Proverbs, Job, the Song of Songs, Ruth, Lamentations, Ecclesiastes, Esther, Daniel, Ezra-Nehemiah (counted as one book), 1 and 2 Chronicles (counted as one book).

227 Ibid., Hiestand, "The Pastor Theologian" 22-24.

228 "Abraham Kuyper," Abraham Kuyper, accessed April 22, 2020,

https://abrahamkuyper.com/).

229 Ibid.

230 James O'Donnell, "St. Augustine," *Encyclopædia Britannica* (Encyclopædia Britannica, inc., February 19, 2020), https://www.britannica.com/biography/Saint-Augustine).

231 The Editors of Encyclopaedia Britannica, "Doctor of the Church," Encyclopædia Britannica (Encyclopædia Britannica, inc., December 31, 2018), https://www.britannica.com/topic/Doctor-of-the-Church.

232 Ibid.

233 Küng Hans, "Great Christian Thinkers" (NY, NY: Continuum, 2006), 143-145.

234 Alan C. Clifford, "John Wesley (1703–91)" Oxford Scholarship Online (Oxford University Press), accessed April 22, 2020, https://www.oxfordscholarship.com/view/10.1093/acprof:oso/9780198261957.001.0001/acprof-9780198261957-chapter-4).

235 Ibid., Vanhoozer & Strachan.

236 Ibid., N.T. Wright.

237 Ibid., Hiestand, "The Pastor Theologian".

238 Ibid.

239 "Dr. Mark Chrionna," Mark Chironna, accessed April 22, 2020, https://www.markchironna.com/).

240 Ibid.

241 David Coghlan, "Ignatian Spirituality as Transformational Social Science - David Coghlan, 2005," SAGE Journals, accessed April 22, 2020, https://journals.sagepub.com/doi/10.1177/1476750305049967).

242 John Macmurray and John Macmurray, "The Self as Agent" (Amherst, NY: Humanity Books, 1999), 86.

243 Ibid., Reason & Torbet.

244 Ibid.

245 Ibid.

246 Ibid., Geivett & Pivec, "A New Apostolic Reformation" 21.

247 Brad Christerson and Richard W. Flory, "The Rise of Network Christianity: How Independent Leaders Are Changing the Religious Landscape" (New York, NY: Oxford University Press, 2017.

248 Bob Smietana, "The 'Prophets' and 'Apostles' Leading the Quiet Revolution in American Religion," ChristianityToday. com (Christianity Today, August 7, 2017), https://www. christianitytoday.com/ct/2017/august-web-only/bethel-church-international-house-prayer-prophets-apostles.html).

249 Ibid.

250 Ibid., Smietana, "The 'Prophets' and 'Apostles' Leading the Quiet Revolution in

American Religion.

251 "Robert Morris," People, accessed April 22, 2020, https:// gatewaypeople.com/staff/robert-morris).

252 Doug Beacham, "Rediscovering the Role of Apostles and Prophets" (Franklin Springs, GA: LifeSprings Resources, 2004.

253 Wagner, "Apostles Today" 428 Kindle.

254 Ibid., 405-410.

255 Ibid., 396.

256 Ibid., 384.

257 Ibid. 432.

258 Ibid., 1152-1155.

259 Ibid., Jenkins, "The Next Christendom" 133, 135. He also says earlier in the book, "Many churches include the word "Apostolic" in their title, indicating a sense of direct continuity with the believers of the New Testament era and with the powers manifested by the Christians of that age."

260 Restoration Ministry, International, is the largest network in Brazil with over 25 thousand pastors, 3000 apostles and about 6 million followers. "Restoration Ministries,"

Restoration Ministries, October 9, 2018, https://restorationministriesbrazil.com/).

261 Andrew R. Burgess, "The Ascension in Karl Barth" (Abingdon, England: Routledge, 2017), 680.

262 Ibid.

263 Hans Urs von. Balthasar, "Explorations in Theology" (San Francisco: Ignatius Press, 1993), 139-140.

264 Ibid.

265 Ibid., Reed, "Kerygmatic Communities" 9.

266 Ibid.

267 Gary S. Greig, Kevin Springer, and James Innell Packer, "The Kingdom and the Power: Are Healing and the Spiritual Gifts Used by Jesus and the Early Church Meant for the Church Today?: A Biblical Look at How to Bring the Gospel to the World with Power" (Ventura: Regal Books, *1993*).

268 "Our Team," Bild, accessed April 22, 2020, https://bild.org/about-us/team).

269 Ibid., Hirsch.

270 Ibid. Geivett & Pivec, "A New Apostolic Reformation".

271 See the book Crossing Cultural Frontiers by Andrew Walls page 14, published by Orbis books copywrite 2017.

272 Lance Ford, "Unleader: Reimagining Leadership-- and Why We Must" (Kansas City: Beacon Hill Press, 2012.

273 Ed Delph, "Church@Community" (Lake Mary, FL: Creation House, 2005).

274 By common or creation grace I am referring to the fact that God graces all humanity with certain assignments and gifts for the sake of coherence through the providential administration and distribution of people with various gifts and abilities to serve throughout civilization; hence there is a difference between "saving grace" and "common grace."

275 Related to community transformation, one of the biggest mistakes the Evangelical Church in the USA has made is

to only target moral issues and political elections without a multi-generational plan to transform culture. Since culture trumps politics and ideology, we may win an election but will continue to lose our children if we do not have a bottom-up approach in which Jesus followers fill and influence every aspect of culture. Since young people are inculcated by all forms of media, popular trends and secular humanistic college professors, Christ-followers need to fill and affect those realms without neglecting the political and public policy realms.

About the Author

Dr. Joseph Mattera is an internationally known author, consultant, and scholar whose mission is to influence leaders who influence nations. He leads several organizations including The United States Coalition of Apostolic Leaders. He has a DMin. from Bakke University, THD from Antioch University, and is a PhD candidate.

instagram.com/josephmattera

facebook.com/josephmattera

twitter.com/JosephMattera

Joseph Mattera

Other Books by Dr. Joseph Mattera

The Purpose, Power and Process of Prophetic Ministry

The Jesus Principles

Walk in Generational Blessings

La Bendicion Generacional

Poisonous Power

Understanding the Wineskin of the Kingdom

25 Truths You Never Heard in Church

The Divided Gospel

Cutting Edge Leadership

An Anthology of Essays on Apostolic Leadership

Ruling in the Gates

Travail to Prevail

Kingdom Revolution

Kingdom Awakening

To order his bestselling books or to join the many thousands who subscribe to his acclaimed newsletter, go to www.josephmattera.org.

Made in the USA
Middletown, DE
06 November 2022

14296903R00214